DEVELOPER RELATIONS

HOW TO BUILD AND GROW A SUCCESSFUL DEVELOPER PROGRAM

Caroline Lewko
James Parton

Apress®

Developer Relations: How to Build and Grow a Successful Developer Program

Caroline Lewko
Vancouver, BC, Canada

James Parton
London, UK

ISBN-13 (pbk): 978-1-4842-7163-6
https://doi.org/10.1007/978-1-4842-7164-3

ISBN-13 (electronic): 978-1-4842-7164-3

Managing Director, Apress Media LLC: Welmoed Spahr
Acquisitions Editor: Aaron Black
Development Editor: James Markham
Coordinating Editor: Jessica Vakili

Distributed to the book trade worldwide by Springer Science+Business Media New York, 1 NY Plaza, New York, NY 10014. Phone 1-800-SPRINGER, fax (201) 348-4505, e-mail orders-ny@springer-sbm.com, or visit www.springeronline.com. Apress Media, LLC is a California LLC and the sole member (owner) is Springer Science + Business Media Finance Inc (SSBM Finance Inc). SSBM Finance Inc is a **Delaware** corporation.

For information on translations, please e-mail booktranslations@springernature.com; for reprint, paperback, or audio rights, please e-mail bookpermissions@springernature.com.

Apress titles may be purchased in bulk for academic, corporate, or promotional use. eBook versions and licenses are also available for most titles. For more information, reference our Print and eBook Bulk Sales web page at http://www.apress.com/bulk-sales.

Any source code or other supplementary material referenced by the author in this book is available to readers on GitHub via the book's product page, located at www.apress.com/978-1-4842-7163-6. For more detailed information, please visit http://www.apress.com/source-code.

Printed on acid-free paper

Caroline:

To Mom and Dad (posthumously) for letting me carve my own path.

To Alain, my spicy frog, because it's already been discussed.

James:

To my parents for their love, security, and patience.

To Michelle, Jacob, and Holly – everything is for you and because of you. x

Without you, this book wouldn't have been possible:

Anikó Bukta – illustrations

Phil Leggetter – technical reviewer

Dana Fujikawa – for his big red pen

Carlo Longino (posthumously) – a key contributor of many of the early DevRel frameworks and ideas

Thank you for your contributions and support:

Andrew Oliver, Jason Nassi, Russell Buckley, Ameer Badri, Jon Bradford, Matthew Revell, Thayer Prime, James Governor and the Flyless community, Judy Hamilton, Rod Burns, Ana Schafer Muroff, John Denniston, Bear Douglas, Stephen Millard, Suzanne Nguyen, Anthony Fabbricino, Bryce Keane, Ben Blume, Martin Isaksson, Steven Pousty, Linda Streb, Desigan Chinniah, Rand Hindi, Ben Gamble, Andreas Constantinou and the SlashData team, Tony Fish, Chrysanthos Chrysanthou, Jake Ward, Tyler Jewell.

There are hundreds more. Thank you one and all.

Contents

About the Authors

Caroline Lewko is an accomplished visionary and entrepreneur who has spent over two decades helping develop groundbreaking technology and nurturing community connections and innovation. She started WIP, the first boutique Developer Relations agency in 2006, after founding a community and incubator for mobile startups. She'd led consulting engagements and developer events in over 20 countries, spanning a wide range of platforms and technologies, from edge computing and machine learning to mobile. She's a regular keynote speaker and conference moderator.

Now as CEO of Revere Communications, she continues to work with the top ranks of the Fortune 500 and Global 500 to fast-growing startups, with a focus on training and mentoring the next generation of DevRel leaders.

When not speaking, training, or traveling, Caroline can be found gardening, biking, and wine tasting in her beloved Vancouver, BC.

https://twitter.com/CarolineLewko

https://www.linkedin.com/in/carolinelewko/

https://www.stateofdeveloperrelations.com

https://www.reverecommunications.com/

James Parton created and ran Developer Programs for O2 (O2 Litmus) and Telefonica (BlueVia) before joining Twilio in 2012 as their first hire outside of the United States to launch and run their European business. He did that successfully for five years, leaving just after Twilio's IPO in 2016. James has held board positions with the Application Developers Alliance and the Mobile Ecosystem Forum where he championed the needs of developers with industry and government. He regularly advises startups, corporates, and venture capital firms on their Developer Relations strategies via his boutique agency Land and Expand.

In addition to his Developer Relations activities, James is the Managing Director of the Bradfield Centre in Cambridge, which provides entrepreneurial opportunities for students at the University of Cambridge and acts as a tech community hub for Cambridge and the wider east of England region. He is also a cofounder of the Triple Chasm Company, which provides data-driven tools, training, and content to help companies successfully scale.

https://twitter.com/jamesparton

https://www.linkedin.com/in/jamesparton/

https://www.landandexpand.net/

About the Technical Reviewer

Phil Leggetter has a broad experience of Developer Relations, from hands-on execution through to strategic planning with C-level executives, justifying multimillion-dollar budgets and successfully achieving multimillion-dollar revenue targets. He has led DevRel teams within startups through growth, acquisition, and accelerated growth at a publicly traded enterprise. Phil supports the DevRel community through actionable knowledge sharing such as the AAARRRP DevRel Strategy Framework that has helped numerous Developer Relations teams map company-level goals through to team activities that bring value to a business. He continues to lead DevRel teams in addition to holding Developer Relations and experience advisory roles at a small number of startups.

Foreword

In the 1990s, Java was a young, exciting programming language that made it possible to write portable applications easily. I was overjoyed and spent the better part of the six years after university graduation training, educating, and promoting this world-changing technology to anyone who would listen.

These efforts were given a platform (and at the time an amplifying megaphone) at BEA Systems, the market leader in Java application servers, where I carried the title of Chief Evangelist. Developers, at the time, were seen as fickle, idiosyncratic, and with low influence authority in the IT decision-making structure.

Little did I know that "evangelism" was how early technology companies were establishing a Developer Relations function. At the time, we were thrilled when developers attended our workshops to acquire new skills or when our articles outlining innovative techniques in Java programming were published in hip trade magazines. Evangelism was, in many respects, fun because while we were spreading essential technology insights, it kept our own knowledge growth curve piqued.

In the following 20 years, developers have become an economic force. Businesses that build products sold to or consumed by developers generated $40B in 2020 annual recurring revenue, putting developers at the center of the multitrillion-dollar IT industry. More than 1200 companies have created commercial products within this landscape, and it's growing 19% annually. With more than 20 million professional software engineers, and 250 million knowledge workers transitioning into civilian developers through low-code technology, the influence of developers will be increasingly as important as advertising in the Super Bowl or the reach of TikTok.

Developer Relations has emerged as the professional practice by which organizations build sustainable and endearing relationships with developers in their new role as economic influencers.

The industry's understanding of Developer Relations is in its infancy. Only 24% of the Fortune 500 companies have established developer program management offices, and cursory scans of job boards show DevRel positions available in only the best-funded venture capital technology startups. And, in the companies that I've invested in, only one third have established DevRel programs even though it's always highlighted as essential in the boardroom!

When Caroline Lewko told me that she was combining her and James Parton's many years of Developer Relations experience into a book that outlines a recipe for creating, building, and growing a Developer Relations group, I knew that their efforts would have a profound and lasting impact upon marketing, product, and customer success organizations.

Well-run DevRel groups have a significant impact on the bottom line. By reaching developers to facilitate solving their technology problems, businesses can expect a lower customer acquisition cost, lower support costs which improve gross margins, and lower customer churn rates improving the net retention rate.

In *Developer Relations, How to Build and Grow a Successful Developer Program*, Caroline and James provide a blueprint for organizations to build high-performing DevRel organizations.

In Part I: Develop a Common Understanding, they define Developer Relations and articulate how it is different from B2B and B2C techniques by laying out a framework that combines education, marketing, experience, and success, and emphasize the value of the Developer Economy.

The definition of a developer changes with the nature of technology, and with low-code systems making nearly every knowledge worker a developer, there may be up to 500 million reachable professional developers in the coming decade. In Part II: Key Differentiators, Caroline and James provide the constructs necessary to define, segment, and identify different categories of developers, and the companies they work in, which inform the nature of how your marketing and education investments will be made, and the type of monetization strategy you might deploy.

Developers as buyers are more likely to buy from companies implementing a Product-Qualified Lead motion rather than the traditional, sales-heavy Sales-Qualified Lead process. In Part IV: Go-to-Market, Delivering Your Strategy, Caroline and James codify the PQL experience from discovery through activation and scaling. It delves you into the mindset of the developer to help you address key questions that must be addressed at every stage of engagement with developers. Combined with Part III: Alignment on Goals, they also emphasize, whether it's a Product-Qualified Lead or a Developer Relations Qualified Lead, the importance of collaborating with the sales and other teams inside your organization.

Successful DevRel programs are tribes that leverage the collective experiences of team members and your user community to become stronger together. In Part V: Managing and Growing Your Program, Caroline and James provide actionable processes, frameworks, strategy, and tactics to measure and grow your DevRel team and investments.

This book is more than a how-to guide for DevRel professionals. It'll help your organization gain years of knowledge without the years of trial and error so many groups have gone through previously. I hope it becomes a reference that you turn to frequently as you build and grow your DevRel team.

—Tyler Jewell

Managing Director, Dell Technologies Capital

Formerly product at BEA, Oracle, Quest, Red Hat, and MySQL

Formerly CEO of three different developer-led businesses

Investor in 15 developer-led businesses

https://www.linkedin.com/in/tylerjewell/

Introduction

What Is Developer Relations?

This is a question of fierce debate within the DevRel community and one not well understood outside the DevRel community. That this question has yet to be conclusively answered reflects the multifaceted nature of DevRel. We must also recognize that DevRel is a relatively new endeavor, with its origins in the Apple Macintosh marketing team of the early 1980s.

There is a growing body of work that's been created by DevRel professionals to improve the strategy and tactics of the practice. This work has been driven forward by various DevRel books, podcasts, events, and communities including WIP, DevRel.net, DevRel Weekly, and others. There is also specialist research and data from a new breed of industry analyst firms focused on the Developer Economy like SlashData, RedMonk, and EDC.

We want to support the drive to further professionalize DevRel as a practice and achieve board-level recognition for it. We believe any company with a developer program or an ambition to engage with the Developer community should appoint a Chief Developer Relations Officer. The CDRO role would represent the voice of the developer at the executive team level and ensure the DevRel effort is coordinated and connected to the core strategy and objectives of the company.

To support this goal, we have created, updated, and tested frameworks and tools for DevRel professionals. We've used our 20 years each of experience and combined it with the experience and input of the wider DevRel community, who graciously supported the development of this work.

If you are a practicing DevRel professional or aspire to be one, this book will equip you to create and pitch your strategy. It will also teach you how to engage developers, build a DevRel program, hire a team, and measure your activities' impact.

If you are a stakeholder in a business that has an existing Developer Relations program or is thinking of creating one, this book will define and demystify the activities of DevRel and show you how to ensure alignment with your overall corporate objectives.

We have open-sourced all of the included frameworks, and we look forward to seeing them adopted, adapted, and extended by the community.

—Caroline Lewko and James Parton

This Book Is for You If…

- Your company wants to **start a new developer program**, and you've been tasked to lead the initiative. You need to understand how to get started, hire a team, how to sequence the investment, and how to maximize the program's chance of success.

- Your company has an existing developer initiative, and you want to **audit and benchmark** the program's activities to increase its impact and to justify its continued existence.

- Your company has an existing program and wants to **launch a new product or tool** successfully.

- You need standardized language and tools to set and manage your **internal stakeholders' expectations**.

- You come from a business background and need to understand **how working with developers is different**.

- You **come from a technology background**, and you need to have a **better handle on marketing to developers**.

- You think you might want to **become a Developer Relations practitioner**, and you want a better understanding of what it is all about and the tools needed to be effective.

Good news!

The strategy and many of the tactical challenges around engaging developers are common regardless of company size, type of product, or business maturity. Whether you have the luxury of a blank sheet of paper in an early-stage startup or are trying to turn around a supertanker, this book is for you.

Let's get started!

Develop a Common Understanding

To get your Developer Relations initiative off on the right foot, everyone involved must have a common understanding.

The "everyone" translates to you and your stakeholders. This shared understanding starts at the top of your organization – the CEO and your board of directors. It also includes departments that will interact and support the Developer Relations activities such as the CTO office, marketing, product, customer support, and others. It may also include teams external to your organization, such as marketing agencies, PR firms, or other contractors, and of course your team needs to be on the same page too.

As we outlined in the Introduction, we strongly advocate for the Developer Relations team to report directly into the executive team to aid this alignment. However, we recognize that this is not always the norm at the time of writing this book.

Therefore, ensuring everyone is on the same page is crucial, no matter your starting point – a brand-new program, launching a new product, or reviewing/rebooting an existing program. This ensures that overall corporate goals and messaging are aligned. It also ensures there is an understanding and recognition for the Developer Relations effort in the company, one which has a relevant place and priority and contributes to the overall company objectives.

You can establish these relations via one-on-one interactions, but we recommend you host a kick-off workshop to get all your stakeholders together simultaneously. This type of gathering ensures consistency of message and allows interdepartmental questions and issues to be tabled and resolved up front.

Alignment is not a one-off activity. Invest in maintaining and strengthening these crucial relationships and alliances that support your activities, including regular meetings to cascade program updates.

The shared understanding includes the following:

- What is Developer Relations – its components and differentiators.

- Who are developers, and why they are relevant to your business.

- How Developer Relations is activated in your organization, as a separate program or integrated into other functional departments.

- What the business model of Developer Relations is, and which variation is specific to creating value for your business.

We walk you through these in turn in the upcoming chapters.

What Is Developer Relations?

The focus on developers as a route to market[1] is a relatively new field. As such, it's not currently recognized or taught in universities or postsecondary schools, and there is no professional body or association. This immaturity means there is a lack of standard definitions, frameworks, measurements, and tooling for Developer Relations practitioners to adopt. It also accounts for the lack of awareness and understanding of Developer Relations in the broader business world.

Perhaps more challenging for professionalizing this nascent field is the misconception of executives who have limited exposure to the world of Developer Relations. The classic proverb "*A little knowledge is a dangerous thing*" holds true here. To them DevRel is simply hack days, hoodies, and laptop stickers. As we will discover, it is so much more than that.

---

[1] A route to market is the strategy and tactics used to get your product or service to your target customer and/or end user.

© Caroline Lewko, James Parton 2021
C. Lewko and J. Parton, *Developer Relations*,
https://doi.org/10.1007/978-1-4842-7164-3_1

In general, practitioners in the field have agreed on "**Developer Relations**," shortened to "**DevRel**," as the all-encompassing term. This term includes developer marketing, developer evangelism, developer advocacy, developer support, Developer Experience, developer education, developer success, developer community relations, and the management of developer programs.

Throughout the book, we interchange Developer Relations and the abbreviated "DevRel" to talk about the profession overall.

Developer Relations is both:

- The **professional practice** of engaging with developers as the primary user of a product, generally outside of one's own company[2].

- **The program or set of activities within an organization** that interact with Developers on their journey with your product and company.

Let's review the core components of DevRel before we dive into the rest of the book. Often the terminology is confusing, as the relationship between distinct areas and how they all fit together can overlap or be ill defined in an organization. Let's start to clear this up.

The Core Components of Developer Relations

Creating a single diagram that describes the individual components and their relationships was perhaps one the most time-consuming tasks in writing this book. To increase the chance of adoption by the profession, we strove for something to simplify a complex subject while being memorable.

After hours of debate and prototype designs, there was an epiphany around the idea of a stylized tree to represent the **Developer Relations Framework** and the core elements of successful Developer Relations Programs as seen in Figure 1-1.

Around the core of "**Developer Experience**," there are three main areas of the practice (the branches of our tree):

- **Developer Marketing**
- **Developer Education**
- **Developer Success**

---

[2] There are some DevRel activities that work with developers inside one's company.

The final component, which gives the tree and your program life, is the **Community**, represented as the tree trunk and roots.

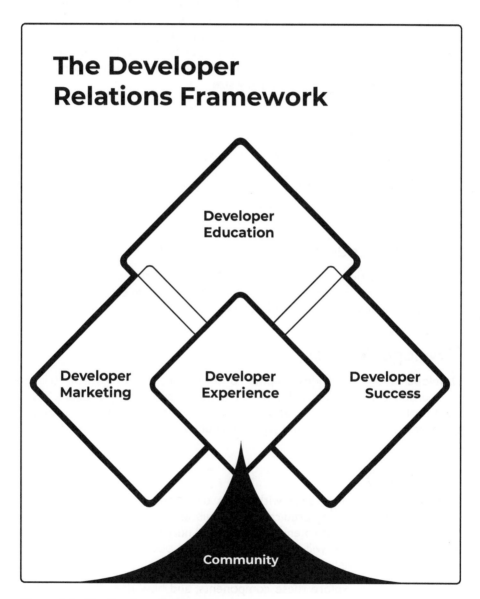

Figure 1-1. The Developer Relations Framework

Let's review these components.

Developer Experience

At the heart of the tree, or the core of any successful developer endeavor, is the Developer Experience, also referred to as **DX**. It is the equivalent of User Experience (UX) where the user of your product is a developer. DX includes their interactions with your product, developer hub, and documentation as they learn and begin to build. Functionally, DX sits with Product or sometimes the CTO office depending on company size.

Developer Marketing

Developer Marketing is the set of outreach activities designed to create awareness as developers discover and evaluate your product and program. Functionally, developer marketing can sit in the marketing department but often overlaps into product. Sales activities also interplay here.

Developer Education

Developer Education, also referred to as **DevEd**, is critical to the adoption of your product. You will need to provide a comprehensive set of content and learning resources in a variety of formats.

Developer Success

Developer Success provides support to developers as they go from trialing your product to building a full-blown commercially scaled product. As a functional role, Developer Success varies and may overlap with product, engineering, sales, support, and your community team.

Community

Critically, a tree cannot exist without its trunk and roots, analogous to a successful program being predicated on a vibrant **community**. The whole point of your program is to engage, serve, and nurture your community. This is what your success will be built upon. Without a healthy, sustainable community, you have little chance of success.

We'll continue to explore these components, and how they work together, throughout the book.

Summary

We've established that DevRel is multifaceted, containing the functional areas of Developer Experience, Developer Marketing, Developer Education, and Developer Success. A vibrant community gives life to the whole framework.

In essence:

Developer Relations is enabling a developer to be successful with your product, while aligning with your corporate goals.

Next, let's see what influences Developer Relations and where it fits in an organization.

Where Does Developer Relations Fit?

In this chapter, we'll take a deeper look at the multiple roles Developer Relations plays, where Developer Relations sits within an organization, and how you can determine its influencers and influences.

Confusion over roles and responsibilities can creep into DevRel, especially in larger organizations. To the untrained eye, elements of the DevRel role can be perceived as overlapping with existing departments' activities. In this chapter, we will look at the different functional areas of DevRel, some common functional reporting structures, and the vital role DevRel plays as an information valve.

Functional Activities

If you come from a product background, understanding your target customers' needs and designing a compelling product experience for them is the norm. But you might believe that your support ends as soon as the product is shipped. That's not the case in DevRel.

© Caroline Lewko, James Parton 2021
C. Lewko and J. Parton, *Developer Relations*,
https://doi.org/10.1007/978-1-4842-7164-3_2

If you come from an engineering background, you might think marketing, or heaven forbid, sales, is something you have no interest in at all and that it couldn't possibly be related to anything to do with developers. You might believe that as long as the product is strong, and you continue to build in new features, the company will find success. But, have no doubt, there is commercial intent behind the vast majority of DevRel activity.

If you come from a marketing background, much of what you see in a typical Developer Relations program will look very similar to traditional **marketing and sales** efforts in either B2B (business-to-business) or B2C (business-to-consumer) companies. So you might believe that you can stick to your traditional tactics, but as we'll discover, developers are an entirely new audience to understand.

If you work in **community management**, you might think Developer Relations is the same, in that the style of the interaction is more akin to one friend helping out another to solve a problem or enhance their creativity, rather than making them feel they are a sales prospect. Talking directly to your customers and potential customers in a direct, friendly, nonsales, noncorporate way and amplifying and showcasing your customers' work, achievements, and community contributions are not exclusive to any one business model.

You'll soon see the differences in how and where value is created and adoption occurs in Developer Relations' business models as well as in its sales funnel. These differences affect the way DevRel community management is undertaken.

Developer Relations shares traits with all of the preceding business functions, but also has distinctive characteristics. As we dive deeper in the book, you'll see that DevRel differs from the traditional style and tactics used in sales and marketing efforts, and from an engineering support perspective, the audience is different from what you might be used to in a partner or ISV[1] program. You'll see there are also subtle differences in the type of community interactions because of the business model. We will look deeper into these distinctions in Part II.

Functional Reporting

There is no one dominant functional reporting structure for DevRel within a company, according to studies and our own observations. This aspect of DevRel is perhaps unsurprising given it's a new field and as it sits at the intersection of several traditional roles.

Figure 2-1 shows data from the State of Developer Relations Report 2020 showing that overall marketing has a small lead in functional reporting; however,

---

[1] An ISV is an Independent Software Vendor.

the CTO Office/Engineering is a close second.[2] However, Marketing's lead should not be misinterpreted. If the Engineering and Product results are combined, they demonstrate a majority of organizations have DevRel reporting into technical departments, rather than marketing departments.

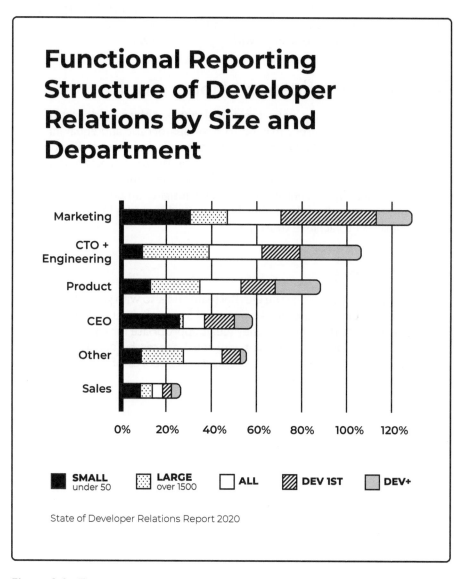

Figure 2-1. The reporting structure for Developer Relations per the State of Developer Relations 2020 Report

---

[2]State of Developer Relations Report 2020.

Regardless, there is no single blueprint that defines how your DevRel program should be structured. It will skew toward certain functional areas depending on variables like the type of organization or the maturity stage of the product or company.

What is important is to have a good understanding of which functional areas influence Developer Relations to aid and tune your strategy, discussions, decision-making, and relationships within your organization.

Department Influence Mapper Tool

Do you know which way your program leans – either by department or function? Initially, your intent may be to have democratic and equal influence from all departments. However, that is normally unrealistic. Plotting the influence various departments or functions have on your program is a useful exercise to complete. We've created the Department Influence Mapper Tool to give you a clear visual representation. This insight can be helpful once you understand the overall goals of your business and how the DevRel effort can aid your business to achieve those goals.

How It Works

Complete this exercise within the DevRel team and also with your stakeholders to help uncover bias, misalignment, potential for conflict, and allies. Ask each participant to score the influence they feel is appropriate for each department on the program. You can then plot individual scores by department or, as shown as an example in Figure 2-2, the aggregate scores of the DevRel team members and the other stakeholders.

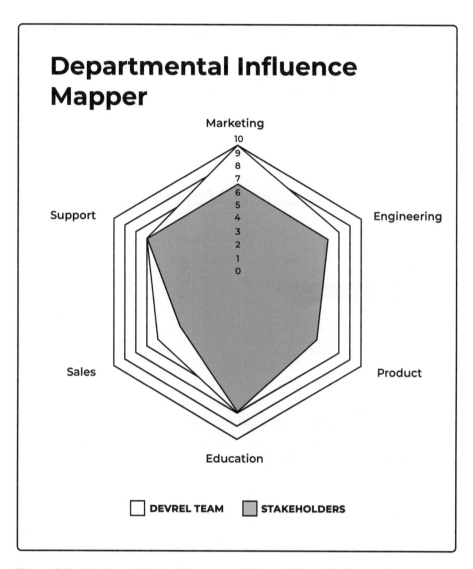

Figure 2-2. Developer Relations Department Influence Mapper Tool example

Using the Tool

This exercise is perfect for the program kick-off workshop we recommended you hold. We also strongly recommend regularly revisiting the exercise to assess how effective your internal interactions have been, to ensure you still have alignment, and to uncover any changes in influence, changes in the strategy, or changes in sentiment toward your program from other departments. It can help you decide on your direction, information you may need to gather to inform everyone, as well as staffing decisions.

An Information Valve for Your Company

One role that DevRel plays is as a critical liaison between the company and the external community of developers it serves. This community may include influencers, prospective customers, active customers, previous customers, partners, and even media. Figure 2-3 outlines the type of information flow that DevRel facilitates.

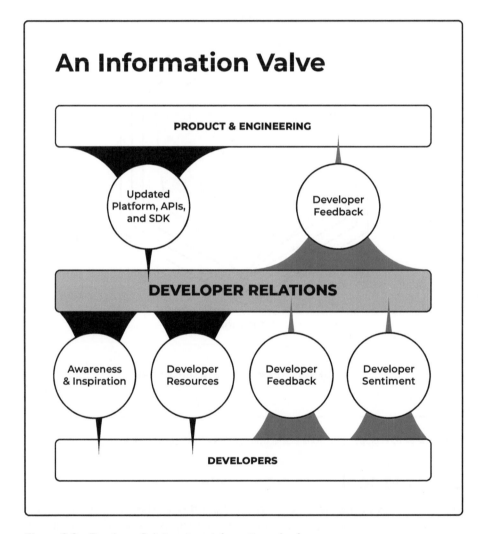

Figure 2-3. Developer Relations is an information valve for your company

In her book,[3] Mary Thengvall attributes this quote to Ewan Davis:

"To the community, I represent the company

To the company, I represent the community

I must have both of their interests in mind at all times"

Because of this vital role, DevRel practitioners must be sensitive and skilled at cross-team communication and collaboration. However, it is essential to note that the internal effectiveness of the DevRel team is not only predicated on their skills and style. Their reporting structure and line management also influence it. Their department's internal influence and reputation affects how much attention and priority the DevRel team receives and the results they are able to achieve. This is another key reason why we believe DevRel needs to have C-level authority.

If you are not quite sure if you should be reading further, or you are questioning if you are indeed working in DevRel – here's a test for you.

The Developer Relations Test

Am I in Developer Relations?

☑ **Your primary target audience is developers**

☑ **Your strategy & tactics are designed to change developer behaviour**

☑ **Your internal definition of success is predicated on developers**

Did you check all 3?
Congratulations - you are in DevRel!

Figure 2-4. The Developer Relations test

---

[3] *The Business Value of Developer Relations*, Mary Thengvall.

Review your results:

1 – Your primary target audience is developers.

The choice of "primary" is deliberate. There is no ambiguity in this statement. Developers are the target you are trying to reach. You may also have secondary audiences as part of your marketing activity, for example, nontechnical corporate decision makers who control or influence the buying decision, but developers are your primary focus.

2 – Your strategy and tactics are designed to change developer behavior.

Just because you want developers to use your product, it doesn't mean they will come to you. There are hundreds of developer-oriented companies offering thousands of tools, all trying to reach the same people as you. Not only do you have to cut through the noise, but you also have to convince the developer to take that leap of faith and try your product. Then you must support them through experimenting, prototyping, and building, which hopefully leads to them releasing something meaningful into production. Fine-tuning your Developer Experience to remove friction at all stages is critical to your success. This is no small undertaking. Understanding the creative and technical development processes of people and companies within Developer Relations is critical for differentiating it from traditional functional areas.

3 – Your internal definition of success is predicated on developers.

If you and your program are measured by something other than your developers' actions and results, you have a severe misalignment in your program. We've seen organizations attempt to measure or benchmark their developer program against more mature departments. If left unresolved, it will likely be terminal for your program, as you will never be able to match expectations.

If you weren't able to check "Yes" to the questions in Figure 2-4, you might still be in DevRel, but you'll need many of the strategies and tactics in this book to align the goals of your company and program.

Summary

There is no one size fits all for Developer Relations roles, nor a standardization of functional reporting in the corporate structure. However, the data demonstrates that DevRel typically aligns with Marketing, Engineering, or Product. One aspect is certain – the DevRel team acts as a crucial information valve for your company and, with this in mind, requires the authority that comes from having a C-level leader.

Due to the variety of DevRel programs and responsibilities, the Departmental Influence Mapper Tool is helpful to visualize your key internal influencers. If you are in any doubt if you are in DevRel – take our test!

By now you are probably wondering – if the role is so variable and complex, how did DevRel get started? We're glad you asked. Our next chapter looks at the history of where Developer Relations started and how and why it is growing in significance.

The Origin of Developer Relations and the Rise of the Developer

Establishing Developer Relations programs, which organize the activity of engaging and influencing the behavior of developers, has been around longer than the World Wide Web. However, the recognition that developers represent a direct and significant commercial opportunity is a relatively new phenomenon.

© Caroline Lewko, James Parton 2021
C. Lewko and J. Parton, *Developer Relations*,
https://doi.org/10.1007/978-1-4842-7164-3_3

The recent developer gold rush has led to a plethora of developer-oriented products, tools, and services, with their associated developer programs and developer-led marketing. Interest and investment have followed. For example, Crunchbase, which lists more than 1200 "Developer API" companies that have raised $6.9bn in venture funding, 13% of which have been acquired, represents just a small part of the developer-led economy.

In this chapter, we turn back the clock and explore its origins inside Apple during the 1980s. We then look at six key trends over the past two decades that drove the need and adoption of Developer Relations for hundreds of companies around the world today.

The Apple Didn't Fall Far from the Tree

Apple was the first company to use "Developer Relations" and "Evangelist" as formal job titles in 1982, coined by Mike Murray of the Macintosh Division. They built the first recognized developer program in the late 1980s and early 1990s.[1]

Apple's Chief Evangelist at the time, Guy Kawasaki, published the seminal book *The Macintosh Way*[2] in 1990. This book left such an indelible mark on Developer Relations that the language and many tactics are still used today, such as:

- A theology-based lexicon such as "evangelism," "spreading the gospel," and now overused phrases like "making the world a better place" and "winning hearts and minds."

- Tactics such as nurturing the community (referred to back then as user groups), focusing on demos rather than pitches, etc.

- Empowering employees to directly help customers.

- Thanking customers through random acts of kindness like handwritten notes.

- Emphasis on the imperative that the top leader in the organization has a passion for what you are doing and provides air cover.

- Playing a long game that allows for big ethereal ideas.

---

[1] Based on desk research and collective knowledge.
[2] https://guykawasaki.com/books/the-macintosh-way/

- A powerful demonstration of scrappy new entrant/ challenger brand positioning. The intent was to disrupt the dominant market players of IBM and Microsoft in personal computing. David vs. Goliath symbolism was used to keep the religious tone, emphasizing taking on mediocrity and the status quo, Good vs. Evil. A key tactic was building community and a halo around the Macintosh.

The longevity of these concepts over two decades demonstrates their power.

Following Apple in the mid-1980s to early 1990s, other technology companies forayed into building developer programs. Microsoft invested significant resources in building its developer offering, as did Intel. In 1999, Salesforce released its first API and a free trial, and Cisco and eBay launched Developer programs in 2000. Many others followed. For more details, we recommend watching *History of Modern Developer Relations by Brandon West*,[3] which provides a great flyby in 30 mins.

The Rise of the Developer

You may be asking yourself how did Developers become "The New King Makers" as coined by Stephen O'Grady. Why and how have developers become so hot?

We have identified six key trends, as shown in Figure 3-1, which when combined led to the rise in importance of developers to modern business over the past 20 years. Together, these trends provided an unparalleled canvas for technical creativity, perfectly captured in the now-famous phrase "Software is eating the world" from an article by Marc Andreessen, of Silicon Valley investment firm Andreessen Horowitz, back in August 2011.[4] Let's take a deeper look into each of these trends.

---

[3]https://youtu.be/vFGDzaLiAnM
[4]https://a16z.com/2011/08/20/why-software-is-eating-the-world/

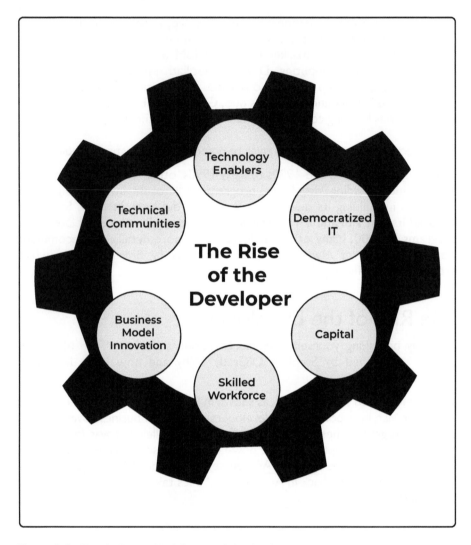

Figure 3-1. Trends that enabled the rise of the developer

Technology Enablers

The technology pieces of the puzzle required to fuel the developer's creativity fell into place between the mid-1990s and mid-2000s and haven't stopped. Internet technologies such as web browsers, HTML, HTTP, and FTP led the way at the start of the new millennium. In parallel, modern programming languages were invented and quickly gained in popularity: Python (1991), JavaScript (1995), Ruby (1995), Ruby on Rails (2005), Go (2009), and Swift (2014). Internet access speeds radically increased and costs fell, jumping from the kilobits of dial-up to the gigabits of fiber. Cellular networks raced through four generations (2G to 5G). New devices appeared with the iPhone and smartphones arriving in 2007, followed by iPad in 2010, and now wearables and XR head-up displays (HUDs).

These technologies, combined with the drop in computing costs driven by the advent of cloud computing led by AWS which launched in 2006, meant the infrastructure was now in place for fast and reliable data exchange anytime, anywhere. This in turn enabled real-time services, distribution of apps, and transactional activity powered by APIs.

Democratized IT

In the 1990s, the high-ticket price of IT infrastructure meant that companies had well-defined procurement processes. There was no way for individual developers in companies to proactively seek out the software and tools they wanted to use directly. Technical teams would contribute their requirements to Request for Information (RFI) and Request for Proposal (RFP) exercises as part of the procurement process. They then sat through hours of vendor presentations and plowed through hundreds of pages of RFI and RFP responses before the purchasing decision was made.

In the 2000s, we saw Software as a Service (SaaS) disrupt the business model for software and drive a significant shift in how companies purchased and integrated technology. Suddenly, you no longer had to commit thousands of dollars and sign complex multiyear contracts to access and benefit from cutting-edge software and tools. This consumerization of B2B software was nothing less than a revolution. Seemingly overnight, the IT department and procurement department gatekeepers were suddenly out of control and easily bypassed, empowering individual developers to experiment with and adopt the tools they wanted to use.

Skilled Workforce

The software developer workforce grew significantly (see Figure 3-2) as demand for technical roles increased, and new languages and frameworks became easier to learn. Web standardization meant technical skills were now more portable than before, making individuals more attractive to prospective employers, a positive move away from vendor-specific training.

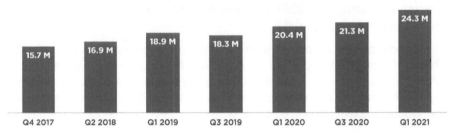

Growth of the global developer population

Active software developers (in millions)

Figure 3-2. Growth of the global developer population 2017–2021, from SlashData

As opportunities grew for technical skills, a greater emphasis was placed on STEM subjects in schools and universities to ensure the pipeline of future technical talent could match demand, propelling the strategic importance of computer science and software engineering to mainstream consciousness.

Capital

As we have seen earlier, infrastructure costs and labor costs were falling year on year, meaning the cost to start new companies was also dramatically falling. Capital could now go further, and when combined with the growing interest in "Tech" attracting more investors, it led to the funding and creation of more and more startups. More startups created a greater demand for more developers, driving the flywheel described in the "Skilled Workforce" section earlier.

The creation of more startups also in turn created the "Technical Founder" or Founding CTO. This was significant for early Developer Relations programs. The Technical Founder was a new category or persona of buyer, motivated by innovation. They could make a purchasing decision without the burden of worrying about interoperability with legacy systems or a significant outlay from their budgets.

Business Model Innovation

Going hand in hand with the democratization of IT, new business models came to market, creating a two-sided opportunity for Developers that:

- Empowered them to become buyers of tools and services.
- Provided them with new channels to market for their own products and services.

Whether employed within a larger organization or in an early-stage startup, developers could now take advantage of free trials, "pay-as-you-go" pricing, self-service, and purchases with credit cards. Inside corporations, this represented an attractive antidote to the frustration and complexity of procuring services as described in the "Democratized IT" section. Increasingly, corporate gatekeepers could be bypassed.

Of course, as developers became empowered to buy direct, appropriate sales, marketing and support activities were required to engage and influence their buying decisions.

The second opportunity occurred when bringing their own products to market. In addition to having their own direct channel (e.g., their API or website), developers now had innovations like mobile app stores that could reach millions of customers without the huge marketing expense of building traffic to their own properties. Startups that offered business apps like Dropbox, Evernote, Box, and Trello spread like wildfire inside organizations, and those startups grew to become valuable companies in their own right.

Technical Communities

The sixth trend accelerated the first five. The increasing importance of technical communities, fueled by technology and startup-centric media like TechCrunch and Hacker News, increased the awareness of new technology, startups, and tools. This awareness led to the hype around "hot" technologies and FOMO (fear of missing out), driving the desire to participate. Perhaps the poster child for how ridiculous things got was an API, that simply sent the word "Yo", that gained attention and raised $1.5m in funding.[5]

Stack Overflow, GitHub, and other communities grew during this time, adding to the heightened awareness of developers, and developers as community influencers. Being recognized as a leading contributor in your community of choice boosted your industry profile and influence, leading to career opportunities.

Attending, sponsoring, speaking, and exhibiting at community meetups and conferences became integral to the go-to-market strategies of Developer Relations programs.

---

[5]https://techcrunch.com/2014/06/18/yo-yo/

The Rise of APIs

The popularity of APIs can be traced back to the three trends of Technology Enablers, Democratized IT, and Business Model Innovation. As APIs have, at times, become synonymous with Developer Relations, we believe they justify further investigation.

The concept that software building blocks could be integrated with other software originated with service-oriented architecture (SOA) in the late 1990s. Breaking down previously complex and inflexible software into logical representations of business activity triggered a revolution in software design. It also paved the way to microservices and modern web APIs that used lightweight web technologies like REST and JSON and were cloud-hosted. For a deep dive into the history of APIs, we recommend watching *A Brief, Opinionated History of the API* by Joshua Bloch.[6]

The pivot point for Developer Relations came around 2000. Rather than just create these services exclusively for a company's internal use, why not put them in the cloud and let any developer use them. This strategic shift led to companies "opening up" and exposing their capabilities outside their organization for the first time. Early pioneers were eBay, Amazon, and Salesforce.

In 2005, ProgrammableWeb started to catalog and analyze the API economy, launching the first API directory, which contained 40 APIs. Fourteen years later, the directory has almost 24,000 listed APIs; see Figure 3-3. It is important to note, however, not all of the 24k APIs listed are still active.

---

[6]https://youtu.be/LzMp6uQbmns

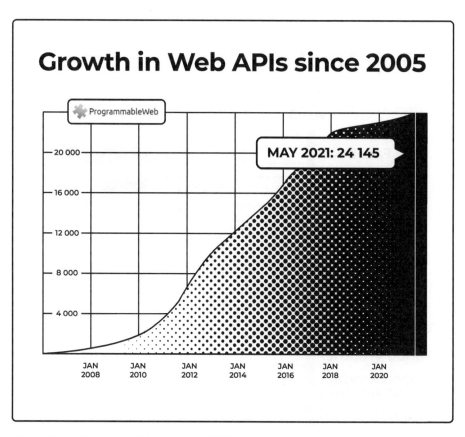

Figure 3-3. Growth in Web APIs since 2005 by ProgrammableWeb

While this explosion is impressive, like most industries, the few tend to dominate the space. Seven of the ten most popular APIs of all time have remained the same, demonstrating the power of brand, reach, and utility/value exchange. (see Figure 3-4)[7] In 2019 ProgrammableWeb also found a 30% growth rate over the previous four years[8] inferring APIs are still a growing technology force. To achieve success, API companies are solely dependent on developers adopting their technologies and driving transactions through their platform. Constant usage and high volumes are crucial. Stimulating this is the job of Developer Relations.

---

[7]https://www.programmableweb.com/news/which-are-developers-favorite-apis/research/2019/10/24

[8]https://www.programmableweb.com/news/apis-show-faster-growth-rate-2019-previous-years/research/2019/07/17

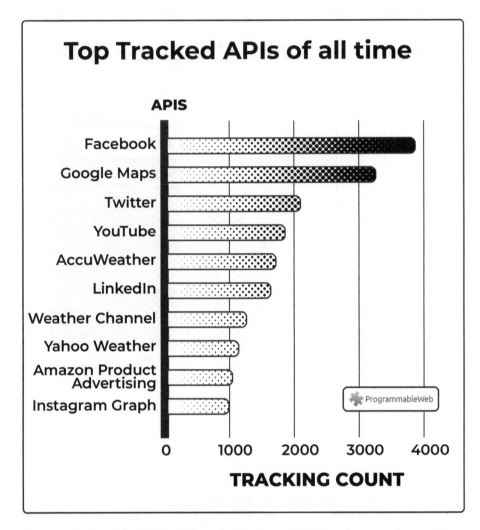

Figure 3-4. Top tracked APIs of all time by Programmable Web

Interestingly, these early API leaders all had a core business focus that wasn't predicated on APIs or developers. Companies included an online marketplace (eBay), a social network and advertising platform (Facebook), online retail (Amazon), and online video (YouTube). However, these companies realized that APIs and developers could enhance their businesses. We define this type of company as "Developer Plus" companies and expand this definition later in Chapter 7.

The next logical step on this path was the birth of a new generation of companies built *exclusively* around their API, wanting to serve one kind of customer – the developer. We define these companies as "Developer First" companies, and again we delve deeper into this topic later in Chapter 7.

Today, it sounds unbelievable that the poster child for API and developer-centric companies – Twilio, founded in 2008 – struggled to raise its early-stage financing because VCs didn't believe software developers could write checks to pay for services.

Twilio Cofounder/CEO Jeff Lawson's insight was that developers represented a vital part of the decision-making process to buy new technology. As well, the developer could be inside a larger established company or part of an early-stage company. This breakthrough spurred on other companies to bring developer-oriented products, tools, and services to market with their associated developer programs and developer-led marketing.

The Growth Continues

Over the last 15 years, many businesses and products like newspapers, music, and more have been "vaporized" as described by Robert Tercek,[9] as software enabled new products and new business models to be created. Today, over 2.5 quintillion bytes of data are created every single day,[10] and it's only going to grow from there. We are at the start of "Industry 4.0," which will see billions of users, apps, and sensors combined for an infinite number of connections. Innovation is seeing opportunities arise in almost every vertical and industry, from startups and corporates alike. Watch for advancements in IoT, Big Data, AI and machine learning, edge computing, extended reality (XR, including augmented reality (AR) and virtual reality (VR)), robotics, and esports – the list is endless.

Code is the foundation of innovation today, and these innovative projects are enormous. Consider that a Porsche Panamera has 100 million lines of code, an MRI scanner has 7 million lines of code, a combine harvester has over 5 million lines of code, a modern boom lift has 40 sensors and 3 million lines of code, and a drug infusion pump has more than 200,000 lines of code.[11] This phenomenon has changed the staffing requirements in companies. Nike, for example, now employs more software developers than shoe designers.[12]

---

[9] https://vaporizedbook.com/
[10] https://www.visualcapitalist.com/wp-content/uploads/2019/04/data-generated-each-day-full.html and https://www.domo.com/learn/data-never-sleeps-7
[11] https://www.aitrends.com/iot/how-new-business-models-are-combining-the-iot-and-services/
[12] https://twitter.com/twilio/status/910067091025354753?s=20

This leads us to the "so what" of this chapter. The common denominator in all of these opportunities is the creators – the developers. To create, developers need tools. These tools need strong, experienced, and robust developer programs to meet the goals of the companies that bring them to market.

Summary

Over the past 40 years, six key trends created perfect conditions for developers to flourish. Consequently, "Tech" has never been so vital to our economy, with companies like Google, Facebook, Instagram, Twitter, Spotify, Airbnb, Uber, and Tesla becoming household names.

In the process, the developer has risen to become a key influencer, buyer, and creator of technology. As recognition of this has risen, the need to organize sales, marketing, and support activity to address this new customer persona necessitates the demand for Developer Relations.

Developers are the creators of innovation.

To create, Developers need tools.

Developer tools demand Developer Relations.

DevRel's roots can be traced back to Apple's Macintosh marketing team, but its evolution now includes defining and building the tools that developers use and the resources to ensure their success.

Our next chapter tackles the value of the developer-led economy.

The Value of the Developer Economy

Developer Relations is becoming a strategic priority for so many companies due to the recognition of the value Developers can bring to their businesses. However, the total value of the developer-led economy, in terms of the dollars generated by products used, influenced, or purchased by developers, is something the industry hasn't yet been able to fully quantify. Another telltale sign of its relative immaturity. In this chapter, we'll see how the dollar value of DevRel is starting to be captured by new research, as well as illustrate the supplemental value developers contribute to an organization.

Some Numbers

Tyler Jewell, Managing Director of Dell Technologies Capital, released some eye-opening numbers in August 2020, based on his ongoing groundbreaking research, which began in 2009. Jewell has tracked over 1000 companies, "*each company whose products were sold to, purchase-influenced by, or consumed by software developers.*"

The original version of this chapter was revised. A correction to this chapter is available at https://doi.org/10.1007/978-1-4842-7164-3_30

His research values the Developer-Led Landscape at $40 billion, with a 19% annual rate of return (ARR) growth rate, as shown in Figure 4-1. We recommend you check out his blog or GitHub repository for further details.[1]

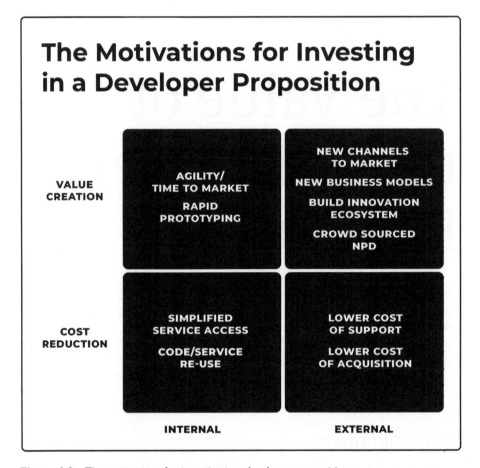

Figure 4-1. The motivations for investing in a developer proposition

His data highlights how it is impossible to ignore the Developer-led economy and how this market continues to grow. This clearly demonstrates the need for your company to have a developer strategy and, when the time is right, a developer offering backed by a strong Developer Relations program to ensure the opportunity can be seized.

[1]https://tylerjewell.substack.com/p/the-developer-led-landscape-20-08-28

Jewell's research doesn't however include the entire value created by the Developer-led economy as his research is primarily focused on software-based Developer Products with a direct revenue model.

For example, Jewell's research excludes "Market and Ecosystem Enhancement" models practiced by the likes of Qualcomm that use their developer program to enrich their product lines, making them more attractive to customers, rather than monetizing developers directly by charging to use their tools. It includes Google's API and Cloud offerings, but leaves out the Android ecosystem. It includes Twilio, but leaves out Infobip, one of their primary competitors, likely due to Infobip's initial enterprise-first rather than developer-first approach.

Jewell's research also leaves out the value created by hardware-centric companies, for example, Apple and Samsung. Apple alone has paid out $155 billion in revenue share payments to Developers since the App Store launched in 2008,[2] meaning Apple's retained share is worth approximately $66 billion. Not bad for a business model that Steve Jobs was against initially.[3]

Away from company-specific revenue, other associated data points act as indicators for the vibrancy and importance of this sector. As mentioned in Chapter 3, Crunchbase[4] lists more than 1200 "Developer API" companies, a small subsection of the developer-led economy. At the macro level, BSA The Software Alliance values the Total Value-Added GDP contribution of software to the economy of the United States at a staggering $1.6 trillion.[5]

As you will appreciate, there is much complexity in calculating the true impact, and much of the necessary data is not in the public domain. We know, for example, that the Ford Motor Company spent $7 billion on R&D in 2020;[6] however, there is no data on the direct or indirect revenues generated by its Developer Program.[7]

---

[2]https://www.cnbc.com/2020/01/07/apple-app-store-had-estimated-gross-sales-of-50-billion-in-2019.html

[3]https://appleinsider.com/articles/18/07/10/the-revolution-steve-jobs-resisted-apples-app-store-marks-10-years-of-third-party-innovation

[4]https://www.crunchbase.com/hub/developer-apis-companies#section-overview

[5]https://softwareimpact.bsa.org/

[6]https://www.statista.com/statistics/260867/fords-research-development-expenditures/

[7]https://developer.ford.com/

We are vocal in our support for better data to quantify the Developer Economy and are working to help provide it. Along with this book, we believe better data will significantly increase the attention of Developer Relations at a board and executive level.

There is perhaps no stronger example of the perils of underestimating the value of developers to your own company and the future of your entire industry than the cell phone operating system wars of the early 2000s, as outlined in the following case study.

Case Study: Mobile Apps – Those Who Didn't Believe

In the early 2000s, the mobile industry moved toward an app store model, which signaled a shift away from accessing the Internet and associated services via mobile operator–controlled portals. This was not a pain-free transition, as the mobile operators fought to maintain control of the user experience and associated service revenues. Established players like Nokia/Symbian, RIM/BlackBerry, and Microsoft/Windows Mobile attempted to placate the all-powerful mobile operators. This compromise only succeeded in delivering a substandard user experience, which ultimately led to their demise.

It was the arrival of the iPhone in 2007 and Apple's entry into the telecoms arena when things changed. You had a handset manufacturer that understood the power and potential of software and had the confidence that the demand for their product would empower them to dictate how things would work from this point forward.

The mobile operators were largely removed as the "gatekeepers of the walled garden," and Apple embarked on establishing new relationships with app developers to build for iOS. This strategy has delivered back \$155 billion in revenue to developers, while all the original power brokers in the mobile industry have seen their control crumble.

The power of a two-sided marketplace was evident. The most desirable phone had the most comprehensive choice and the highest quality of apps with premium positioning in the market, which created a flywheel of success. Despite having a five-year head start on Apple and all the advantages of being the incumbents in a high-margin world, the mobile operators and existing handset manufacturers were caught cold by the new market entrant who embraced a philosophy of co-creation with software developers. This was in stark contrast to the defensive and control-oriented mindset of the telecoms industry. You can see the results in Figure 4-2.

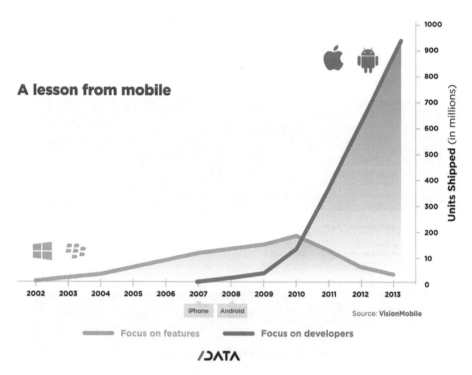

Figure 4-2. A lesson from mobile, by SlashData

Supplemental Value of the Developer-Led Economy

There are other considerations regarding the value of the developer economy and the benefits of launching a developer play for your company other than the direct revenue benefits.

Figure 4-3 shows some additional benefits to an organization for investing in a developer proposition, inspired by a presentation by Jed Ng, Head of Rakuten RapidAPI, on the API Value Creation model given at APIDays London.[8]

---

[8]https://www.slideshare.net/APIdays_official/apidays-london-2019-value-in-the-api-economy-insights-from-the-worlds-largest-api-marketplace-with-jed-ng-rakuten

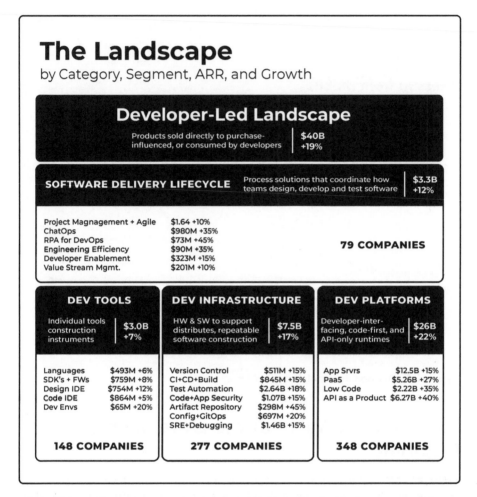

Figure 4-3. Developer-Led Landscape compiled by Tyler Jewell, of Dell Technologies Capital

Let's review these supplemental values in more detail.

External Creation Value

Investing in a Developer Relations play can bring both value generation and cost-saving opportunities. If you are a Developer Plus company, working with developers represents a new channel to market for your organization and provides an opportunity to offer entirely new business models. You may be following a strategy designed to supplement your own internal new product development efforts by enabling third parties to build on and extend your "stack" or "platform." You may also look to make your existing product(s) more attractive to your end users by establishing an innovation ecosystem around it, for example, by providing an app store.

External Cost Reduction

Implementing a self-service channel for developers will lower your cost of sales, meaning – if executed correctly – your customer (the developer) shouldn't need to interact with your people to trial and adopt your product. If you have a self-supporting community (either on your site or somewhere else like Stack Overflow), your cost to serve will also be lower than a traditional product. In many of these instances, the developer will not contact you for help, rather will figure things out for themselves via your docs and by searching historical answers for similar issues.

Internal Value Creation

Architecting to support a developer play presents an opportunity for your own product and engineering teams to reuse the same capabilities, tools, and resources. This not only allows them to be more efficient, it provides the opportunity for them to experiment and bring your own products to market faster.

Internal Cost Reduction

By having this architecture available internally, it may reduce your cost of R&D through the reuse of resources and services as well as simplified access to services via microservices and APIs.

Summary

Thanks to research from Tyler Jewell, we can estimate the developer-led economy to be at least $40 billion, with a 19% annual rate of return (ARR) growth rate. We emphasize "at least" due to the data excluded from his report including developer revenue generated from companies like Apple, those that don't have formal developer programs, or a developer-first go-to-market approach. There are also supplemental ways of assessing value like cost reductions and additional value creation. We've also witnessed how companies that took the approach of implementing developer programs outmaneuvered their competitors.

This part of the book wraps up a common understanding of Developer Relations and its value. Next up, we'll dive into what makes DevRel unique.

Key Differentiators

What Is Unique About Developer Relations

After reading Part I, we hope you now have an understanding of what Developer Relations is and the components of the Developer Relations Framework – developer marketing, Developer Experience, developer education, developer success, and community. More importantly, we hope you have an appreciation for the value of the developer-led economy and why you might want to implement a Developer Relations program in your organization to capitalize on that opportunity.

You might think having a developer strategy is simply adding a few developer-focused messages into your marketing or hiring a developer advocate to deal with developer support questions. Of course, a successful Developer Relations strategy and subsequent program is much more than that.

In Part II, we'll look at what differentiates DevRel and why it requires changes to both your strategy and tactics.

The key differentiators of DevRel we'll review in this part include:

- The target audience and developers as decision makers.

- Categorizing the organizations pursuing a Developer Relations strategy – Developer First and Developer Plus.

- The Developer Relations business model – Business to Developer, or B2D, and its variations.

- The types of developer products.

The Audience: Developers

The target audience of developers is of course one of the main differentiators of Developer Relations. Identifying the right target for your program and engaging developers throughout their journey is your challenge. Success requires you and your team to be experts in their field as well as having the knowledge and appreciation of developers.

In this chapter, we'll explore the size of the developer population and then review the typical characteristics of this audience or "developer truisms" and how they inform your developer program strategy and activities. We will also examine the myths around "it's easy to be a developer today" and introduce one of their key motivations – the sense of pride in saying "I made this."

Developer Market Sizing

How many developers are there? That is a question we get asked regularly from those wanting to understand the developer community as a whole, from those needing market sizing as they segment and build their communities, and from others looking for investment.

© Caroline Lewko, James Parton 2021
C. Lewko and J. Parton, *Developer Relations*,
https://doi.org/10.1007/978-1-4842-7164-3_5

We have witnessed the market size of the global developer population grow with the rise in the importance of software, SaaS, APIs, and other emerging technologies, as we saw in Chapters 3 and 4.

There are several sources you can use to determine the overall market size of developers; each has its own methodology and definitions of developers:

- **SlashData**[1] – Estimated in Q3 2021 that there were 24.3 million active software developers globally, out of which 15.3 million are software professionals.

- **EDC (Evans Data)**[2] – In 2019, estimated 23.9 million software developers worldwide, almost doubling from their estimate of 12 million in 2006.

- **Stack Overflow**[3] – Estimates that 20–25 million developers visit their site every month (professionals and university-level students combined).

- **Statistica**[4] – Estimated 23.9 million software developers in 2019.

Figure 5-1 shows the growth of the global developer population since 2017, according to SlashData.

Growth of the global developer population

Active software developers (in millions)

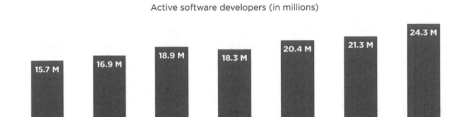

Figure 5-1. Developer population growth, 2017–2021, by SlashData

---

[1]https://dashboard.slashdata.co/
[2]https://evansdata.com/press/viewRelease.php?pressID=278
[3]https://insights.stackoverflow.com/survey/2020
[4]https://www.statista.com/statistics/627312/worldwide-developer-population/

It is essential to note that there is no simple single definition for "Developer." Consequently, there is room for interpretation on the sizing estimates of the number of developers. As such, these current estimates of the global developer population of 20–25 million developers are likely low.

There is a wide variety of titles and professions beyond pure "software developer" or "software engineer," upon which many of the research companies base their data. With the advent of low-code/no-code solutions, there are also many individuals that now use some type of development product in their role or project which could now be legitimate targets for your Developer Program. Many individuals have previously been excluded from the umbrella term of "developer."

Developers could also include product managers, project managers, hardware developers and embedded developers, games and VR artists, UX designers, DevOps and MLOps, data scientists, and machine learning engineers, to name just a few. Stack Overflow has the broadest definition based on the job descriptions of the contributors to its annual Developer research,[5] perhaps explaining why their population estimation is the highest.

It's also essential to realize that developers represent a very diverse market demographically. Therefore, making too many generalizations when you do your market sizing won't be effective and may actually be counterproductive to your DevRel program and your business model calculations.

Here are two simple examples to underscore this point:

- **Using a basic filter of region.**

  As you can see in Figure 5-2, North America has the highest number of software developers, while Europe is close behind. From a go-to-market perspective, it's critical to understand that Europe is not a single market entity, as there is complexity around spoken languages, law, currencies, and culture.

- **Using a basic filter on programming language.**

  Based on SlashData's numbers, if your product was designed to appeal purely to Python developers, your global addressable market falls from 21.3 million to 9 million, a reduction of 57%. If you only wanted to focus on professional Python developers, that reduces your addressable market again to 6.3 million or a drop of 70%.

---

[5]https://insights.stackoverflow.com/survey/2020#developer-roles

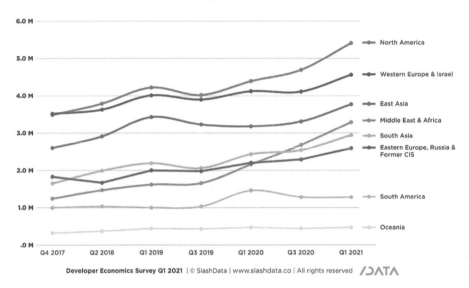

Developer population by region

Active software developers (in millions)

Figure 5-2. Developer population by region by SlashData

These examples start to show just how quickly your addressable market is reduced, encouraging you to be mindful of the breadth of your target, as well as allowing you to be much more targeted in your messaging.

Our chapter on segmentation will show in detail how to create your own segmentation and personas so you can focus on the developers that will be successful with your product.

Demographics and data are one way to look at and understand developers. However, you must also be aware of some general characteristics of developers, so you'll better understand their diversity, personalities, and some of the challenges of working with them. We call these developer truisms.

Developer Truisms

Research and anecdotal evidence shows there are a number of truisms around the general characteristics of developers. For a more in-depth read, we encourage you to read books such as *Coders: The Making of a New Tribe and the Remaking of the World*[6] and *Ask Your Developer*, by Twilio's CEO, Jeff Lawson.[7]

---

[6] https://www.clivethompson.net/
[7] https://www.askyourdeveloper.com/

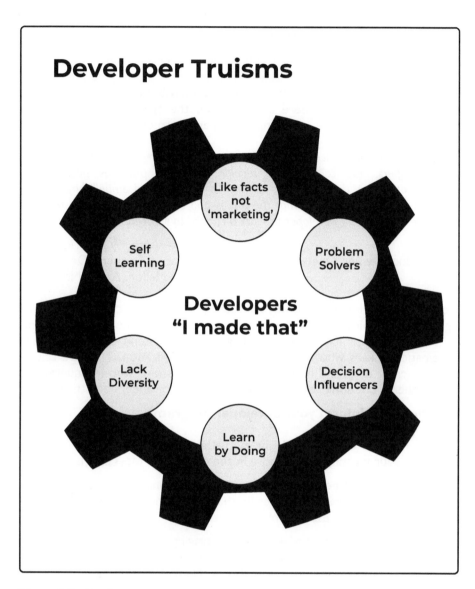

Figure 5-3. Developer truisms

You'll see in Figure 5-3 some of the most important developer truisms. These truisms revolve around developers' main motivator, which is to create something they can be proud of. That gives them the opportunity to say, **"I made that."**

We'll review each of the truisms next and note how you should use them in your approach to strategy and tactics in your Developer Relations Program.

Like Facts Not Marketing

We are not sure any group of individuals "likes" to be marketed to; still, this truism is very relevant to developers. This truism is partially due to a lot of clumsy marketing targeted at developers, generally because of an overall lack of understanding of this core audience and the types of messaging that resonates with them (see an example of what not to do in Figure 5-4).

> *Respect the differences between traditional marketing and marketing to developers. You can't inherit regular marketing practices because developers are different. Tone of voice is crucial, avoid embellishments and provide context for what the tool is and can do. And focus on use cases to give your developer product a chance to succeed.*
>
> —Anthony Fabbricino
> Product Owner, Open Banking APIs, Wells Fargo, Formerly DevRel at Adobe, BNY Mellon, AT&T, Nokia

Professional developers are highly educated (79% hold a bachelor's degree or higher[8]) and typically have degrees in computer science or engineering. Whether it is their nature or schooling, developers tend to be logical and systematic thinkers who value efficiency and optimization. They are critical thinkers, crave data, and have little tolerance for those who masquerade as "one of them," but don't really speak their language or understand their issues.

How does this inform your developer program?

- Err on the side of being factual about your product in your messaging (see more in the chapter on messaging).

- There is freedom for your communications to be much more technical and specific than traditional mainstream marketing. Less fluff, more substance.

- Have developers review your messaging for accuracy and tone before you make it public to avoid potential problems. See an example of clumsy marketing to developers in Figure 5-4.

---

[8]https://insights.stackoverflow.com/survey/2019#developer-profile-_-developer-role-and-gender

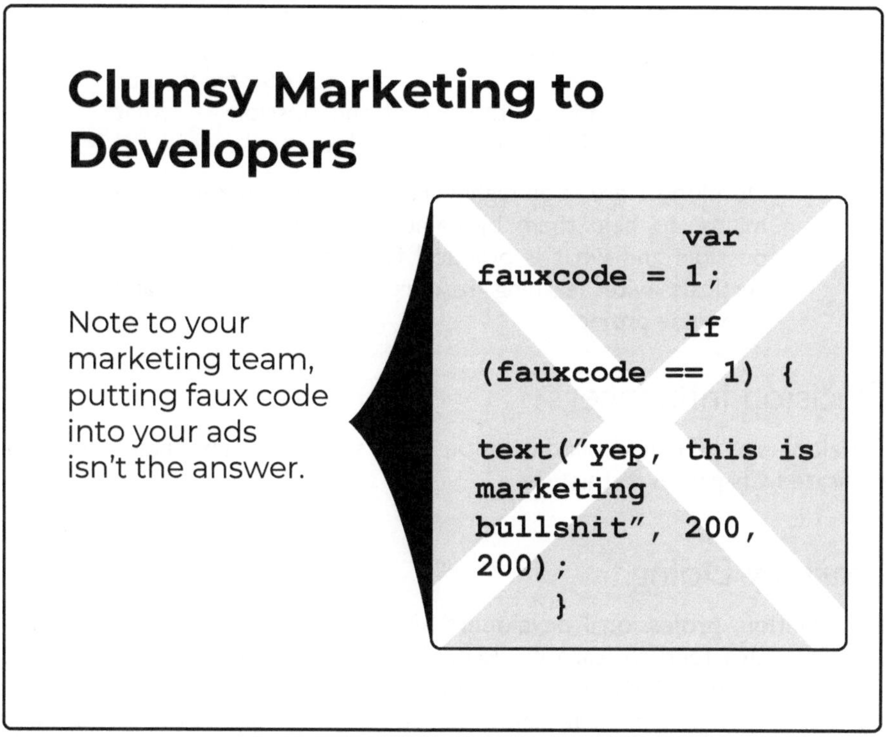

Clumsy Marketing to Developers

Note to your marketing team, putting faux code into your ads isn't the answer.

```
             var
fauxcode = 1;
             if
(fauxcode == 1) {

text("yep, this is
marketing
bullshit", 200,
200);
    }
```

Figure 5-4. An example of clumsy marketing to developers

Developers Are Creative Problem Solvers

There is a belief that all developers are creative geniuses that can create the next world-changing company anytime they put their mind to it. Indeed, developers are definitely motivated by the ability to solve problems. There is also no doubt that significant creativity is required to first imagine the possible and then create, experiment, build, and break in the most efficient and elegant way possible.

However, as creative as coding can be, not all developers are born to create the next big thing. As well, many do not have the necessary levels of experience in either coding or in the particular business vertical they operate within.

How does this inform your developer program?

- Motivation, experience, passions, and types of education combine to vary a developer's ability to create.

- Think about what you can provide to entice developers to engage their imagination and passion with you and your product. Focus on the desired outcomes, not activities. It's about "the art of the possible" – what developers can build with your product.

- Developers aren't all highly creative, and they can't read minds, so help them by painting a picture of what is possible and what is practical for specific industries or verticals with learning resources like use cases and showcase projects.

Decision Influencers

Developers as influencers and decision makers is such an important topic; we dedicated Chapter 6 to this.

Learn by Doing

By definition, professional developers are hands-on with technology every day. They also tend to learn by doing. Developers want to get started and figure things out quickly. Becuase some developers like to work late into the night or may well be in a different time zone to your support team, they need to be able to find answers quickly at any time of the day and learn new things for themselves without needing to contact your company directly.

How does this inform your developer program?

- Provide developers with the means to "see" quickly how your product works by offering code samples, quickstarts, or getting started guides in your documentation (more on this in Chapter 17).

- Peer reviews, recommendations, and showcase projects will be far more compelling than any marketing speak you can create.

- Developers want to be the first to know, but not necessarily the first to try. Incent early adopters to take the plunge. And recognize community members who lead the way for others – and they'll keep doing it.

- Provide more self-service options like sign up for free, no credit card entry required, free credits to encourage immediate experimentation, etc.

These tendencies help explain the popularity of sites like Stack Overflow, which are perceived to be mostly free of sales and marketing messages and instead are solutions-oriented and self-service.

Lack Diversity

Back in the 1950s, most of the first-ever coders were women.[9] Today, developers are upwards of 90% male, according to most surveys.[10] This is starting to change, as there has been a concerted effort to address the gender imbalance, especially in countries like the United States, the UK, and India.

There are also differences when you drill down into specific job roles commonly gathered together in the umbrella term "developer." For instance, in a recent Stack Overflow survey, developers who are data scientists or academic researchers are about ten times more likely to be men than women. In contrast, developers who are system admins or DevOps specialists are 25–30 times more likely to be men than women. Women have the highest representation as front-end developers, designers, data scientists, data analysts, QA or test developers, scientists, and educators.[11]

Diversity of course isn't just about gender. It's important to be mindful of cultural, racial, religious, age, sexual orientation, and disability differences.

How does this inform your developer program?

- If you genuinely value diversity (vs. virtue signaling), position both your marketing messaging, your recruitment, and company culture to appeal to a diverse workforce which will give you a valuable advantage.

Self-Learning

The developer workforce may have less experience than you think, and postformal education is mostly self-taught. Data from the 2020 Stack Overflow Developer Survey[12] finds:

- 17% of developers learned to code in the last five years, 40% in the last ten years.

---

[9] https://www.clivethompson.net/
[10] https://insights.stackoverflow.com/survey/2019#demographics
[11] https://insights.stackoverflow.com/survey/2019#developer-profile-_-developer-role-and-gender
[12] https://insights.stackoverflow.com/survey/2020

- 40% have been coding professionally for less than five years.

- 86.7% taught themselves a new language, framework, or tool without taking a formal course.

Technology is fast moving. For instance, TensorFlow was only released at the end of 2015, so it would be unreasonable to expect a developer to have ten years of TensorFlow experience. When mobile app development started, we recall that certain hiring companies were just lazy, recycling their standard job description template which required developers to have ten years of Android development experience when Android was only two years old at the time!

How does this inform your developer program?

- You must do your research and set expectations based on the experience levels of your target developers.

- You need to help them learn with things like code samples, learning resources, GitHub repos, video tutorials, and workshops.

- Provide low- or no-cost self-service options so they can learn when it is convenient for them, not you.

Is It Easy to Be a Developer Today?

We have high levels of empathy for developers, an important trait for everyone in Developer Relations. Development is not easy, and it takes time. Today, there is a plethora of companies and products available for developers, all vying for their attention. Along with no-code/low-code options and plenty of resources for developers to learn and share knowledge about development, it's no wonder the developer population is growing. However, we believe coding and development are more challenging today than they have ever been, precisely for those reasons – there is more choice and more noise. See the differences in Table 5-1 and let us know if you think development is easier or harder today.

Table 5-1. Is Development Easier or Harder Today?

Is development easier or harder today?

DEVELOPMENT IS EASIER TODAY, BECAUSE:	DEVELOPMENT IS HARDER TODAY, BECAUSE:
Lower barriers to entry - free tools, free trials	More programming languages
Growing recognition for developers	More tools - noise & confusion
	More competition for work
Abstracted code and less code required to achieve your goal	Boom or bust economics and supply/demand issues - extremes of highly paid roles vs. the threat of offshoring
Tools, tools, tools - a tool for most jobs	Unrealistic expectations from leadership
Lots of online learning resources	Low code / no code devaluing skills
Communities to get support	Noise in the industry, FOMO

Summary

As mentioned at the start of the book, the **goal of Developer Relations is about enabling a developer to be successful with your product.** Therefore, remember these tips as you build out your developer program:

- Match your expectations to the experience and capabilities of your target audience.

- Manage developer expectations by providing the best information and learning experience based on their needs.

- Ignite their imagination to create, and then get out of their way by reducing the friction for them to get started and find commercial success.

- **Developers are driven by one primary emotion: the pride to know and say "I made that!"** Once you have helped them create something of value, celebrate their achievements.

Developers As Decision Makers

As the software and technology sectors grow, so does the number of developers. Hand in hand has been the rise of developers' decision-making influence within organizations. Fueled by advances in business models discussed in Chapter 3, many developer tools now have a free entry point or offer low-risk pay-as-you-go pricing. Today, developers can find out about a new tool, trial it, and buy it in minutes, independently of any formal procurement process in their company.

Surveys by many research firms have **clearly proven that developers are a vital part of the decision-making process for new tools**. Developer Media found that 60% of developers can approve or reject a tool purchase.[1] SlashData found that 77% of developers have a say in tool selection.[2] Peter

[1] https://developermedia.com/developers-influence-tool-purchase/
[2] https://www.slashdata.co/blog/developers-purchase-tools

© Caroline Lewko, James Parton 2021
C. Lewko and J. Parton, *Developer Relations*,
https://doi.org/10.1007/978-1-4842-7164-3_6

Levine of Andreessen Horowitz also echoed that – *"Developers are more than just influencers inside the enterprise – they're now buyers, too."*[3]

Whether developers are the actual buyers or the bridgehead to get you in the door for the enterprise-sized sale, your company is probably losing out on significant sales if you aren't considering developers. Who can afford to do that?

This chapter looks at the developer as a decision maker and the criteria used by those who are part of the developer decision-making unit.

The Developer Decision-Making Unit

A key part of developer marketing is to understand how decisions are made around tool or resource adoption within your target customers' organization. Often, we think it's an individual coder merely saying, "I'll use this API or IDE," but that is not usually the case. Organizations come in various sizes and shapes, so a variety of people make decisions on which tools and products to adopt. Once you understand the decision-making process and who is part of that process, you can begin understanding their needs and tailoring your messaging and activities to match.

Who Makes the Decision?

We use a **"developer decision-making unit" (DDMU)** concept to help us map who we need to focus on. We start with these two steps:

1. Consider the **developer organization's structure and context**: Is it a one-person band, is it a startup, a small agency, or a large enterprise?

2. Consider **your product's context**: How widely will it impact the organization and the products it is developing? Is it a tool an individual contributor would choose to use (say, a text editor), or is it a more strategic component that would integrate into a mission-critical application that can only have 00.001% downtime each year?

---

[3]https://soundcloud.com/a16z/selling-to-developers-open-source-business-models

With these steps in mind, we can begin identifying the DDMU's makeup and put names to roles. The roles within a DDMU include:

- **An Initiator** – The person who begins the process by raising awareness internally. This could range from a developer who found your product via a Google search to an internal purchasing or procurement person responsible for sourcing the organization's technology needs.

- **A Technical decision maker** – The person who evaluates the technical aspects, such as compatibility with existing resources and the fit with the company's technical strategy, security, reliability, and so on. This could range from a technical lead on the development team, a Product Manager, someone in DevOps, or the company's CTO.

- **A Business decision maker/budget holder** – The person who evaluates the commercial aspects including pricing, business model, and return on investment and gives approval to make the purchase. This could be the founding team at a startup, a CFO, a specialist procurement person, or C-level management.

- **Influencers** – The people who may not have explicit decision-making authority but can influence the overall decision. This is usually internal developers who have tried your product firsthand and so are in the best position to provide input.

- **An Approver** – The person who makes a final yes/no decision. This can vary widely depending on the organization's size and structure.

Keep in mind that this is a model and that the DDMU will vary across organizations. In some cases, a single person will play multiple roles; in other cases, specific roles may not exist. But using a variation of the DDMU model to match your situation will help you to understand the different stakeholders and values that contribute to the decision to adopt a developer product. Furthermore, the DDMU is fluid, meaning it can change depending on the situation or product, and it can also be very informal.

All of these variables depend on understanding your target developers and the organizations in which they reside. We will help you figure that out in Chapter 12.

Decision Criteria

Once we understand who is making the decisions, we can explore the criteria they use to evaluate your developer product. We can make a general distinction between technical criteria and business criteria, outlined in Tables 6-1 and 6-2.

Table 6-1. Technical Decision Criteria

Technical Decision Criteria pt. 1

Criteria	May be expressed as:
Features and functionality that answer a specific need	Does it do X?
How it compares to other competitive choices in the market	Is it better than Y?
Level and quality of technical support	Will I get the help I need? Is it easy to use? Are there different levels of support we can buy? Are there Service Level Agreements?
Customizations and Customer-integration	Can we get custom modifications specific to our needs? Will they be an expensive "one-off" or "modular"
Credability & stability of the product & vendor	How long has the vendor been around? Who are your reference customers? How long has the product been available? Will it remain available and continue to be updated? Are there emerging products or technologies that will make the offering obsolete?
Community	Who else is using this? Is there an open source component? Is there an existing user base? How active is the community?

(continued)

Table 6-1. *(continued)*

Technical Decision Criteria   pt. 2

Criteria	May be expressed as:
Compatibility	How does this fit with our existing technology stack? Will my development team need training? What risks does this introduce?
Switching costs	How much technical debt will we have? What is the match with existing in house skills?
Internal willingness to embrace	Hesitancy to embrace change or displays of a "not invented here" culture.
How good is it, really?	Cut through the marketing BS, show me real evidence of impact. Let me speak to some of your existing customers.
Does it meet certifications?	Does it satisfy the certifications or regulatory requirements that our organization is bound by (e.g., ISO, financial regulations, health regulations, etc.)?

Table 6-2. Business Decision Criteria

Business Decision Criteria

Criteria	May be expressed as:
Costs for integration and running	What will it cost to start, and what will it cost to operate?
Time and/or money savings over the long run	What will we save by using this, and can we quantify it?
Additional revenue/profit	Can we quantify the monetary benefit?
Contractual terms & conditions	Are the terms agreeable, will legal approve?
Reputation	Is this a brand or technology we feel comfortable being associated with? What is the size and activity level of the community? Is the community sentiment positive or negative?
Overall Return on Investment case	What's the benefit and ROI when we combine all this?

With a good understanding of the various decision makers and what's important to them, you can then focus your messaging to address their individual concerns.

Matching Messaging to Decision Makers

Using the preceding decision-making criteria and your understanding of who the decision makers are, you can then shape your messaging, activities, and education resources to best match their interests and concerns. You can work through this by asking a series of questions about your product and decision makers:

1. **Who has the need for our product or understands its benefits?** Is it the coder, is it the product manager responsible for monetization, or someone else? Make a clear technical and business case available to the DDMU, customized to their specific situation and context. Deliver this through customer presentations, product fact sheets, whitepapers, references in analyst research reports, case studies, example apps, etc.

2. **Who will implement our product?** This could be a coder, a QA specialist, DevOps, data analyst, customer support, integration specialist, etc. To this group, emphasize ease of use and implementation through documentation, forum support, quickstart guides, and example code. Offer practical support like hosting an internal hackathon to get the company's developers hands-on with your tech.

3. **Who is the ultimate decision maker?** Is it the individual developer, a team manager, a CTO? They need to see the summary and outcome of the business and tech cases – the combination of the why and the how. The following can be the most persuasive for the decision maker: testimonials, case studies, cost-benefit analysis, and quantified ROIs.

Completing this mapping exercise up front and having prepared answers to obvious questions will help stimulate trials and close sales. Often, you will use a two-pronged approach to attack a new opportunity. The DevRel team may be forming a relationship with the company's developer and technical teams, while your sales team may be working on the decision makers.

The language, materials, and resources used should be tailored for the audience, be they technical or business. Great sales engineers come to the forefront, where these lines meet and blur. The sales engineers' ability to switch and mix business and technical aspects can be the vital cog in closing an opportunity.

We explore this further in the later chapters.

Summary

Developers are significant decision makers when it comes to trialing and purchasing developer products. Ignore this fact at your company's peril. Understanding the developer decision-making unit (DDMU) and preparing for it will help in the strategic and tactical decisions you will make for your developer program.

Developer First and Developer Plus

Classification of DevRel Organizations

Before we dive into the nuances of DevRel business models, we thought we should dedicate a chapter to classifying and quantifying the organizations which engage in DevRel.

Organization Types

As a DevRel professional, understanding the type of organization you are operating within is an important consideration for a range of reasons. Some reasons are obvious and visible; others are subtle and hidden. Organizational factors include identity, purpose, priorities, and culture. Business factors include the business model and the type of pricing that a company offers, which we review in Chapter 8. These factors can ultimately make or break your program and most definitely affect your strategy and go-to-market activities.

© Caroline Lewko, James Parton 2021
C. Lewko and J. Parton, *Developer Relations*,
https://doi.org/10.1007/978-1-4842-7164-3_7

We have defined two categories of organizations that operate DevRel programs:

1. Developer First
2. Developer Plus

Developer First

Developer First (Dev First) companies create and sell products specifically designed to be used by developers. The product may be a platform that a developer uses to create an application, or it could be something like an API which is a component of their application. Regardless, the entire Dev First company has a single focus in seeing developers as their primary market.

With that, the Dev First go-to-market strategy is aimed at a bottom-up approach in considering developers not only as the main user of their product but as the main decision maker in the buying process of their product.

We recall during the late 2000s, investors were initially reluctant to fund companies which provided developer tools. Eventually, startups like Flurry and Crittercism convinced them and had successful exits. As mentioned in Chapter 3, it wasn't until Twilio blazed the trail, that a developer focus was deemed a viable stand-alone business model.

A few examples of Developer First companies include:

- **APIs** – Twilio, Stripe
- **Databases** – MongoDB
- **HDKs** – Arduino
- **Tools and platforms** – PerceptiLabs, Splunk, Unity
- **Services** – GitHub, Stack Overflow

As you may suspect, life can be sweeter for a DevRel professional inside a Dev First company. Their company's sole purpose is to build tools for developers; therefore, there is little confusion around the simple question "why are developers important?".

Developer Plus

Developer Plus (Dev Plus) companies' primary market is selling products or services for businesses or consumers. In addition, they also have products available to developers, which they believe benefits their strategy in some way.

The reasons for extending their business in this way are many and varied. It may be an opportunity to open new channels to market, extend into new innovative use cases and products, contribute to an innovation strategy, or a method to optimize or enhance existing products.

A Dev Plus organization may go to market with developers as partners, through a marketplace, as a stand-alone product/app, or as an add-on tool to an existing product. The products of Dev Plus organizations may be revenue producing, or they may be entirely free.

Examples of Developer Plus companies range from hardware manufacturers like Qualcomm, Samsung, and Apple to financial institutions like Capital One and Santander. Larger software businesses like Microsoft, Salesforce, Amazon, and Google could be considered hybrid organizations. Although their original business model was not developer centric, they have evolved substantial parts of their companies to serve developers, like Microsoft Azure and Google Cloud. AWS has built such momentum that it now accounts for more than half of Amazon's revenue.[1]

While Developer Plus companies come in all shapes and sizes, by definition their main reason for being is something other than serving developers. Ford sells cars, AT&T sells communications, and Santander sells financial services. It is natural they see the world and prioritize according to their core business. This can create a number of challenges for the DevRel professional. We will explore some of the challenges of corporate alignment in Chapter 10 and make note of issues to consider throughout this book.

How Many Companies Practice Developer Relations?

Indicated in the annual State Of Developer Relations market research from 2020, there are more DevRel professionals working in Dev Plus companies than Dev First companies, as shown in Figure 7-1.

---

[1] https://www.businessinsider.com/andy-jassy-aws-amazon-spin-off-break-up-tim-bray-2021-2

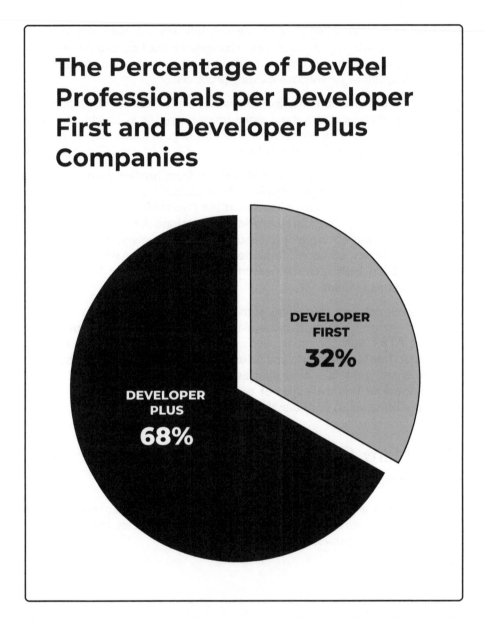

Figure 7-1. The percentage of DevRel professionals per Developer First and Developer Plus companies

So you may be wondering how many Developer Relations programs are there? We've wondered that too. As noted in Chapter 4, Tyler Jewell has tracked over 1000 companies whose products were sold to, purchase-influenced by, or consumed by software developers, but this doesn't directly translate to a conclusive list of Developer Relations programs.

There is a lack of public data on how many companies actually have a DevRel offering (which may or may not have a formal DevRel Program,) so we started an open crowd-sourced directory of DevRel programs to try and fill this gap. Please check it out and add your company's entry. Over time, we hope this grows into a valuable community resource. The directory is hosted at DevRelBook.com.

The Market Leaders by Community

Another way to review this market is to look at the size of the developer community associated with an organization. SlashData lists 22 organizations with communities of over one million developers.[2] We've updated the list in Table 7-1 to include the type of organization. Interestingly, 55% of the 22 are Dev First companies, and 45% are Dev Plus companies.

Note some of the listed organizations do not operate a Developer Program as defined in this book, as they are service providers to developers as opposed to companies that have products for developers. We review these types in more detail in Chapter 9.

---

[2]SlashData – https://www.1milliondeveloperclub.com/

Table 7-1. Developer Communities of over One Million Community Members Noted As Developer First or Developer Plus Organizations

Developer Communities of over one million community members

ORGANIZATION	ESTIMATED SIZE OF COMMUNITY (MILLIONS OF DEVELOPERS)	DEVELOPER FIRST	DEVELOPER PLUS
Github	41	✓	
Apple	20		✓
Stack Overflow	16	✓	
Bitbucket	10	✓	
Hackerrank	6	✓	
Twilio	5	✓	
Salesforce	5		✓
Celebros	5	✓	
J-Frog	5	✓	
Digital Ocean	3.5	✓	
HackerEarth	2.9	✓	
SAP Cloud Platform	2.8		✓
Visual Tools	2.6		✓
Docker	2	✓	
HERE	2		✓
Kaggle	2		✓
Tencent Cloud	2		✓
BrowserStack	2	✓	
Mapbox	1.6		✓
WeChat Apps	1.5		✓
TopCoder	1.4	✓	
Google Cloud	1		✓

Summary

Organizations which practice Developer Relations today are categorized into two buckets – Developer First, whose market is primarily developers, and Developer Plus, in which Developers are a secondary market. Each category comes with its own challenges and directly influences the way they do business which we explore in more detail throughout the book.

Business Models and Monetization Strategies

Business to Developer (B2D)

If the target audience is the first differentiator, the second major differentiator of Developer Relations is the business model. A business model is how an organization captures value. As we read in Chapter 4, value in developer products can come in the form of dollars generated by selling products or services, but it can also be achieved via other means such as through a reduction in costs and time and the community and relationships the DevRel team build and nurture.

A number of building blocks go into creating a business model. If you need to read up on this topic, we suggest reviewing the Business Model Canvas[1] that is especially popular in startup education.

---

[1] https://en.wikipedia.org/wiki/Business_Model_Canvas

© Caroline Lewko, James Parton 2021
C. Lewko and J. Parton, *Developer Relations*,
https://doi.org/10.1007/978-1-4842-7164-3_8

The business model for Developer Relations is called "**Business to Developer" or B2D**. In this chapter, we'll investigate the uniqueness of B2D and its variations in Developer First and Developer Plus organizations. In particular, we observe the differences in the value chain, especially where the value is exchanged or captured.

It's an Input

In B2D, you are not offering a solution or a preformed product.

You are always offering an input into another product.

The Lego analogy is often used when describing the B2D business model. It's not about selling a finished product; rather, component pieces or tools are offered with the promise that something could be created. You, as the input provider, do not necessarily need to know what the developer may be cooking up, in the same way that Lego does not need to know what you might create when they mold a plastic brick. This is a curious situation to be in, as, ultimately, your success is entirely dependent on your customers' creativity and ingenuity to create something that will become popular. Welcome to the world of open innovation! This is described by Henry Chesbrough as business transformation through co-creation.[2]

There are certainly B2B and B2C companies which sell components. However, their marketing and sales process and the value chain are very different which we'll explore in more detail in the following.

The Value Chain

First, let's look at the value chain. A value chain maps out the steps a product goes through to get to its end user.

If we take a close look at a traditional B2C or B2B value chain, it goes something like this:

A product (value) is created by the organization, there is marketing to create awareness, and there is a channel through which to purchase. Once the product is purchased (value exchange) from the channel, there may be some after-sales support or a community to participate in. The gong is rung and the sales team is able to show a sale in their metrics.

---

[2]http://openinnovation.net/about-2/open-innovation-definition/

B2D isn't as straightforward and goes something like this:

> A component or tool is created by the organization. There is marketing to create awareness, but the marketing isn't focused on pushing a finished product. It is centered around inspiring developers in how the component can be combined with other technologies to create or enhance a different product. The priority of DevRel is to remove any friction that would stop or delay the developer's success in adopting the components.

In contrast to the traditional model, the B2B value chain is not yet complete:

> From there, the developer builds or enhances their own product and hence creates value. Once the developer has achieved demonstrable 'success', their endeavors are then showcased and celebrated by the DevRel program and incorporated into their marketing in the form of case studies and other materials to inspire future developers. Additionally, the developer gets ongoing support in scaling their solution and for any future software updates.

Figure 8-1 pictorially compares the traditional activities of B2B and B2C organizations against the activities in the B2D model.

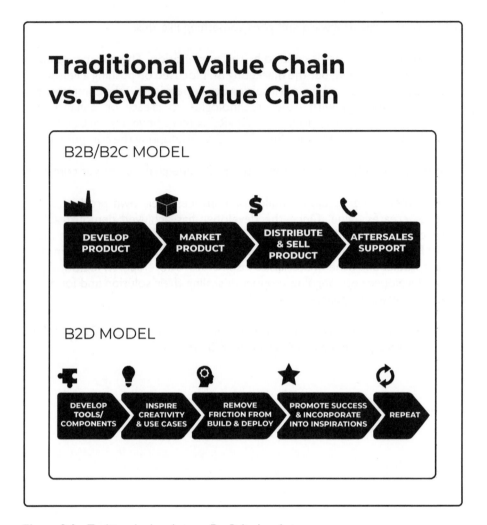

Figure 8-1. Traditional value chain vs. DevRel value chain

Let's drill down into these differences and see how they affect your strategy and go-to-market planning.

B2B, B2C, vs. B2D

Based on the diagram in Figure 8-1, let's break down the key differences between the business models of B2B, B2C, and B2D in terms of sales strategies, value creation, target marketing, and sales cycles. In Table 8-1, we compare the key differences between the three models.

Table 8-1. Differences Between B2B, B2C, and B2D Business Models

The Differences Between B2B, B2C and B2D Business Models

	B2B	B2C	B2D
Sales Strategy	Relationship Driven	Product Driven	Outcome Driven
Sales & Marketing Approach	Benefits & Solution	Features & Aspiration	Community & Relationship led, Enablement & Inspiration
Target	Organizations	Individuals	Both
Sales Cycle	Long	Short	Both
Value Capture/ Success Measure	Product Sold	Product Sold	Component used in new product

In B2B, the product is sold, with sales made to other organizations exclusively. The sales cycles are typically long. The traditional modus operandi for B2B is focused on the sales team building relationships with decision makers in their target accounts or prospects. The salespeople then network within the account to build awareness and trust. Their sales approach is to focus on the benefits of their solution, framed to solve the problems they have uncovered in the target account.

The introduction of SaaS had a direct impact on B2B. It reduced the need for a prospect to speak or interact with the sales team in order to learn more or buy the product. There was a shift to self-service, where the prospect could learn and purchase without ever needing to speak to Sales. This sped up the sales cycle for early trials and small accounts, but bigger accounts still typically rely on the traditional sales process.

In B2C, the product is marketed, and the approach is typically feature driven, based on aspirations. Individuals are buyers, and the sales cycle is short. B2C component products, like a hammer or bag of rice, are marketed to a large segment of consumers with its list of features combined with an attractive price which make them more attractive than competitive options. The marketing will include ideas of what to build or cook, but the prospective purchaser can rarely take the product home and try it out without paying for it.

Ultimately, it makes little difference to the company selling the hammer or rice what the purchaser ends up choosing to do with their product as there is no long-term relationship with the buyer post purchase. The company's focus turns to selling the next hammer or bag of rice. A B2B or B2C business that has a community model attached to it generally uses the community to provide presale and postsale support and encourages user-generated content on social media to supplement their own marketing efforts. **But the product has already been sold.**

In B2D, success is defined by outcomes.
The approach to developers is one of enablement & inspiration.

B2D differs in that you are not selling to the ultimate end user of the product. You are marketing to a developer that will take your product to create or enhance something that they will then sell to *their own* end user. Here, the main marketing push is to developers first, in a bottom-up approach. Additionally, because of the complexity of adopting new technology, the B2D approach requires significant investment in educating prospective users in how to use the technology and inspiring them with suggestions on how they might apply it. Here, learning resources like blogs, case studies, and even tweets can all serve to inspire developers and show what's possible with your product. However, these must be backed by resources like technical documentation and code samples which provide the instructions on which bricks to use and how they snap together, crucial to enabling developers to embellish on your basic blueprints.

The sales cycle can be fast – typically via your self-service developer hub – or longer if you are selling into larger companies in combination with your sales team.

Because of these differences, the **B2D value chain is extended**, and it fundamentally changes the type of strategy, go-to-market plans, support, and community you will need to provide.

B2D Monetization Strategies

You may have noticed up to this point that we haven't mentioned the value exchange for B2D. In other words, **how does the DevRel-focused company make money?**

Over the years, B2D monetization strategies have increased in complexity;[3] however, they all tend to fall into one of four categories:

1. Direct – Revenue Upfront

2. Direct – Revenue Delayed

3. Indirect – Market Enhancement

4. Indirect – Ecosystem Enhancement

See Figure 8-2 which simplifies these models in a visual format. We'll review them in more detail below.

---

[3] For a deeper dive into a range of API business models from the developer's perspective, we recommend you watch this presentation by John Musser, founder of ProgrammableWeb: https://www.infoq.com/presentations/API-Business-Models/

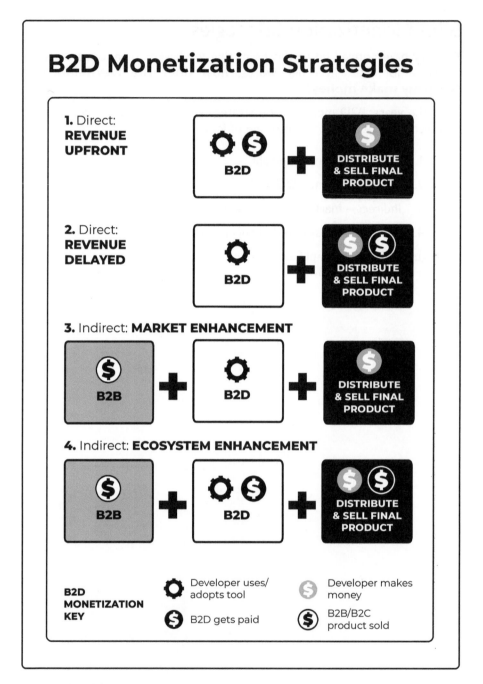

Figure 8-2. B2D monetization strategies

1. Direct – Revenue Upfront

The direct monetization strategy is the most straightforward. The DevRel organization is paid directly by the developer. This value exchange takes place somewhere in the Build stage of development, when the developer has started building their proof of concept or has started to scale their product into production. In many ways, this is the same as a traditional B2B or B2C model, except there is usually some limited opportunity for the developer to trial the product free of charge during their evaluation phase, often to make a simple "Hello World." The developer is supported as they build and later celebrated for their success.

There are variations in the pricing models of DevRel products, including per transaction, monthly or yearly subscription fees typically tiered by usage volume, or a licensing model. Examples include Netlify and Cloudflare.

A small twist on this approach is where the developer only pays for services attached to the product. Red Hat has made this model famous, where the product is free and open source, but if you wish to scale effectively, they sell subscriptions for support, training, and integration services.

2. Direct – Revenue Delayed

While the developer still pays directly, the revenue is not received up front in this model. Rather, the Revenue Delayed strategy means payment is delayed until the developer has finished building their product and has gone to market themselves and captured their own value in some form.

Examples of this method are used in marketplaces, in revenue share models, and advertising platforms. Examples include Stripe and Smaato.

3. Indirect – Market Enhancement

A Market Enhancement approach, sometimes called a two-sided business model, is only used by Developer Plus companies. In this model, the company has already made money from the sale of their primary product, and their **B2D product is used to enhance that product, increasing its value/ attractiveness.**

Qualcomm provides a great example here. Their primary products are processors for mobile phones and other devices. Having made their money from selling their processors to the device manufacturers, their Snapdragon SDKs are used by developers to make apps that will run "better" on a Snapdragon-powered device, for example, being optimized for better power efficiency.

There is no direct payment received from the use of the SDK. Rather, the strategy behind this is that these "better" apps help to showcase the superior performance of the Snapdragon processor, and the greater variety of apps makes Snapdragon devices more desirable with consumers which is good for Qualcomm, the device manufacturer (like Samsung), and the developers of the apps.

There are often additional supplemental values (as described in Chapter 4) associated with this model. For instance, support costs may decrease as the developer educational material created by the DevRel program indirectly supports the primary product. As well, we see marketing pulls initiated by developers for the B2B product. This pull happens as the developer discovers the B2D product first and understands how it enhances the B2B product, thus influencing that purchase.

Other companies that use this model include IBM, Intel, ARM, and others.

4. Indirect – Ecosystem Enhancement

An Ecosystem Enhancement approach is also used by Developer Plus companies. In this model, like the preceding indirect example, the B2B company has made money from the sale of their primary product. **Their B2D offer is used to encourage an ecosystem of new products (e.g., plugins, applications), thereby increasing the overall value and extending the utility of the primary product.** You can also argue it saves the company money by outsourcing elements of their product development and innovation, allowing them to focus on what is strategically important to them.

Salesforce is a good example here. Their developer program provides tools to build apps that plug into or supplement their main products, thus enhancing them, while developers are rewarded by selling into the popular Salesforce ecosystem.

Apple's App Store is perhaps the ultimate example of an indirect means to market its existing range of products. They not only retain 30% of revenue from app sales made, they also charge developers to be part of their developer program.

Getting this model right makes participation in the ecosystem more attractive to prospective developers and makes the primary product more attractive to purchasers due to the increased richness of the offer.

Maturing Your Model

As a developer program and product mature, companies typically broaden their product offer by adding prepackaged versions of their most common use cases, termed "moving up the stack." For example, after a few years of offering purely APIs, Twilio observed the demand for two-factor authentication (2FA) use cases using their text and voice API. Rather than every customer having to build it from scratch, via the acquisition of Authy[4] Twilio could now offer a prebuilt 2FA solution to supplement the API approach. To continue the Lego analogy, this is the equivalent of buying Lego's Millennium Falcon. Sure, you could buy all the individual bricks and figure it out for yourself, but you save considerable time knowing you have everything you need in the box, with a clear set of instructions. But of course, you pay a premium over the baseline building blocks for convenience and packaging.

For API or platform-based companies, there can be a tension between your ambition to further develop your own products and services and staying a pure-play tools provider. There is a potential trap that you either intentionally or unintentionally use your Developer Community to test the market to find winning use cases and then release your own products to capitalize on those insights, directly competing with your own community. Twitter is a famous example of this struggle to figure out where the line should be drawn. In the article "Twitter's 10 Year Struggle with Developer Relations" by Vassili van der Mersch, found on the Nordic APIs site, the author provides a nice summary of Twitter's turbulent history with Developers.[5]

With the move to selling "solutions," you open up new sales opportunities to a new type of buyer. No longer are you exclusively targeting Developers, for the first time, "business decision makers" become targets as you are no longer exclusively operating at the code level.

Depending on your chosen business model, you need to be mindful of your revenue mix and an overreliance on a few large customers, aka "don't have all your revenue eggs in one basket." Your investors or corporate stakeholders may be concerned if large percentages of your revenue are not protected or predictable.

Twilio experienced this in its early days with a perceived dependency on two or three key customers – Uber, WhatsApp, and Airbnb. Twilio used a pay-as-you-go per-transaction pricing model, with no long-term lock-in. When Jeff Lawson announced he expected revenues from Uber to fall as they switched from SMS notifications to in-app notifications, Twilio's stock fell 30%.[6]

---

[4]https://www.twilio.com/press/releases/twilio-acquires-authy-to-accelerate-strong-authentication-and-identity-adoption-for-web-and-mobile-apps
[5]https://nordicapis.com/twitter-10-year-struggle-with-developer-relations/
[6]https://techcrunch.com/2017/05/02/twilio-stock-takes-a-nosedive-in-after-hours-trading-on-weak-guidance/

A Numbers Game

When the developer takes your input to create something themselves, they are adding value to the next stage in the value chain. However, just because a developer is using your product does not guarantee that the value for the DevRel company is realized at that point, or indeed ever.

You may have done a great job of inspiring them, enabling them, and walking them through how to integrate it into their offer, but if their product is not successful in its own right, it is unlikely they will generate enough transaction volume or licenses to deliver meaningful revenue back to you.

Take, for example, the pay-per-transaction model, popular with many B2D models, especially with APIs. Your own sustainable business can't be built on the back of a string of "flash-in-the-pan" use cases. Nor can you afford to have friction in the developer journey. For example, if Uber incorporates Stripe as their payment API, Stripe rides the wave as Uber's popularity (and the number of transactions) explodes. From a marketing perspective, it's much like the Artists and Repertoire (A&R) department at a record label. The A&R team has to scout and sign hundreds of unproven bands playing in small clubs in front of a dozen people in the hope a few of them develop into the next U2 or Coldplay, therefore subsidizing the losses sustained from supporting the bands that never make it and turning an overall profit for the record label.

You may also experience many developers using your product just to learn something new, or they just aren't ready to build a commercial product.

You can start to see how building a Developer Program becomes a numbers game. You are forced to play the percentages, knowing that only a small proportion of your users will ever lead to meaningful revenue generation.

Summary

There are fundamental differences in the Business to Developer (B2D) business model when compared to a B2B or B2C model. Your relationship with the developer doesn't end with one purchase or value exchange, so consequently it affects the flow of activities, given the long-term relationship required to support the developer's success in building and scaling their own products.

As we discussed in earlier chapters, building a successful developer program is a long game. Any barriers you put in place will affect the overall outcome. Those who understood that and built their program on the right strategies and tactics have come out on top.

Developer Products

Determining Value and Finding Fit

As mentioned at the beginning of the book, you may be starting a Developer Relations program, benchmarking your program, launching a new product, or just trying to learn more about DevRel. You may sit in a marketing role, or product development, or be a sales support engineer. No matter which scenario or role you fall into, ground zero is getting to know the product you are being asked to promote and support. Let's see what you need to know.

Treat Your Developer Offering As a Product

It's vital to have a company-wide understanding that your developer offering is a product. As with all products, they need a combination of the following to be successful:

© Caroline Lewko, James Parton 2021
C. Lewko and J. Parton, *Developer Relations*,
https://doi.org/10.1007/978-1-4842-7164-3_9

- Strategy
- Team
- Budget
- Business model
- Documentation
- Users

- Outreach
- Learning resources
- Support
- Product development
- Community

Finally, and critically, a product and the developer program that supports it require a commitment from the executive level in your company. This point is further discussed in our chapter on corporate alignment.

If you are asked to work with a developer product without adequate resources or commitment, you're likely to fail. A developer product also needs patience and the commitment of time. A minimum of one to two years is required to demonstrate traction as you build a critical mass of developers using your tool, and they demonstrate their own success with it.

Types of Developer Products

There are a wide variety of offerings presented to developers, as shown in Figure 9-1. These developer products require the support of a Developer Relations program.

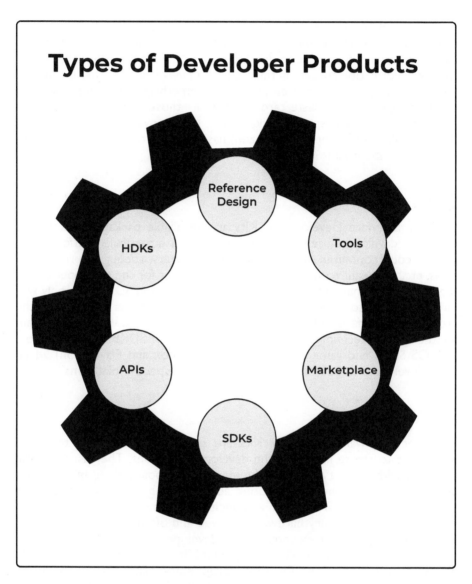

Figure 9-1. Types of developer products

Let's review a few examples to understand the breadth of what is offered.

APIs

APIs (Application Programming Interfaces) have become one of the most prevalent Developer Products and are offered by both Developer First and Developer Plus companies. APIs are a programmatic interface between two software applications or hardware to invoke an action between them. An example is a weather organization that has an API detailing information about today's weather. An application developer could invoke the API, so the latest weather information appears in their app or a news feed. Another example is online shopping. If you've ever purchased something online and chosen a payment option like Mastercard or PayPal, those organizations, or an intermediary payment specialist like Stripe, have provided payment APIs so that the online merchant (e.g., Amazon) has a way to collect your money. We wrote more about APIs in Chapter 3.

SDKs

SDKs or Software Development Kits are installable packages of software tools that developers use to build applications for a particular platform. The package could contain an API, a compiler, a code library, a debugger, proprietary tools, etc., all meant to work together, so it is easier for the developer to use the SDK rather than individual tools. In many cases, the SDK is the only way for developers to develop for a particular platform, as it contains the proprietary interface and tools necessary to communicate with and program for the specific technology in question. Examples of SDKs include Android and iOS SDKs and game console SDKs (e.g., Xbox and PlayStation) which allow developers to build applications for those respective platforms.

HDKs

HDKs or Hardware Developer Kits are similarly a package of tools for developers to create hardware and develop applications. They usually come packaged with some type of development circuit board along with various ports, interfaces, connectivity options, additional debugging facilities such as special status LEDs, JTAG ports, and additional memory. They are common when there is proprietary hardware involved and often work in conjunction with a specific SDK. For example, in IoT development the Arduino HDK or the Qualcomm Robotics RB5 Development Kit[1] allows developers to build hardware and applications for those proprietary platforms. In the game development world, console manufacturers like Microsoft and Sony provide sophisticated HDKs often costing hundreds of thousands of dollars. Often, the game hardware is an early-access prototype offered under very restrictive NDAs due to the fiercely competitive nature of the game console industry and subject to change which makes the developers' job challenging. These HDKs are made available to game developers long before the console is released to enable developers to build a selection of games ready for the

---

[1] https://developer.qualcomm.com/qualcomm-robotics-rb5-kit

hardware's launch. The growth in video game development, Internet of Things (IoT), and wearable tech has increased the number of HDKs available for developers.

Reference Designs

Reference designs are another type of developer product. They can be specs or technical blueprints which developers or engineers use to create hardware products like mobile phones, robots, or AR glasses. They can also exist as a *completed* example product, showing what a product built around a specific platform (e.g., processor) might look like and how it could work. Note, in this form, they typically also serve as an HDK. For example, Qualcomm's Smart Headset Reference Design is a Bluetooth-enabled headset demonstrating how their QCC5124 chip works while providing developers with an HDK consisting of an additional circuit board for development and testing.

Tools

Developer Tools, Development Tools, or Dev Tools is a large umbrella category and encompasses everything from debuggers and test suites to libraries, engines, scripts, IDEs (integrated development environments), low- and no-code platforms, DevOps solutions, and many others. Perhaps the most famous example is Microsoft's Visual Studio IDE. Much loved by developers spanning web apps to Xbox games, Visual Studio has matured over the last few decades to support building for a variety of platforms, a user-friendly GUI, strong scalability, and a myriad of integration options.

Marketplaces

Marketplaces, such as app stores, are another form of developer offering. They are typically offered as a platform ecosystem complete with APIs, SDKs, and testing and monitoring tools for developers to create an application or plugin. The developer's app is designed specifically for that marketplace. Examples include Google Play, Apple App Store, Salesforce AppExchange, Slack App Directory, and others.

Developer Services

There are a growing number of services being targeted at developers which we think is important to mention and differentiate here. The arrival of companies "serving" an industry is an important signal of increasing maturity and opportunity.

Developer services are similar to developer products in that they share a target customer – a developer. Therefore, the marketing and messaging employed by developer services companies share the same principles we describe in this book, and they also build their own developer communities.

However, services differ from products, in that they don't require the same type of technical documentation, technical learning resources, and support.

Let's look at some examples of developer services to help illustrate the point.

Services like HackerRank[2] and Stack Overflow Talent[3] will help you identify, test, and hire software developers. They target developers to join their community so they can connect them to career opportunities. Both companies have been very successful at doing this. According to SlashData research we saw in Chapter 7, Stack Overflow has a community of 16 million developers, and HackerRank has more than 6 million.

Social coding and code repository sites are also popular examples of developer services. Services like GitHub (41 million strong developer community) and Bitbucket (10 million) enable collaborative coding, code publication, and sharing, while NuGet is an example of a .NET marketplace and NPM for the JavaScript community.

Other examples of developer services include hackathon and coding prize organizers like Major League Hacking and DevPost and companies like Udemy, Pluralsight, Code Academy, General Assembly, and others in the software developer training space.

Product Scope in Organizations

The following charts, from the 2020 State of Developer Relations Report, illustrate the scope and scale of the products DevRel professionals are responsible for advocating (as opposed to product managing). As you can see, the range is huge.

Figure 9-2 shows the range of developer products offered by organizations to developers. The survey clarified that a product was considered a distinct entity with its own identity, resourcing, documentation, support, and maintenance needs and included developer tools, APIs, SDKs, HDKs, or marketplaces.

---

[2]https://www.hackerrank.com/
[3]https://stackoverflow.com/talent/en

According to the respondents, 50% of companies offered ten products or less, and just 9% of companies manage a single product. On the other end of the scale, 19% of DevRel teams advocate for over 100 developer products.

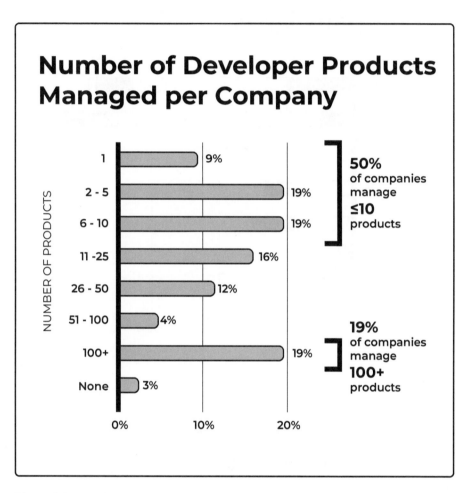

Figure 9-2. Number of developer products managed per company

Figure 9-3 breaks this down further to view the number of products offered by team size. The variations in ratios highlight the discrepancy in how developer products are resourced. Teams we have worked with who have a large product-to-team ratio organize their efforts by technology buckets, time frames, corporate goals, or important announcements. Many rely (sometimes not so successfully) on other departments for marketing, content, forum support, or doc creation support. This discrepancy in the ratios certainly points to the need for a strategic look at your team complement, as well as the importance of collaboration as a fundamental skill of DevRel professionals.

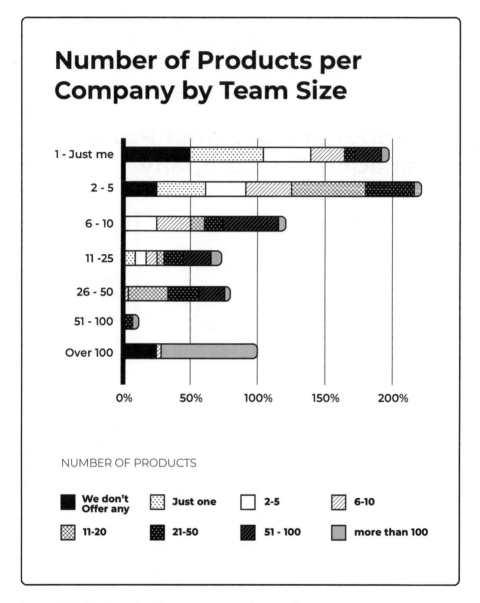

Figure 9-3. Number of products per company by team size

Product Value Proposition to Developers

When you are ready to take your product to market, each product must have a value proposition that speaks to developers. The value proposition should answer the deceptively simple question as shown in Figure 9-4 – **why does a**

developer want to use your product? Nailing down the value proposition will help you formulate your go-to-market strategy, how you support your developers, how the product is priced, and even the type of community you want to create around it.

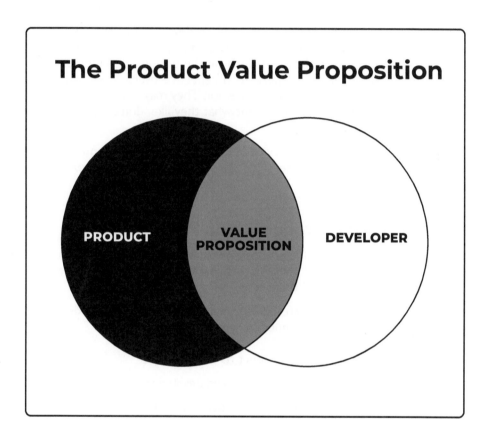

Figure 9-4. The product value proposition

Understanding this value via research with prospective users is the first step – or at least should be. This research may happen before the DevRel team is in place, by the product and/or marketing team. It's often completed in conjunction with a market research firm, for additional insight and expertise.

The DevRel leader may be tasked with running this research depending on when they join and the development stage of the product, so it's important to be prepared!

Either way, it is critical that your company has validated its assumptions before building the product and continues to ask these types of questions periodically to ensure they are keeping pace with the latest trends and developer sentiment. We do recommend the DevRel leader take an active role in this process.

Unfortunately, engaging in research doesn't always happen. You may find you are working with a very enthusiastic product development team who gets very glassy-eyed telling you about all of the great product features and the long list of enhancements already defined on the product development road map without ever thinking to speak to prospective users about what they think is essential and what they would pay for. They may also not think about surveying their current users to find out what they like, don't like, and would like to see next.

Shockingly, 72% of product or service innovations fail to deliver on customer expectations.[4] This failure rate underlines why nailing down your value proposition is so important.

Determining the Product Value Proposition

Determining the product value proposition is all about getting to the bottom of what your product's real value is to a developer and how you stack up against the competition (and there is always competition!).

Take a look at Figure 9-5, which shows three different inputs into a developer product value proposition and questions to ask to determine:

- The relevancy of the product to the developer
- The benefits of the product to the developer
- How your product is differentiated for the developer over their other options

---

[4]https://www.strategyzer.com/canvas/value-proposition-canvas

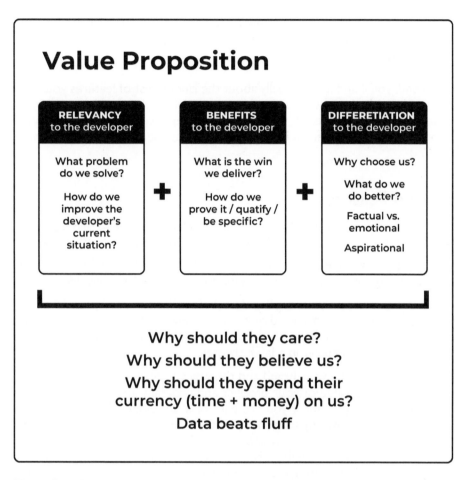

Figure 9-5. The components of the developer value proposition

There are many ways to go about developing your value proposition. A popular example is the Value Proposition Canvas by Strategyzer.[5] Split into two sections, it guides you to define:

- Your customer's major jobs to be done.

- The pains they face when trying to accomplish their jobs to be done.

- The gains they perceive by getting their jobs done.

---

[5] https://www.strategyzer.com/canvas/value-proposition-canvas

- While mapping your products and services, how they solve pain points and how they increase benefits and drive better outcomes.

In the end, you'll find it's not really about the laundry list of features your new product has; it's about what a developer can build with it and how you make their life better if they use it. Essentially, why they should choose you. And as mentioned in the chapter on Developers – making them proud to say, "I made that!".

Beyond Features

A differentiated value proposition is not always achieved by having better features. You can win the "hearts and minds" of developers in other ways.

One way is to have a great Developer Experience, especially with documentation and learning resources which you'll read more about in Chapters 16–19.

Another way is to have an exceptional level of service across all your developer touchpoints, from forums to direct engineering support. Having a vibrant community that you nurture is a third way to differentiate your program. We dive more into community in a later chapter.

Emotional factors like your brand and the way you make developers feel also contribute to the value of your product and program. Brand considerations are particularly important if you are part of a Developer First company, as chances are your company brand and product value proposition are one and the same in the eyes of the developer (e.g., Stripe is seen as a payment API and a company interchangeably). For companies with many competitors like the Communications Platform as a Service (CPaaS) space which includes the likes of Twilio, Nexmo, RingCentral, Infobip, and many others, simply having a great product offering isn't enough to differentiate.

In combination, this all adds up to a fully rounded product and a great developer program proposition. One that is hard for developers to ignore, and your competitors to copy.

A Long-Term View

We hope your product and developer program is set up for the long term. Here are a few issues to be mindful of.

Deprecating and Sunsetting Product and Code Breaks

History is littered with deprecated APIs and sunsetted SDKs from companies which made big claims to be developer-friendly. If you search ProgrammableWeb for "deprecated," you find nearly 50 APIs from the likes of eBay, Google, Microsoft, IBM, Amazon, PayPal, and Facebook. In the cell phone industry, companies like Nokia, Palm, Microsoft, and RIM all spent millions of dollars on devices trying to appeal to and serve mobile app developers in the early to mid-2000s.

There is also a constant flow of new product versions released which "break code" for developers. This can happen directly within your own product or downstream in an interconnected tool which developers have come to rely on in their production code, which now no longer functions as expected without any warning.

There are an endless number of ways in which you can "break" your product from changing your functions' input parameters or changing which REST verbs you support on your endpoints, deprecating certain class methods in your next library build, or modifying how your tools organize or generate the data necessary to use your product. There's also those seemingly "innocent" changes behind the scenes (e.g., how data is stored), which can also break the "contract" (i.e., interface and expected behavior) of your API or tool interfaces and send your developer community scrambling for a solution.

Such breaks can also occur upstream when the tools, SDKs, and other resources you depend on for your product are modified, deprecated, or cease to exist. The problem can be further exacerbated when relying on "sketchy" resources such as tools or APIs managed by a small team or individual who ceases to support it, but it can occur when relying on a reputable company that has a history of pulling the plug on an interface without regard for the implications. That's why it's important that your selection of technological dependencies be scrutinized for their likelihood of long-term support or breaking changes, just as your customers will do with your product(s).

While improving and replacing products with better ones is not necessarily a negative thing, it's essential to appreciate that many companies downstream in your value chain will have placed significant bets on your developer products as ingredients to their own product and propositions. If they are pulled, or significantly changed, the implications can be significant, especially in today's ecosystem of cloud-based offerings, where breaking changes can have an immediate impact on your customer's live online offering.

Popular third-party social media apps like Tweetbot and Twitterific were affected when Twitter pulled its API in 2018, ironically while Twitter simultaneously recognized its best innovations had come from third-party developers. This came after several u-turns, broken promises, and PR gaffes by the company toward its developer community.[6] There was a similar issue when Netflix closed its API program in 2014.[7]

In the early days of the "API economy," this was one of the main criticisms that detractors felt would hold back mainstream adoption of APIs – why would you integrate technologies from small venture-backed companies that could be here today and gone tomorrow? Those types of sentiments kill any positive value proposition you have going for you.

While software companies deprecating and/or changing products has been an issue since the dawn of software, the widespread adoption of web-based APIs due to their low-entry barriers (free trials, cheap pay-as-you-go transactional business models) and wide distribution (the cloud) and public platforms for customers to complain (social media) make these closures seemingly more impactful. This is due not only to the numbers of developers directly integrating the APIs but also to many end users of the developers' products depending on the functionality.

You can see how broken promises, withdrawal of services, and other poor community behavior can quickly sour your reputation within developer circles. If you work at a large company with a long history of previous developer engagements, beware of what came before you. You may be unaware of historical baggage that will hamper your plans to try reengaging again – once bitten, twice shy. The community has a long collective memory.

When you deprecate or change a product, it adds complexity to your messaging, content management, site navigation, and support. You may have groups of users spread across multiple versions of your product, so unless you decide to remove access entirely to previous versions, consider the knock-on effect to your customers in that scenario.

Make it clear and explicit that you have multiple versions available and what the differences are (i.e., changes and removals between versions). If you plan to make a product version unavailable at some point or break one, this needs to be communicated well in advance.

Do consider that **developers love to see your product road map**, as it gives them confidence that you have thought about future development, you plan to be around for a while, and they have the opportunity to provide feedback on it. We discuss this further in Chapter 17.

---

[6]https://insights.dice.com/2017/02/10/twitter-developers-dont-matter/
[7]https://mashable.com/2014/06/19/netflix-public-api/?europe=true

Pricing Changes

Breaking their code is one thing, breaking the developer bank account is another. In the same way that a developer makes a commitment to your technology and doesn't want to see breaking changes, they are also committing to a cost model at the price point you advertised at the point of their adoption. The developer will not want to see drastic shifts in pricing that could make their continued usage, or even their business as a whole, untenable.

Product-Market Fit

In discussing developer product value earlier, we primarily looked at the time frame of a product launch. It's highly unlikely you will get your value proposition absolutely right the first time. Also, as you gain more users and make changes to your product, the value proposition of your product might need to be modified. Finding that product-market fit is exactly as it sounds – determining the value of what the market is looking for with what your product provides to them. It's not rocket science, it's Business 101, so consider this an ongoing exercise of testing to find the best fit. Testing, as mentioned, includes talking to your users, assessing their usage of your product, getting feedback on your product road map, as well as testing and assessing different marketing messages and channels.

Summary

As we've seen in this chapter, developer products come in many varieties. Some organizations have only one product to manage, while others look after hundreds of products. To be successful requires understanding what your product does and determining the value it provides to developers with a view for the long term.

However, before you use this information to determine the goals and activities of your DevRel program, you must ensure there is a fit with the overall company goals. Let's read about that in the next chapter.

Alignment on Goals

Setting and agreeing to goals is common for all organizations and is the next step in setting up your Developer Relations program. DevRel is often misunderstood, and we have observed this is often self-perpetuated to some degree by the lack of consistency across DevRel programs on goal setting.

Understanding your company's direction and setting program goals that link your activities to the things that are important to your company while demonstrating DevRel value can be hard.

In Part III, we look at both corporate goals and program goals and offer some insight to help you gain that crucial alignment between them.

Company Goals and Alignment

Now that you have a good appreciation for DevRel and the value of the product you are supporting, it's time to ensure there's alignment with your organization's high-level company goals. In this chapter, we'll look at how to identify company goals, issues for consideration, and ways to align your program's goals, which are vital to the success of your program, your team, and you.

Identify Company Goals

Regardless of your company type, as a leader of a program, it is critical that you understand your business's strategic direction and its associated priorities. If you are not the DevRel lead, it's still vital to know what the company goals are so you have a better appreciation for your team fit in the organization.

Hopefully, you will be given the company goals as part of your onboarding, or you can ask your line manager. If you don't have them, or you are seeking additional detail and color, you can find information on company goals from various sources such as all-hands meetings, company yearly kick-off meetings, company conferences, your Intranet if you have one, departmental briefings and meetings, press interviews with your senior team, etc. If you work in a

© Caroline Lewko, James Parton 2021
C. Lewko and J. Parton, *Developer Relations*,
https://doi.org/10.1007/978-1-4842-7164-3_10

large public company, you can also learn enormous amounts from S1 filings and quarterly investor calls.

Being aware of the goals is only the first step. Understanding the company goals is an essential input into the creation of your developer program goals and subsequent tactics. If you work in a Developer First business, your company's sole mission is to provide great tools to developers. Therefore, it is usually fairly easy to draw a line between how your developer program activities positively contribute to growing the company's market share and bottom line. However, in a Developer Plus business, for example, Walmart, it might be less obvious why launching a developer play is beneficial to growing the bottom line, so there is more work required to uncover the links and identify all of your stakeholders.

To really understand the goals, it is vital you put yourself in the shoes of your stakeholders. Consider how the goals influence their attitude to your program and how they set their own priorities. For example, if they have a challenging revenue target to hit, they will likely be asking you questions about the contribution your program will be making to that target. Organizations often have long-term and short-term goals, and company goals often get muddied by the individual goals of departmental and line managers. It's important to know and understand all of these influences in combination so you can align with them appropriately.

The Importance of Company Alignment

So you might be asking – why is understanding this so important? And you might be thinking that you need only care about delivering the best possible experience for your developers and have no time for, or interest in, corporate BS and politics.

The reason simply boils down to support and air cover for you and your program. If it's not you directly, then someone in the organization needs to make the business case for investing in a DevRel program and demonstrate why that investment was – and continues to be – a prudent use of resources.

Every company, regardless of size, has intense internal competition for how to deploy its people and where to spend its money. Job security rests on placing the right bets to grow a company's market share. This is especially true inside a Developer Plus company where the internal competition for resources will be much more diverse, and most "asks" will be unrelated to serving developers.

Let's take a look at aspects to consider when reviewing company goals and achieving alignment with them.

Alignment Considerations

Connect to Core Company Goals

Within a **Developer First company**, the focus from the top is building tools and services for developers. Therefore, it makes sense to launch a DevRel program to increase your product's awareness and adoption. Company commitment is unlikely to waver or change over time. Generally, in these companies, friction arises over a lack of communication between departments, disagreements on go-to-market tactics, metrics, or a lack of understanding of what "good" looks like, rather than disagreement over the need for a DevRel effort. However, if you are savvy, you'll keep an eye on the company's investors, who may not fully understand DevRel and may be misinformed on some DevRel strategies and tactics.

In **Developer Plus companies**, the environment can vary enormously, but always be aware that your activity is likely not viewed as core to the business. Therefore, your job is to educate your stakeholders to ensure you have the air cover you need to flourish. Find ways to connect your endeavors to the core goals and priorities of your department and the company. Connect the dots and make the case that a dollar spent on your program provides a better return than a dollar spent elsewhere (see Chapter 4 on the Value of DevRel if you need some ideas).

Hiring, firing, and restructures are the norm in larger startups and the corporate world, so never get complacent. Your stakeholders will change over time, often every six months. Even though you convinced the last set, there is no guarantee that the new faces coming in will support you. This type of disruption also happens in early stage startups, whether due to founders still identifying product-market fit, new hires as you move into high growth, or a new round of investors with new ideas. New entrants to a company often want to make a statement that they are shaking things up and typically recruit people they have worked with before. Your program will be under constant scrutiny, and disruption and distraction could be hiding around the corner, even when things seem to be going well.

Be Attuned to the Company Culture

One of the most significant challenges for DevRel inside Developer Plus companies with a more "old-school" attitude is a lack of fit with the corporate culture. Cultural issues can appear in startups too. For example, a new senior hire may bring a "that's not the way things are done" attitude with them and be intent on following a strategy that has previously worked for them, which may extend to hiring people they have worked with before to execute that plan. For DevRel to be successful, there has to be openness and a willingness to share information, receive and act on feedback, be supportive and collaborative, and have a partnership approach. If you are with a new Developer First company, make the effort to instill this type of culture from the beginning.

Sometimes bravely, but naively, a DevRel effort springs up inside Developer Plus companies that are just not geared to nurture such endeavors. While the DevRel champion may build enough momentum to start and launch, they will find themselves in a debilitating war against corporate antibodies that are there to attack and kill anything they don't recognize as belonging inside the host. Departments and individuals will either deliberately or unconsciously grind away at any activity deemed to be outside of the norm.

Because of the lack of understanding in the broader organization, mistakes and compromises will be made that are perhaps trivial individually but collectively create a terrible Developer Experience and produce a friction-filled developer journey. Examples we have seen in Developer Plus companies include legal departments requiring developers to sign complex jargon-filled contracts before they can use APIs, small partners or consultants having to agree to the same supplier terms as companies the size of IBM or Microsoft, developer revenue share payments being paid out after 90 days rather than appreciating the importance of cash flow to small independent developers, the inability to use social media authentically, the inability to make use of developer communities such as Stack Overflow, and the list goes on. In Developer First companies, the disconnect tends to occur when the CTO is overly focused on product development to the detriment of the overall Developer Experience and the growing awareness and community – a "build it and they will come" mentality.

Changing your company's culture should not be on any DevRel job description. While you may have some positive influence, you shouldn't be burdened with that impossible task. You already have enough to do. However, you shouldn't put your hands over your ears and pretend there isn't a problem. Do your best to educate your stakeholders, but we would recommend you seriously reconsider launching a program at all if you already know the cards are stacked against your success.

Be Aware of Company Antibodies

Large organizations are complex to navigate by their very nature. They become even more challenging when you attempt to launch a new innovation initiative like a developer program because of corporate antibodies.[1] Depending on where you sit in an organization, you might see the corporate antibodies as naysayers or those responsible for risk reduction. Either way, having an understanding of them and how to protect your program is important.

---

[1] The people and processes that extinguish a new idea as soon as it begins to course through the organization – https://hbr.org/2012/05/get-the-corporate-antibodies-o

At each layer of the organization, every decision maker and stakeholder has a set of parameters they work within, including:

- **The company** – They will have formed a mental construct around their own role in relation to the overall company mission and vision.

- **Their department** – They have pre-agreed priorities set within their department structure by their line management. These are typically set once a year.

- **Their individual objectives** – They have their own personal objectives upon which their performance will be measured.

Individuals in the company likely have financial compensation, like an annual bonus, linked to company, department, and individual performance measured against preset quarterly or annual targets.

Risk and disruption are typically not things large companies rush to embrace. Innovation gets stifled because of the fear of the unknown and the avoidance of risk. The further a new initiative is away from their parameters or core competence, the riskier the project will be perceived. With the wrong company culture, executives stand to gain by keeping their heads down and sticking to the status quo. Why would an executive back your idea if it poses a risk to their internal reputation, or to their ability to achieve their objectives (and bonus), or keep their job?

As well as the "fit" and "compatibility" of your idea to the existing strategy, you have to consider the implications of your idea.

Therefore, it is vital to ensure you understand every person's motivations in the organization that you need to support your proposition. Then tailor your pitch to maximize the chances of winning them over. Put yourself in the other person's shoes by asking yourself questions like, "What risk am I asking them to take by supporting my idea?" or "By supporting my program, how will it help them achieve their objectives and those of the company?"

The fear of cannibalizing existing revenue streams is real. If you are in a company with a star product, you may see the complacency creep in. See Kodak as a prime example.[2] Companies get addicted to cash flow and develop arrogance around their market position. When you are at the top, you forget what it is like to have to fight and scrap, you forget what it is like to be chasing the top dog, and you forget what it is like being the challenger seeking to disrupt vs. being the leader seeking to defend. When you are number one, you have a lot to lose and very little to gain by taking risks.

---

[2]https://en.wikipedia.org/wiki/Kodak#Shift_to_digital

Understand Innovation Disconnects

Sometimes, internal resistance isn't down to a misalignment with strategy and can simply be due to a "not invented here" culture and internal politics. Often specific individuals or teams within the organization feel they "own" innovation and seek to control or block anything that doesn't originate from them. Read *Cutting the Cord*,[3] which tells great stories of how the cell phone nearly didn't happen because of that type of culture.

Another classic example of internal politics that regularly appears in complex organizations is the creation of a centralized function that sits above the business units. There is a strategic cycle that rotates between two sets of logic, typically every five years:

- Innovation is better delivered centrally to achieve benefits of scale.

- Innovation is better delivered decentralized as the business units are closer to the needs of the customer.

This constant friction from the rotation leads to confusion, duplication, and frustration with teams competing for resources and recognition at a business unit level vs. centralized level. Significant resources and internal energy are burnt simply identifying competing projects and attempting to align them, rather than delivering innovation to affect customers and the bottom line.

The board of a company gets pitched hundreds of ideas a year, and very few get past the feasibility stage. This is why it is essential not to get 100% engrossed by your concept and consider the implications and the environment you are proposing to operate within. Painting the big picture, identifying, understanding, and countering these corporate antibodies are key to your success.

Brand Reputation Matters

Every company we have ever worked with cares about their brand and their perception in the market. Competition in all sectors is fierce, and often it is not enough to compete on features alone. You will need to demonstrate to your stakeholders that you understand how your program will enhance brand perception to get the backing you need to execute successfully.

You also need to demonstrate you understand that the moves you make with your developer program have external ramifications. We saw in the chapter on the value proposition how products that aren't created for the long term can adversely affect a brand. Poor marketing execution also falls into this bucket, referenced by the infamous $1 million hackathon run by Salesforce

---

[3] *Cutting the Cord*, Martin Cooper, "Father of the Cell Phone."

which was dogged by controversy.[4] As you will likely already know, developers are not shy about expressing their opinions publicly, and the tech media also loves to pick up on these types of stories!

Launching Is Only the Beginning

So good news!

You have figured all of this out, have successfully achieved the backing for your program, and have launched it into the market.

Well, don't pop too many champagne corks just yet. This isn't a one-shot deal. As you attempt to grow your program, you now face the next set of challenges within the innovation agenda that mainly happens inside larger organizations:

- **The reorg** – Every 12 months, perhaps every 6 months, some part of the company will be restructured. This means a new stakeholder(s) to build a relationship with and restart the internal evangelical mission on why your project is vital to the company's future success. Of course, these reorganizations are incredibly impactful when they happen in your direct department. Your new boss may come in with preconceived ideas or a set of new priorities, or they might not buy what you are selling. Being armed with data and other evidence to show your impact is your best friend in these situations. If you are a startup, these changes often occur during a new round of investment and the entry of new board members with new ideas.

- **Measurement disconnect** – Your program has launched and is a live product, but your company's **success measurements are not calibrated to recognize disruptive innovation**. Typically, success in a company is measured by revenue and return on investment. If you are delivering innovation in a new field for the company, time needs to be invested up front in building credibility and trust. Demonstrating the impact and success of this against traditional criteria can be especially tough. The DevRel leadership may also not be perceived as senior enough to be around the table when budget reviews happen, due to DevRel often being rolled up under other departments like engineering or marketing. When project impact is assessed via spreadsheets, you don't always have the opportunity to provide the strategic color. You can

---

[4]https://techcrunch.com/2013/12/02/salesforce-hackathon-tie/

easily have a line put through your program at any point in time as, outside of your direct team, there is unlikely to be an emotional attachment to your program.

The following is a personal story from James' time at the BlueVia program that drives home many of these points.

BLUEVIA (TELEFONICA DEVELOPER PROGRAM) AND FAILING TO SET INTERNAL EXPECTATIONS

I was in the room where the financial performance of the 2 year old BlueVia developer program was being discussed. Despite the relative lack of maturity of the program, it was already delivering tangible results with tens of thousands of developers signed up globally and delivering double digit millions of dollars in revenue.

Had this been at a startup, it would have demonstrated more than enough product market fit to raise millions of dollars in venture capital. This "success" was achieved despite no previous in-house experience of operating a developer program, combined with the major hindrance of a negative brand perception issue with developers that needed time to overcome and establish trust.

The program's progress had gained global recognition from the industry analyst community as the most innovative program in the telecoms sector and we had competing mobile operators coming to the table requesting to partner.

The BlueVia team was operating, shipping, and measuring success like a startup. We felt we had made impressive progress, but our executive stakeholders were evaluating our "success" through the prism of the traditional business. When considering the investment case for year 3 of the program, there was a dismissive comment that Telefonica could make more money from shaving a penny off the price of SMS without expending any effort or resources in something they didn't really fully understand.

Because of our emotional investment, and the encouraging progress delivered inside a hostile environment, the immediate reaction of the BlueVia team was defensive. However on reflection, we had failed to set the internal expectations of our stakeholders and to clearly demonstrate why the program shouldn't be measured in the traditional way.

We had also failed to educate our stakeholders on the market context, and how success in this area would deliver significant strategic and brand benefits in addition to cash generation. A little more than 12 months later, the internal antibodies had effectively killed the program.

—James Parton
while BlueVia Head of Marketing at Telefonica

The preceding BlueVia story is all too familiar.

History is littered with developer programs, APIs, and other developer products that have been launched to a huge fanfare only to be retired, sunsetted, or insert other phrases that marketing dreamt up to avoid using "closed," "shut down," or "failed". This is precisely why so many developers and DevRel professionals are wary and cynical about new developer offers from Developer Plus companies – they have had their fingers burnt once too many times.

Solutions for Company Alignment

So there really is good news in the form of solutions to the issues that come up with aligning your developer program with your company goals. Table 10-1 shows some of the common challenges for starting and nurturing a DevRel program, with some examples of how to address them.

Table 10-1. Company Alignment Challenges and Solutions

Company Alignment Challenges and Solutions

CHALLENGE	SOLUTION
DevRel is seen as a non-core activity (Developer Plus companies)	Frame your pitch to align with the priorities of your company, demonstrating how your program contributes.
Lack of a common under-standing of DevRel, developers as customers, metrics, etc.	Educate and workshop internally within your stakeholders. Give them this book!
DevRel job titles and seniority do not open doors or carry enough weight	Understand your reporting structure, and ensure there is a senior sponsor that has the internal gravitas to provide air cover and open doors. Longer-term, our hope is this book contributes to increasing both recognition and seniority of DevRel leaders.
Lack of specific DevRel skills within the organization	Identify and train existing staff across the organization. Hire full-time employees.
Restrictions on hiring	Create a DevRel culture and utilize resources from across the business. Use DevRel contractors or consultancy services to increase your activities.
Company patience is low	Understand your market share and brand reputation. Be clear up front about the investment and time required to move the needle.
The company culture is not conducive to DevRel	Proceed with caution!

These considerations may help explain why it is so hard to turn a supertanker and why a startup with a single focus can achieve more with smaller budgets and fewer people – because they have an **aligned common purpose**.

Summary

This chapter isn't simply telling you to read up your company goals. Rather, we wanted to paint a realistic picture of what managing a developer program can be like – the environment you operate in, the competitive nature of securing resources, and the varying motivations and agendas that may be in conflict with yours. Take them to heart, but don't be discouraged. If you arrive with your eyes open, and seek support from the wider DevRel community and of course this book, we are sure you will find success.

In our opinion, there has never been a better time to be in DevRel due to the growing recognition of the value of the developer economy and rising awareness of DevRel as a profession.

So with that behind us, let's take a look at setting goals for your Developer Relations program and your team next.

Program Goals

Setting Your Strategy and Plans

You've been chosen to lead your organization's Developer Program. Congratulations! Starting something new is super exciting, and there is the desire to hit the ground running.

To recap, you've gained an understanding of Developer Relations, you've had a chance to learn about developers, and you have a good appreciation for the B2D approach. You have a critical opinion of the product you are supporting and its value proposition to developers. You have secured the backing of the executive team, and you understand the relationship between your DevRel program and the high-level company goals.

OK, what's first? Time for a hackathon! Right??

We've run into this scenario more times than we care to recall. That, or the one where you immediately rush to hire a developer advocate. Our response is always the same – slow down, where's your plan?

Let's look at the pieces you need to build a solid plan and set your program's goals.

© Caroline Lewko, James Parton 2021
C. Lewko and J. Parton, *Developer Relations*,
https://doi.org/10.1007/978-1-4842-7164-3_11

Setting Program Goals

Planning starts by setting your goals, so that you and everyone else are clear on what you want from your program. Ask these four deceptively simple questions:

- What is the purpose of your developer program?

- What do you want your developer program to achieve?

- What value will it bring to your organization?

- What value will it bring to the developers you want to serve?

See Figure 11-1 for a few ideas of what you might want from your program.

Figure 11-1. What do we want from our developer program?

Suzanne Nguyen is a veteran when it comes to DevRel, starting as part of the Sun Product Marketing team for Java ME. Here are some tips she shares for building a sustainable program:

> When I start with a new program, I always identify an ROI goal. I also review the product to understand the current state, understand the current developer journey and determine what needs to be improved.
>
> Unfortunately, most companies hope for instant results from their DevRel Programs, not realizing that it's a longer-term play of 3-5 years. They don't invest that long and thus have problems with gaining momentum and adoption. I've definitely seen this in product launches, where too many promises are made, upgrades are not backward compatible, or the product is too quickly moved to end of life. This breaks trust with developers, which is very hard to rebuild. There is also a push to chase new developers, but what's really needed is the increase in nurturing the current community that has tremendous value to give.

—Suzanne Nguyen
Senior Director, Brand and Communications, Angora

Formerly DevRel at Samsung, Immersion, T-Mobile, Adobe, Sun

Long-Term Program Goals

You'll want to have one or two long-term goals, something to strive for over the course of two to five years. Sometimes, these are called top-line goals. We recognize that your corporate culture might dictate whether those goals are practical or grandiose. The big striving goals are sometimes called BHAGs, or Big Hairy Audacious Goals – think of NASA striving to put a person on Mars. The best BHAGs require building for the long term and exude a relentless sense of urgency. In a more practical business context, that motivation may come from overtaking a rival or by disrupting a market that is stale and starved of innovation.

Long-term goals are often driven or at least influenced by corporate goals. If you are a startup, one of your long-term goals might be contributing toward a corporate transaction like an investment, acquisition, or an IPO. In a Developer Plus company, the goals might be to support an overarching innovation agenda or a new product strategy.

Short-Term Program Goals

Depending on your situation, shorter-term goals can be anywhere from three months to two years. Here are a few examples:

- To contribute to the company's revenue by growing the size and reach of our program

- To increase our reputation with developers and/or become a thought leader in our field

- To remove the friction in our Developer Experience

- To lower our support costs while improving the support experience

- To improve and speed up the feedback loop for product enhancements and new product development

- To gain knowledge and expertise in running a developer program

You might be tempted to add in things like attend more events or write more blogs. Don't. Those are tactical activities that help you achieve your goals rather than the program goals themselves. Those will come later.

> At this point in your planning, focus on nailing down your long term and short term program goals. These will give you and your team direction, and your stakeholders the confidence in your plans.

Some of your goals may also be very specific to the situation of your program. For instance, your goal might be to establish your team with its own budget, if you have a brand-new program. Or you may wish to improve the level of recognition your developer program receives within your company.

It's always best to focus on a tight set of three to four goals; any more and you will be spread too thinly and lack focus. As well, **at least one of your goals must contribute to bringing value to the business either in revenue or other means**.

Clarity and Realism in Goal Setting

Sometimes, the direction from your stakeholders may be hard to comprehend. This can lead to unrealistic goals that are hard to implement or worse risk damaging relations and reputations. Here are a few examples we have seen to look out for:

- More apps (popular in the early mobile days when device companies and operators just wanted more apps and often paid developers for them, to the detriment of the developer program trying to manage this and lowering the overall quality of submissions).

- New ideas (it's great to be creative, but without context this can just waste time and money).

- Better partnerships (be careful about alienating current partnerships).

- Someone to debug our code and fix our documentation (that's just not nice).

- More efficient employees (it's not the job of Developer Relations).

- Make us look innovative (it's better to actually be innovative than look innovative).

- Make a stakeholder look innovative (pet innovation projects are common with executives looking to curry favor for a promotion, and they often zero in on the latest thing).

- We need to be more like Slack, or Twilio, or Uber or fill in the blank with the name of the current media darling.

- Our company needs to undergo a digital transformation to boost our stock price.

Be careful what you are being asked to do, and aim to understand the intent and get clarity.

Metrics for Measuring Goals

Speaking of gaining clarity – we must make a short mention here on metrics. All goals should have a number and time period attached to them or some way to measure progress toward achieving them. Otherwise, how do you know if you have attained your goal? It's great to say you want to grow your program, but it's more effective to declare: we will grow our program to 500,000 developers by increasing the number of active developers by an average of 15% quarter on quarter for the next 12 months.

Knowing how to identify the best metrics in which to measure and monitor your goals can be challenging, as there is no shortage of things to measure. We'll do a deeper dive on setting program metrics in Chapter 26.

Influences and Gaps

Many programs we've seen can be solely focused on a number to hit they fail to review their goals in the wider context or consider what might influence their goals. These influences will affect the scope of your goals, the tactics required to execute on them, and will have a direct influence on being able to achieve your goals.

Your role is to uncover these influences, determine the gaps between your current situation and your intended outcome, and then set your program plan accordingly. Use your strengths to overcome any weakness and grab the opportunities.

Identifying these influences and their scope will come from your own research and analysis. Tools helpful for reviewing your strengths and weaknesses include a SWOT[1] analysis. Talking directly to your developers whether in direct conversations or surveys can uncover valuable information. And of course, reviewing your metrics when you finally have them.

Some of the variables to be aware of that will influence your goals and planning include:

- Corporate goals
- Number of products you must support
- Number of staff on the DevRel team
- Skill set of the DevRel team
- Where DevRel sits in an organization
- Whether you are a Dev First or Dev Plus company
- The business and pricing models of the DevRel products
- Is the Developer program a cost center or profit center
- Timing of any corporate announcements or expectations
- Geographical considerations, like product availability or localization
- Age of your program
- Status/age of your products (new to the market or sunsetting)
- Status of competitive products
- Your program budget

---

[1]https://en.wikipedia.org/wiki/SWOT_analysis

When you've reviewed the influences on your situation, you'll certainly uncover gaps to overcome. Table 11-1 outlines a few of the ones you might encounter.

Table 11-1. Gaps to Attaining Program Goals Examples

Gaps to Attaining Program Goals Examples

EXTERNAL	INTERNAL
Competition just launched a new product	Product not ready for release
	Friction in the Developer Experience
Lack of awareness of brand (new company or new market)	Documentation incomplete
	Lack of budget
	Lack of resources
Lack of awareness of program or product	Team skills mix
	Interdepartmental collaboration issues
Developers don't understand product value	Competing DevRel initiatives within company

We recommend making thinking visible. Having your goals and the gaps visible to all of your stakeholders and team makes everyone aware of your direction and situation. Here is an example of how you might present your goals and gaps in Table 11-2.

Table 11-2. Program Goals and Gaps Example

Program Goals & Gaps Example

GOALS & GAPS PROGRAM: QUTE CORP'S DEVELOPER PROGRAM	
PRODUCT	**QUTE MAGICAL PLATFORM (QMP)**
Goals	Within 6 months Start Program and gain 1,000 active Developers in first 6 months Gain knowledge and expertise in running a DevRel program
Gaps	Developers don't know Qute has a Developer Program Developers unfamiliar with the new product (QMP) Developer Hub not ready Team complement not ready Product still in beta

Keep these influences in mind as you read the rest of the book and consider your own balance of variables. We'll mention many times in the book that Developer Relations is not finite, so there is no "one" plan to rule all plans.

Summary

Program goals are a reflection of the overall company goals and a means to clarify the purpose and value your Developer Program will bring to your organization. At least one of your program goals should show how the developer program is contributing value to the business. There are a number of variables that affect your ability to create a plan for your Developer Program and to set your goals. Uncovering them and being mindful of the gaps will make your goals and tactics more realistic and achievable.

PART

IV

Go-to-Market

Delivering Your Strategy

Once you've identified your program's goals and influences, there are still a few things to get in place before you can deliver on your go-to-market strategy.

In Part IV of the book, we transition into the execution side of DevRel. We'll do a deeper dive into the components of the Developer Relations Framework – Developer Marketing, Developer Experience, Developer Education, Developer Success, and Community. These are the disciplines that the Developer Relations program and team are typically responsible for or directly influence.

Along with having a functional product, having the basic pieces of the Developer Relations Framework in place are the table stakes of starting a program. Developers, or rather the right developers, won't come without these pieces.

As developers interact with the components of your program, your high-level objectives are **Awareness**, **Activation**, **Engagement**, and **Retention** as outlined in Figure P-IV. In this part, we'll review some best practices and tactics for you to achieve those objectives. We start with identifying your target audience via Segmentation and Personas.

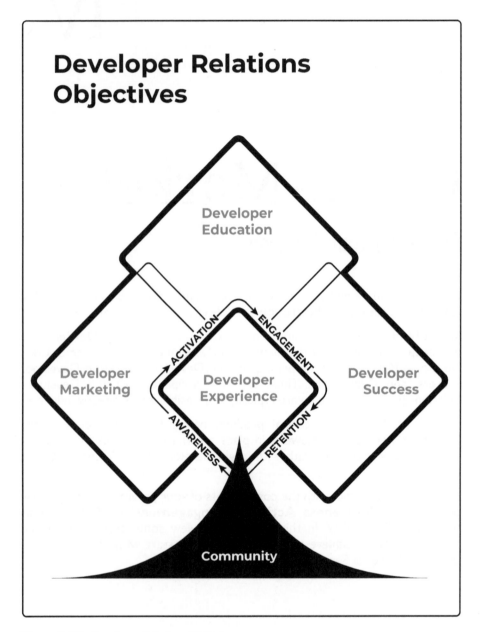

Figure P-IV. Developer Relations Objectives

Developer Segmentation

Based on your developer program's goals and objectives and the product you are supporting, it's time to decide which developers are your target audience. Who do you want to use your product and become part of your program and community?

To effectively reach developers, you must first understand several things about them:

- **Their motivation** – Why do they do what they do?

- **Their skill set** – What tools and resources do they currently use, and what gaps do they have?

- **Their goals** – What do they want to achieve?

- **Their mindset** – How do they evaluate and make decisions?

- **The demands on their time** – Where and how do they need support?

© Caroline Lewko, James Parton 2021
C. Lewko and J. Parton, *Developer Relations*,
https://doi.org/10.1007/978-1-4842-7164-3_12

- **Their limiting factors** – Skills, budget, existing infrastructure choices?

- **The demands on their attention** – Who are you competing with for mindshare?

To be successful, you must use this insight in conjunction with your product in a way that achieves your own goals and measurables. To start, we do this through a process called Segmentation.

Segmentation answers this question:

What type of developer will find success with our product?

Why Is Segmentation Important?

When we hear people say, "We're targeting developers," or "We're targeting the long tail,"[1] our reaction is they are setting themselves up to fail.

Here's why. As we noted in Chapter 5, there are millions of "developers" out there in the world. These developers have differing skill levels and authority. They use different technology stacks and programming languages. They speak different languages and live in different geographic regions. They work for different types of companies, are at different stages of their education or professional career, and are working on different use cases. You can't expect the same message to resonate with them all. You can't expect to find them all in the same place. Nor do they all want or need your product.

The sheer variety of traits that make each developer unique quickly adds to a combinatorial explosion of attributes that create colossal diversity. At the same time, your product was likely designed for a specific audience. It's not effective or necessary for you to target "all developers," and you likely don't have the resources to attempt such a feat even if you wanted to.

Segmentation is about focus.

By creating your segments (or target groups) and, subsequently, your developer personas (more on that in Chapter 13), you will be able to make your messaging more precise, tailored, and aligned with your go-to-market strategy. Focus is required because the alternative is unrealistic. To succeed, you must pursue targeted opportunities rather than the entire market.

For example, perhaps you offer a Java SDK that mobile developers in a specific country can incorporate into their Android application to access a cloud-based repository of locale-specific information that your company publishes.

---

[1] https://www.wired.com/2004/10/tail/

Clearly, such an offering is targeted to a particular market segment, namely, Android developers in a specific region who implement their solutions in Java.

Today, as shown in Figure 12-1, 19% of DevRel programs do not implement any kind of segmentation, according to SlashData research. Others simply differentiate by professional developer vs. student or hobbyist. You can do better!

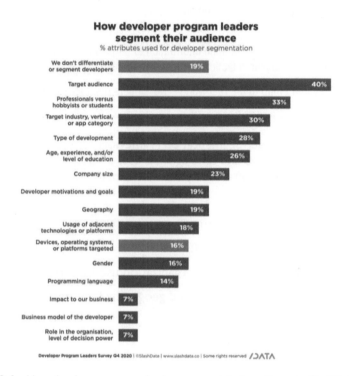

How developer program leaders segment their audience

% attributes used for developer segmentation

- We don't differentiate or segment developers — 19%
- Target audience — 40%
- Professionals versus hobbyists or students — 33%
- Target industry, vertical, or app category — 30%
- Type of development — 28%
- Age, experience, and/or level of education — 26%
- Company size — 23%
- Developer motivations and goals — 19%
- Geography — 19%
- Usage of adjacent technologies or platforms — 18%
- Devices, operating systems, or platforms targeted — 16%
- Gender — 16%
- Programming language — 14%
- Impact to our business — 7%
- Business model of the developer — 7%
- Role in the organisation, level of decision power — 7%

Developer Program Leaders Survey Q4 2020 | ©SlashData | www.slashdata.co | Some rights reserved /⊃ΛTΛ

Figure 12-1. How developer program leaders segment their audience by SlashData

Developer Segmentation Framework

Clearly, a strategy and framework is needed to focus your target audience.

You'll need to base your segmentation on several sources of information. This will include qualitative sources like feedback from your community, colleagues, and peers in the industry and the tech press. It may also include quantitative data from reports and surveys like those published by Stack Overflow, SlashData, or your own community surveys.

Pulling all of this together in a format that is actionable by you and your team can be a challenge. That's why it's essential to use a framework that is comprehensive and that takes developer-specific considerations into account.

COMMON REASONS WHY MANY SEGMENTATION FRAMEWORKS DON'T WORK

- They aren't practical enough.

- They aren't specific enough to *YOUR* business and product.

- They only go part way (using only a single filter or just demographic data).

- They don't give you enough information to target your developer audience and plan a tactical strategy adequately.

- They don't map to the real world – Developers don't identify with them.

We created the Developer Segmentation Framework, as shown in Figure 12-2. It has proven effective time and time again. It uses a series of filters to help you narrow down the criteria in which you will segment your developer targets. The four filters are:

1. Technical (product focused)

2. User (developer focused)

3. Organization (customer organization/use case focused)

4. Market (industry vertical and geography focused)

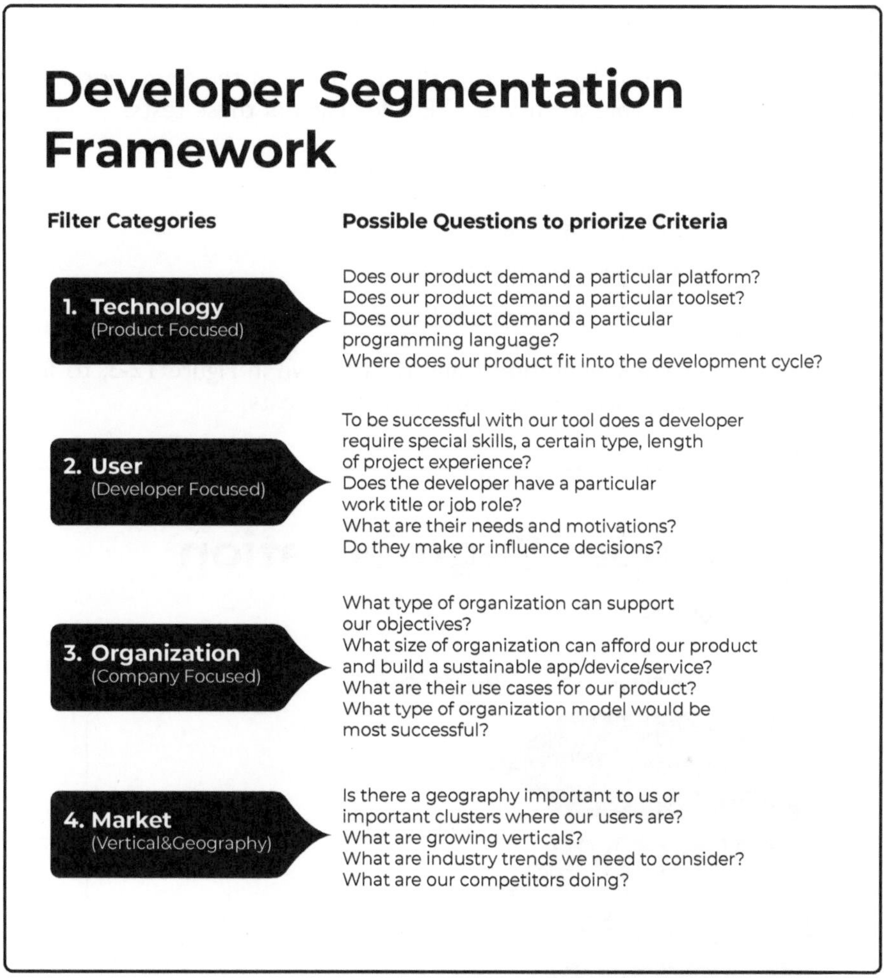

Developer Segmentation Framework

Filter Categories	Possible Questions to priorize Criteria
1. Technology (Product Focused)	Does our product demand a particular platform? Does our product demand a particular toolset? Does our product demand a particular programming language? Where does our product fit into the development cycle?
2. User (Developer Focused)	To be successful with our tool does a developer require special skills, a certain type, length of project experience? Does the developer have a particular work title or job role? What are their needs and motivations? Do they make or influence decisions?
3. Organization (Company Focused)	What type of organization can support our objectives? What size of organization can afford our product and build a sustainable app/device/service? What are their use cases for our product? What type of organization model would be most successful?
4. Market (Vertical&Geography)	Is there a geography important to us or important clusters where our users are? What are growing verticals? What are industry trends we need to consider? What are our competitors doing?

Figure 12-2. Developer Segmentation Framework

We've posed several questions for each filter category here, but of course there are many more. Feel free to adapt it to what makes sense for you. Think about what is important for your product and company right now. You may not have criteria for each category, and the relevance will vary from product to product, and company to company, but that is the point after all!

Tests for Segmentation Criteria

As you list your criteria by answering the questions in the framework, your criteria must also be able to answer "YES" for each of these tests:

1. Is the segment relevant to our business?
2. Is it a large enough segment?
3. Is it a valuable enough segment?
4. Can we target this segment based on our resources?

Use our Developer Segmentation Canvas, as shown in Figure 12-3, to fill in your criteria, making sure they pass these priority tests.

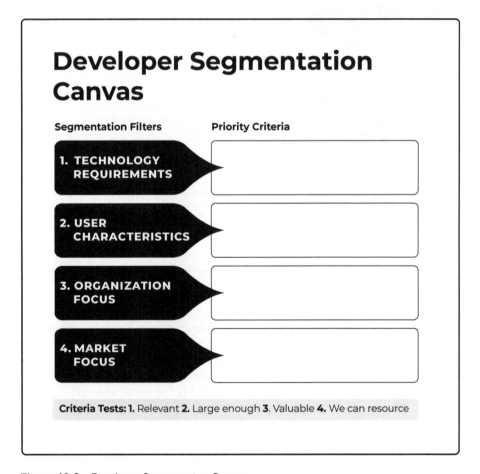

Figure 12-3. Developer Segmentation Canvas

If you've listed more than two or three criteria in a particular category, we suggest you rank them. Then plan your messaging and activities with those ranked most important first.

Developer Segmentation Canvas in Action

We thought it would be helpful if we walked you through an example of completing a segmentation canvas. For this example, we will use a never-before-seen developer SDK that helps mobile game developers utilize artificial intelligence (AI) to create real-time immersive environments in their games.

Of course, we need to answer the question: What type of developer will find success with our product? Let's go through each filter to identify the best criteria:

1. **Technical**

   This product is only focused on the Android mobile operating platform and also integrates with Unity. Developers can use Java or C++ programming languages for the integration of our tool. The implementation takes place after the game has been designed and builds on top of Android's Telecom Framework, so the developer should have some understanding of telecommunications protocols. It includes a number of pretrained TensorFlow models for generative imagery at the edge.

   Our Technical criteria are: Android, Unity Java/C++, 4G, WiFi6, and TensorFlow models

2. **User**

   The implementation of our SDK is fairly complex, so we would expect the developer to have around five years of mobile gaming development experience. This is a crucial technology for a game, so we would expect our developers to have the knowledge and authority to make the decision to adopt our SDK.

   Our user criteria are: Mobile game developer, 5+ years of experience, key decision makers

3. **Organization**

   These complex types of games and technology are likely created by big game studios; however, it is likely that a well-funded Series A startup with experienced developers may also be motivated to attempt this type of game.

Our organization criteria are: Companies that would be most successful with this type of game are (1) large game studios and (2) Series A startups. Their use cases are creating large branded mobile games.

4. **Market**

The industry for our product is Entertainment and Media, notably games. However, we have seen the Education market, specifically because of the home-schooling trend, become more interested in these types of mixed-reality apps. Regionally, the larger game companies are based in the United States (San Francisco), Canada (Vancouver and Montreal), France, and South Korea. It makes most sense to start with our home market of San Francisco, where our CEO is connected.

Our Market criteria are: Industry (1) Entertainment and Media (games), (2) Education. Geography – San Francisco, Vancouver, Montreal, France, Seoul.

In Figure 12-4, we have completed a segmentation canvas for you based on our filtering exercise earlier.

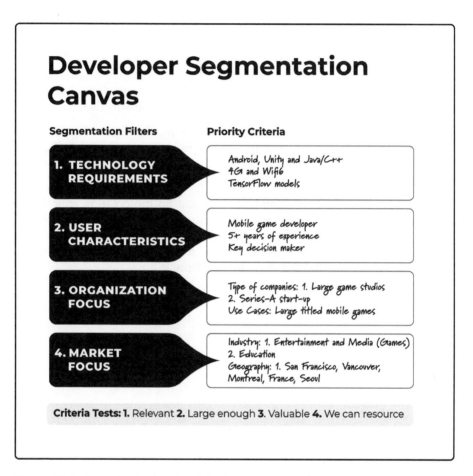

Figure 12-4. Example of a completed developer segmentation

With your segmentation complete, the insight it provides will be used to develop personas (discussed next) to create effective messaging and activities for your developer audiences.

■ **Important point** Segmentation is not a one-time exercise. To start, it's most important to focus on your current situation over the next 6 to 12 months. However, what's important today may change in the future, as the market changes (e.g., new entrants, developers' experience), or your situation changes (e.g., updates to your product or business objectives).

Summary

Targeting "developers" with your product is a recipe for failure. With such breadth and diversity across the entire Developer community, your product is highly unlikely to appeal to everyone, and even if you wanted to, you will not have enough resources to reach so many people and be effective.

The first step in honing your marketing effort is Segmentation. Segmentation is a crucial exercise for a Developer Relations program to undertake as it focuses the target audience while keeping in mind the goals and resources of the company.

This is step one and, once complete, sets you up for creating your target Developer personas which bring your segments to life. With your segmentation and personas in place, you can then move on to step three, creating messaging that effectively articulates the value in your product tailored to the distinct set of people that will find the most benefit from it.

Developer Personas

After you have completed your segmentation, you can start to create personas. Personas are a way to personalize your targets (i.e., put a name and face) to help you and your teams think more personally about your users.

Personas are most effective if used by everyone on the DevRel and product teams and other stakeholders so everyone is creating for and thinking about the same target audience.

Personas make it easier for everyone, whether you are creating your product and documentation or writing your messaging. The more specific you can be, the easier your job gets – for example, a mobile developer named Tom, who works at an ISV in London developing Android apps, is much more compelling than "we are targeting developers," or "we focus on developers in Enterprise companies".

Persona Criteria

We typically create three to four personas, although this may vary based on your product range. When putting together your personas, you'll use the criteria you gathered from your segmentation exercise and add additional personal descriptors.

© Caroline Lewko, James Parton 2021

C. Lewko and J. Parton, *Developer Relations*,

https://doi.org/10.1007/978-1-4842-7164-3_13

Additional information we use for personas includes:

- Name (ensure these are representative of different cultures, ages, and genders)

- Photo

- Job title/type of developer

- Type of company and industry where they work

- Type of technical skills they have

- What they are working on and for who (use case)

- Type of experience they have relevant to your product

- Their particular issues and pain points as developers

- Their level of decision influence

- Where they look for information about new developer products

- Their awareness of your company and product

- Their particular interest in your product (what will it help them solve)

Pricing thresholds if applicableYou may also have others that are applicable to your company or product, but these are the main criteria.

Important note   You may have noticed that we don't include additional personal or demographic information such as marital status, type of music they listen to, etc. That may be important for B2C segmentation and personas, but it's just a distraction for you. As well, there is no need to include the many accepted developer traits as reviewed in Chapter 6. You already know your target is a developer; hence, most of those traits are a given and not useful for this exercise.

Developer Persona Frameworks

There are a number of ways to layout your personas from tables to pictograms to canvases. Choose the one that works best for you and your team, when you need them.

We've included two examples for you that we've created and used. The first, the Developer Persona Canvas, is a great way to visualize your personas, one developer at a time. The second, the Developer Persona Framework, is in table form, allowing you to compare a number of personas side by side.

Developer Persona Canvas

Our Developer Persona Canvas, shown in Figure 13-1, is effective to visualize a developer's needs, on a single sheet of paper. Create one canvas for each persona. We have seen Developer Persona Canvases printed off and taped up on office walls. Then marketing and product teams alike can look directly at the person they are creating for and think: Would this work for "Mark"?

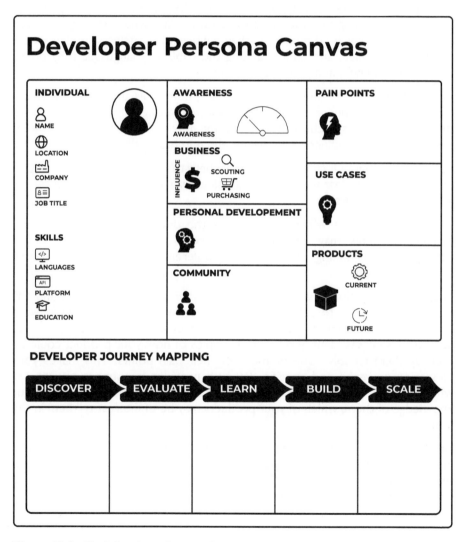

Figure 13-1. Blank Developer Persona Canvas

Let's run through the parts of the canvas and the information included in each.

The canvas starts with information related to the individual – a photo, their name, location, the type of company they work for, and their job title. Next, we establish their skills, especially how those skills relate to using your product. This includes their primary programming languages, frameworks, and platforms of choice. We then document their educational and vocational training, qualifications, and where they go to stay up to date on their skills.

Moving right, we measure how much they know about your company and product. Combining information on the canvas like where they go to learn new skills and which communities they participate in helps you plan where and how to engage, and understanding the tools and languages they prefer informs your DevEd and product activities.

We next assess their influence on purchasing new tools and products. This is of course vital to understand for sales and marketing. Firstly, we categorize their influence on searching or scouting for new technologies in the market and secondly their influence on making the purchasing decision.

Personal development captures how and where they learn new skills. Examples could include peer learning, self-paced online training, books, conferences, or formal training courses.

Community assesses which communities the developer self-identifies as a member of. This may include active participation or lurking in online communities, attending meetups and conferences, making open source contributions, etc.

In the far right column, we look at understanding their pain points and any problems they need to solve. This information will be vital to take forward into the development of your messaging, to ensure it resonates with the persona. Use cases identify relevant examples of how your product could be used by them to solve one or more of their pain points. This makes your messaging powerful and specific. Product provides an opportunity to tag which of your products the developer is using today and, based on your knowledge of them, which of your products may be of interest to them in the future.

Finally, we map "Mark" to his own Developer Journey (see Chapter 15), indicating where he goes to research information on new technologies, and the particular elements of your Developer Experience such as sample code or video tutorials that will most resonate with him.

To see the Developer Persona Canvas in action, we have created an example for you in Figure 13-2. In this example, we've based it on a collection of "never-before-seen" developer products as follows:

- An OAuth API that enables a developer to easily add login capability including third-party services like Google and Facebook login.

- An Out-of-Band Authentication (OOBA) SaaS offering that provides APIs to integrate OOBA into your app and the back-end infrastructure to coordinate OOBA processes (e.g., sending two-factor authentication codes via SMS).

- An HDK that includes a reference design board on which to prototype new devices. The HDK is backed by a collection of SDKs to implement and optimize apps on certain aspects of the hardware, along with hardware-specific compilers, debuggers, and profilers.

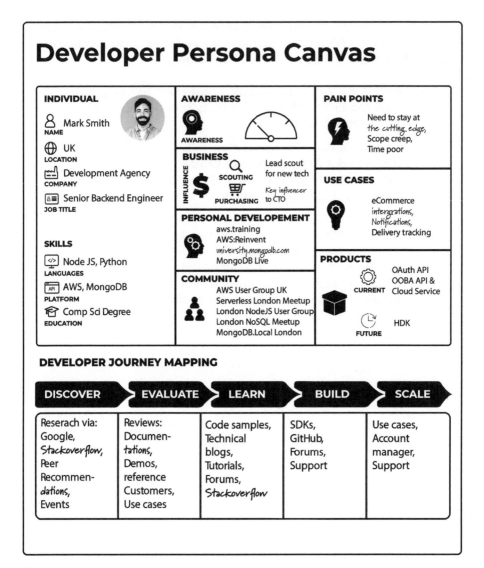

Developer Persona Canvas

INDIVIDUAL

👤 Mark Smith
NAME

⊕ UK
LOCATION

🏚 Development Agency
COMPANY

📇 Senior Backend Engineer
JOB TITLE

SKILLS

`</>` Node JS, Python
LANGUAGES

API AWS, MongoDB
PLATFORM

🏫 Comp Sci Degree
EDUCATION

AWARENESS

AWARENESS

BUSINESS

🔍 SCOUTING   Lead scout for new tech
INFLUENCE
🛒 PURCHASING   Key influencer to CTO

PERSONAL DEVELOPEMENT
aws.training
AWS:Reinvent
university.mongodb.com
MongoDB Live

COMMUNITY
AWS User Group UK
Serverless London Meetup
London NodeJS User Group
London NoSQL Meetup
MongoDB.Local London

PAIN POINTS

Need to stay at the cutting edge, Scope creep, Time poor

USE CASES

eCommerce intergrations, Notifications, Delivery tracking

PRODUCTS

⚙ CURRENT   OAuth API OOBA API & Cloud Service

🕐 FUTURE   HDK

DEVELOPER JOURNEY MAPPING

DISCOVER	EVALUATE	LEARN	BUILD	SCALE
Reserach via: Google, Stackoverflow, Peer Recommendations, Events	Reviews: Documentations, Demos, reference Customers, Use cases	Code samples, Technical blogs, Tutorials, Forums, Stackoverflow	SDKs, GitHub, Forums, Support	Use cases, Account manager, Support

Figure 13-2. *Example Developer Persona Canvas in action*

Developer Persona Framework

Developer Personas summarized in the form of a table, as shown below, can be useful to quickly compare all your personas at a glance. You would typically present three to four personas in this manner.

To see the Developer Persona Framework in action, we've completed Table 13-1. For this table, we've used the product from our Segmentation exercise the "never-before-seen developer SDK that helps mobile game developers utilize artificial intelligence (AI) to create real-time immersive environments in their game" as the example.

Table 13-1. An Example of Developer Personas in a Table Format

Developer Persona Framework
pt. 1

Category	Jackie Game developer, Large Game co Montreal	David Senior Backend Engineer, Agency London, UK	Raj CTO, Startup San Francisco
Company Type Vertical and Geography	Fortune 500 company	3ʳᵈ Party Development Agency, under 100 employees	Startup, small company, Round A funded
Issues/ Pain points	Super busy, no extra cycles; tight deadlines Learning done after hours Limited knowledge of AI	Need to stay on leading edge Time poor, tough customer demands	Need an easy, flawless solution Cash poor
Tech Skills and experience	C++, Unity, TensorFlow, Java	Mobile; platform-specific (iOS/Android), Python, AR experience, Some AI experience	Previously at large gaming company Mobile; platform-specific (iOS/Android), TensorFlow, New to VR and AR, Specialized AI experience
Use case - type of Development/ product	Created popular VR game on Oculus, wants to make interactions with environment more realistic using AI	Custom work for clients (e.g., contracted by game publishers to implement or port part or all of a game).	Gaming for enterprise use cases, health care especially, interested in VR and AR implementations

(continued)

Table 13-1. (continued)

Developer Persona Framework

pt. 2

Category	Jackie Game developer, Large Game co Montreal	David Senior Backend Engineer, Agency London, UK	Raj CTO, Startup San Francisco
Decision Influence	Low – decisions made higher in org but dev is an influencer; team is building off of an existing core game engine with dependencies on existing/legacy technology that weights heavily on decisions around technology adoption.	Lead scout for new tech, key influencer Not usually bound by legacy systems, so able to recommend new technologies. Given the significant role of backend systems, David's recommendations often dictate what products must be used by the front end.	Decision maker Not bound by legacy systems as the product is still in development; able to pivot quickly on technologies as requirements or the target market are being solidified.
Where they find info on new products / Personal Development	Unity newsletter, TensorFlow forums, Reddit, Unity Unite, FB, Stack Overflow, GitHub sample repos, hardware vendor (e.g., Oculus) websites, special interest groups.	Google, Stack Overflow, Android developer, QDN,	Google, GitHub, SFVRCC, industry conferences, special interest groups. memberships in industry alliances
Existing awareness of us and what we offer	Yes/High – aware of us internally, but devs may not be aware of our software/tools	Low	No interest as yet because of lack of awareness

Summary

Creating developer personas is the next step from the work you did on segmentation. They bring personality and help your entire company understand and "see" the developers that you are targeting.

Combining all these data points together will inform your marketing and community strategy as well as your product, Developer Experience, and developer education direction. You will start to understand which cities and countries to target, which technical communities to be active in, which events and conferences to attend, which vendors to integrate with, how to enhance your docs, which code samples to write, what use cases are most relevant, the types of learning resources to create, and how and why your personas buy.

You'll see how your personas work with your Developer Journey in subsequent chapters. In our next chapter, we focus on how this data shapes your messaging to developers, making it specific to maximize your chances of cutting through the noise.

Messaging

"An easier way to develop!"

The preceding sentence is a tagline[1] used by many developer programs. It may seem concise and catchy, but, unfortunately, it's not effective.

In our chapter on segmentation, we took a *product-centric approach* to identify the type of developer required to make your product successful. With messaging, you must take a *developer-centric approach* driven by your personas. Both your segmentation and personas are used to pinpoint what will entice developers to give your product a chance, engage with it, and adopt it.

In this chapter, we'll explore the key factors to keep in mind as you create your messaging, where messaging is used, and how to start creating your messaging. We'll review the difference between messaging and a message. We'll also help you understand why that opening tagline message is not effective.

What Is Messaging?

The term "messaging" can get a bit confusing in Developer Relations, especially as many of us with a tech background think of messaging as specific technology like iMessage or text messages.

---

[1] A tagline, also called a strapline in the UK, is a single short concise sentence used as a catchphrase to distinguish a brand or product.

© Caroline Lewko, James Parton 2021
C. Lewko and J. Parton, *Developer Relations*,
https://doi.org/10.1007/978-1-4842-7164-3_14

Messaging in a marketing context refers to the way you communicate about your product and company with your intended audience. It includes what you say (the message), how you say it, the format, and where and when the message is delivered.

It's often thought that messaging is just for marketing. But that is not true.

You will definitely message to your developer audience when you engage with them in your outreach activities such as advertising, social media, blogs, and other promotions. You will have messages for your events and hackathons and on your T-shirts.

There is also messaging in Developer Experience, the more technical interactions with your developers, such as emails, documentation, YouTube tutorials, and your support options. There is also messaging within your product.

Anytime a developer interacts with your company, there is messaging involved, which is why it is important that it is on point, consistent, and that everyone involved knows what it is.

Key Factors of Developer Messaging

Messaging to developers is different than messaging to either consumers or business. We described many of the differences of working with developers in Chapter 5 and how the business models vary in Chapter 8. These differences affect the type of messaging you create and use.

Several key factors are listed in the following for you to consider as you create your messaging.

Keep It Developer-Friendly

A "Developer-friendly" approach tends to be very practical. As mentioned previously, developers don't want to be marketed to. They want to understand very quickly if your product is for them. To do this, your messaging should help developers decipher questions like these:

- What type of product is being offered?
- What does it do?
- How does it make a developer's life easier or better?
- Why should a developer use it?
- Why should a developer choose it over competitive offers?

When we look back at the opening tagline – "An easier way to develop!" – we see that it fails to answer many of the preceding questions, so it will ultimately be ineffective in enticing developers to try your product. It's best to be clear and concise. Refrain from using superlatives around benefits. Instead, speak to their needs and emphasize the product features and specs that will make a difference to them.

Tone and Voice

It's crucial to find the voice you want to use as your identity. It could be professional, serious, fun, geeky, or edgy. Any one of those styles is OK, as long as you are comfortable with it, it resonates with your developer personas, you remain consistent, and it's authentic to your company culture and people. As a note, developers tend to respond better to a voice that is down to earth and not too corporate. You may find that your company's corporate voice is different from the voice you use with your developers. This difference is perfectly OK and encouraged.

You'll also want to define the reading level[2] that will best align with your audience. You may have noticed differences in the complexity of language used by brands and products. For example, a magazine like *The Economist* has a higher reading level than *People* magazine. Approximately 75% of developers worldwide completed at least the equivalent of a bachelor's degree or higher,[3] so you certainly don't want to use overly simplistic language. At the same time, a PhD level may not resonate well with your potential audience either and may be judged as too stuffy.

Using "you" in marketing communications, which is now common, is especially effective when communicating to developers and communities. So lose the desire to talk about "we," that is, "We are Trustworthy.", "We have the best tools.", or "We deliver." Instead, talk to developers about how they will succeed, without the marketing speak that can trigger their bullshit detectors. They don't care how good you say you are. They care about what you can do for them. Referring to your Developer Persona Canvas from Chapter 13 is especially effective here, so you can look Mark in the eye and say: *You will be able to do XX with our product.*

---

[2] You can read more about reading levels here: https://en.wikipedia.org/wiki/Flesch%E2%80%93Kincaid_readability_tests
[3] https://insights.stackoverflow.com/survey/2020#education

Targeting Other Decision Makers

In addition to developers, elements of your messaging will likely need to target executives or other decision makers as they are often required to support or approve the adoption of your product, especially if your segmentation has identified larger and more complex organizations as opportunities. In this case, indicating the product's business benefits is important, but avoiding the superlatives is still important unless you can prove what you claim.

It's also important to be clear to your audience about who your message is directed to. Separating developer-centric and stakeholder-centric messaging and marketing is sensible. As many technology companies mature their offering, you start to see signposting on their website to allow visitors to self-identify (Developer vs. Business) to get the content they feel is most appropriate to them. Companies will often have multiple social media profiles, again allowing for better relevance of communication. We've seen developer websites be incredibly direct, for example, content labeled "How to get your manager to approve this," making it very obvious to whom the information is targeted.

Timing and Trust

Be realistic about your promises and be transparent about any issues. It's best to set expectations. For example, launch something in beta first, rather than building up unrealistic expectations of a fully released product, which will lead to issues and loss of credibility further down the line if your product is buggy or fails to deliver on your claims.

Being helpful when developers need it will establish trust. To extend this further, being helpful when it's not even related to your product will boost the community standing and reputation of your people and, by association, your company. Examples include organizing community meetups or conferences, helping to troubleshoot at hackathons even if the developer is not building with your product, writing books, contributing to open source projects, etc.

If you've come from a B2C or B2B environment, we recommend you ease up on the volume of messages you send. Growth hacking tactics that revolve around regular social media outreach, retargeting ads, and gated content (where you need to enter your email address to access something like a whitepaper or webinar) which then release a relentless automated email campaign are annoying and will turn off developers. If you recall in the section on business models and funnels, the length of product adoption for developers can be very long. Poking them to adopt your product faster often provokes them to move to the competition.

Of course, the preceding tactics can be useful if used appropriately and timed properly. For example, an email that reaches out with a simple getting started guide two days after they register with you can be helpful. To be successful, you need to understand the relationship between where your developer currently is on the Developer Journey (Chapter 15) and how your messaging, or intervention, can help them move to the next stage of the journey.

Messaging Styles and the Developer Journey

To gain results, you will discover you need different styles of messaging at different times and for different activities as shown in Figure 14-1. If you map your messaging to the developers' stage in your developer journey, you can be more focused and relevant. For example, in the Discovery phase you want to appeal and convince them to give you a chance. In the Evaluate and Learn stages, you need to be educational. Switch to a celebratory tone when they have launched into production, which gives you an opportunity to congratulate and showcase them as a customer.

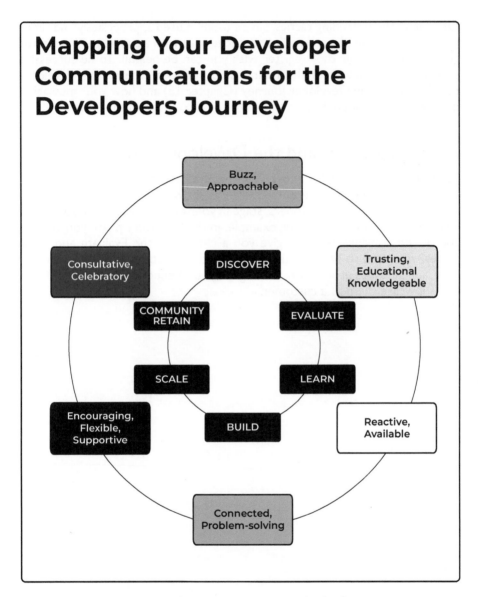

Figure 14-1. Mapping your developer communications to the developer journey

Feedback and Communication Loops

As with everything you do, a feedback loop is essential. Provide your developers with a means to get their questions answered and to tell you how you are doing. Talk directly to your users to find out how you are doing, regularly find out their needs (as they may have changed), and ask them what they like or do not like in your messages and about your product. You can do this by social media, email, regular surveys, focus groups, in-person, or forms on your site.

Developer Messaging Framework

Once you understand the factors of Developer Messaging and you have your Developer Personas in front of you, it's time to create your messaging. The pieces to gather and develop include:

- Tone and voice (as discussed earlier)
- Heroes, halos, and stories
- Keywords – Features
- Keywords – Benefits
- Differentiation
- Key statements

You'll use these headings to create your own Developer Messaging Framework as shown in Figure 14-2. Adopting the Developer Messaging Framework will ensure consistency in your messaging, acting as a reference point and "source of truth." This is especially helpful in larger organizations where many people and teams are involved, making alignment challenging.

Developer Messaging Framework

	PERSONA 1	PERSONA 2	PERSONA 3
Tone/Voice			
Hero			
Key words - Features (1-3)			
Key words - Benefits (1-3)			
Key words - Proof (1-2)			
Key statements (1-3)			

Figure 14-2. Developer Messaging Framework

Heroes, Halos, and Stories

One aspect of messaging that ties into your differentiation is heroes, halos, and stories. Stories, especially if they capture attention and sentiment, are easier to remember than a straight-up product pitch. Most of us recall the story of Hewlett Packard and their start in the garage and how Facebook started on a college campus. Your company might have a story that's interesting too.

On a more practical basis, stories can also be told around marquee customers (like a Fortune 100) or a significant customer success story, where your product solved a major issue in a particular industry segment. These stories tend to become case studies, but they can also be used in your messaging. In that way, we label them a "hero," where they help drive adoption with other companies that have the same issues or are in the same industry segment.

When the hero story becomes well known, it can create a "halo" effect where your products are viewed as being effective in solving other problems, in other industries.

Messaging Keywords

Messaging keywords are simply that – the words used to describe what your product is and does. In this context, these messaging keywords should not be confused with Google AdWords keywords or SEO keywords, although this work will inform your ad buying and SEO strategy.

They come in two forms, features and benefits. Both are important, but 80% of the words you use in messaging should be based on the features of your product, given the practical nature of what helps the developer make a decision about your product as described earlier.

Messaging Keywords: 80% – Features

Keywords based on features come directly from the words you used when creating your segmentation and from your product specs. They are practical and factual. Let Developers know what you offer and what they can build with it backed with any tech specs that are relevant.

For example, if your tool is a machine learning modeling tool, you must say that so it's clear what you offer. If your tool is only for Android developers, you must say that so iOS developers don't waste their time. Developers want to see these words so they can be confident that what you offer is what they are seeking. Use those words directly in your messaging and activities, across the journey. They will provide clarity and confidence in your offering and clarity in what developers can build with it.

Messaging Keywords: 20% – Benefits

Benefits are the words that describe what your product can do for the developer. It's important to be as descriptive as you can, in an honest and authentic way. Again, refer back to the pain points and use cases you identified on your Persona Canvas to connect the dots.

Let's go back and review the message at the start of the chapter – "An easier way to develop." The statement brings up more questions than it answers. What type of development is easier? What part of the development process is easier, all of it? Define easier? Why is it easier? Because the developer will use tools they already know, it's important to be as specific as you can.

Differentiation

Differentiation is the next piece to sort out in your messaging. Differentiation, based on your product and your company's value proposition, primarily comes down to your unique selling point (USP), or your "secret sauce." What exactly sets you apart from all the other choices your target Developer may have? Is it the product, your service, a process, or results you have that no one else has, or that you do the best? Identifying it helps you and your developers understand why they should care and believe you and ultimately why they should spend their valuable currency (time and money) on you. In this case, data beats fluff – always back up any claims with evidence. From recent client work in the CPaaS market, it's evident that not much of this analysis is happening. Of six leading providers, the majority duplicate messages around reliability, security, and ease and simplicity of development.

You may find yourself in a product space that is commoditized, where many companies offer almost identical products with similar claims. In this case, you may be able to differentiate on the service that is wrapped around your product like having the best Developer Experience, docs, the best technical support, or by having the most marquee customers, etc.

Finally, you may be able to differentiate on sentiment. Developers certainly want clarity on what you can provide, but they are also influenced by the way you make them feel and the way you operate in the community. Getting your company culture right along with hiring and training great people is key. It's particularly crucial that your frontline staff like advocates, technical support, and sales engineers are helpful, friendly, and available. Their disposition goes a long way to creating positive sentiment for your company. People like to work with people they like!

Regardless of which messaging you use, and whether the developer knows you or not, your product still needs to be able to deliver.

Developers don't care how good you say you are, they care about what you can do for them.

Key Statements

Once you've narrowed down your keywords and determined the tone of voice you will use and any heroes you have, you can start to put your words into statements. Typically, to start you'll want a tagline or short statement (10 words or less) and longer statements of 25, 50, and 100 words to use for various purposes.

If you get stuck or aren't quite sure if you have the right keywords or statements, we find it helpful to ask – "What does this mean to a developer?" If you can't answer that question, you better get back to the drawing board.

Summary

Messaging is a key part of your strategy when setting up a developer program, and it must be completed before you activate your tactics. All parts of Developer Relations need to be aligned with messaging – it's not just for marketing. Start creating your messaging with your personas in front of you and remember the key factors for being successful in messaging to developers.

Summary

The Developer Journey

In this chapter, we will take a look at what a developer journey map is and how to use it in your program.

All great journeys start with a map, a formal way of understanding how to arrive at a destination or achieve a goal. As such, the Developer Journey Map is an invaluable tool in your Developer Relations program. As developers are increasingly influencing or making decisions about which technologies to adopt, it's important that you formally map out the journey they take from initially discovering your company and product all the way through to scaling with it. Once you've created your map, you must do your best to deliver that journey and experience to them in the most frictionless way possible.

What Is a Developer Journey Map?

Like a customer journey, the Developer Journey Map is a visualization that identifies the ideal path and experience a developer follows across different key stages as they increase the level of interaction with your brand, your team, and your product. It's a tool that helps you to think holistically about the experience from the **developers' perspective**.

© Caroline Lewko, James Parton 2021
C. Lewko and J. Parton, *Developer Relations*,
https://doi.org/10.1007/978-1-4842-7164-3_15

Those interactions, or developer touchpoints, are used to map **the developer's experience – how they engage, what and who they engage with, how it makes them feel, and how they react to those touchpoints at each stage**. Organizing these touchpoints into a map helps you identify shortcomings or friction, creating a better overall experience.

Stages of the Developer Journey

A typical developer journey maps across these key stages a developer travels: **Discover, Evaluate, Learn, Build, and Scale**, shown in Figure 15-1.

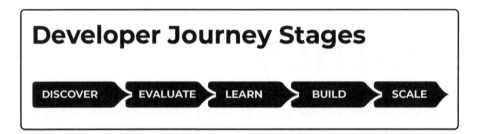

Figure 15-1. Developer journey stages

> **The stages indicate significant changes or stage gates in the developer's intent and actions, but do not imply elapsed time.**

A developer may well complete the first three or four stages on the same day if they invest the time, and you have provided a friction-free experience. Conversely, the adoption cycle to become a user may take a year if the developer hasn't yet found the right use case to build with your product. It can also depend on the product. Identifying and using an API is typically a shorter process than developing with an SDK or HDK.

Developers may also start the journey at different stages depending on their background and persona – it's not always a sequential start on the left, finish on the right. For example, developers engaging with you for the first time are looking for "getting started" style messages as they Evaluate. They should know from your landing page, particularly above the fold,[1] within a few seconds what your product does and where they can find what they're looking for. Practically, it's critical to be aware of how and where developers are accessing their information via a mobile or desktop experience and optimize the information accordingly.

---

[1] The upper half of a web page that is visible without scrolling down the page.

Developers who are already customers may be looking at either how they improve what they have already deployed (e.g., quality, performance, etc.) or how to extend their app by adding more use cases and features to what they already offer. In this case, they may dive right into a Build stage, even though it might be a year or more since they have visited your site.

The right touch points need to be accessible at the right time – when the developer needs them.

In Figure 15-2, you will find a Developer Journey Map framework we created that aligns to the stages, which you are welcome to use. On the map you'll notice the key goal or needs of the developer are outlined at each stage. If the goal is achieved, they move on to the next stage of adoption. Each goal has three key questions you need to answer for the developer to achieve the overall goal of the stage in question. It's your job to develop and optimize each of the "touchpoints" to ensure you meet the goals for each stage of the journey and that developers have all of their questions answered effectively.

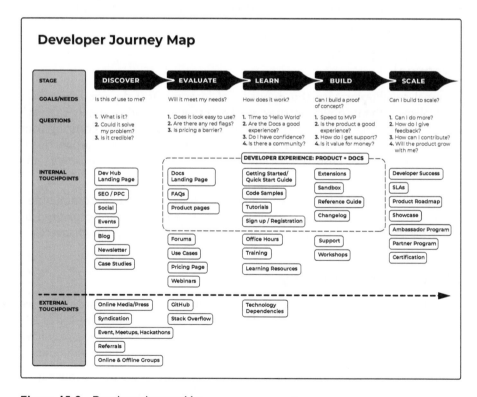

Figure 15-2. Developer Journey Map

Touchpoints of the Developer Journey

As mentioned, touchpoints are used to map the developer's journey. Their experience along the journey includes all the touchpoints they come into contact with including your product, marketing, sales, and support; how it makes them feel about your company, your people, and your product; and their actions or reactions to those touchpoints.

You'll note that the touchpoints are divided into these two categories:

Internal

These are the properties and content that your company owns and controls. You have complete control over what it is, what it does, and how it contributes to answering the developers' questions and achieving the overall goal of the related developer journey stage.

Examples include your website, documentation, your messaging on social media, your advertising, pricing information, code samples, support, etc., as well as your product.

External

External touchpoints are the opposite of Internal. You do not have direct control over them; however, they are key resources and channels to reach both your existing users and your potential future customers. Ensuring your brand and tools are visible, discussed, and supported on these properties is absolutely vital to ensure awareness grows, reputation is positive, and adoption rises.

Examples include media, industry analysts, blogs, third-party communities, and forums. It also includes meetups and conferences that are organized by other parties. We will cover how you achieve this in subsequent chapters.

Notes on the Journey

On the Developer Journey map, in both internal and external categories, we included 42^2 example touchpoints. This is a pretty comprehensive list of the most important and typical touchpoints, but we recognize that you may have other touchpoints you use. We encourage you to iterate on our example.

We have placed each touchpoint in the most relevant stage of the journey to improve the presentation of the information, but of course touchpoints can be relevant in more than one stage of the journey. We have placed them in the

---

[2] Which is the answer to the ultimate question of Life, the Universe, and Everything!

spot they are typically first encountered, but don't feel you need to be locked in to where they are situated in our example – do what is right for you.

The Developer Journey Map is a tool for you and is meant to be flexible based on your product, type of company, and the needs of your developers.

We encourage you to modify the map in the way that works best for you, as long as you are keeping the needs of your developer at the forefront of your decision making.

The beauty of these Developer Journey Maps is they can be applied at the macro, strategic level of your program, or you can drill into a specific area at the tactical micro-level. As an example of a micro-level application, we have created a developer journey specific to events, which we'll share with you in Chapter 23.

Who Owns the Journey?

We are clear that the DevRel team has overall ownership of the Developer Journey. After all, this is the key document that plots the path of their customer – the Developer. Having ownership and oversight of all the constituent pieces of the puzzle allows DevRel to effectively represent the "voice of the developer"[3] and champion the developers' needs inside the company. We refer back to the role of DevRel as an "information valve" in Figure 2-3.

While we state DevRel owns the journey, you will see there are implications for the wider business, as it involves multiple functional areas. From brand to marketing, to product and engineering, to sales, support, and more. Every individual company will be organized differently. The maturity of the business is a major factor. In younger, smaller organizations, you will find generalists who are responsible for multiple tasks. In larger, more mature companies, things become more complex, with specialists organized into different departments, with potentially different priorities and different points of view. For the DevRel team to maintain overall ownership of the Developer Journey (and the encapsulated Developer Experience), they will have to be adept at building internal relationships and managing their stakeholders. We cover some of these challenges in Chapters 10 and 27.

---

[3] The feedback from your developers on their needs, preferences, experience, and expectations of your company and product.

How to Find Out If Your Journey Is Working

We recommend you use this Developer Journey map at the initial creation of your program and periodically to audit the effectiveness of your journey with ongoing reviews and tests. The key is to remove all the friction from your journey. You should have a laser focus and obsession to identify and remove anything that slows the developers' progress through the stages. Getting this right will form the heart of your competitive advantage. Assuming what you offer has intrinsic value, a smooth and seamless experience will bolster your reputation and lead to referrals and advocacy in the community.

Here are three ways to identify friction in both quantitative and qualitative ways to understand if your journey is working optimally:

1. Ask Your Community for Feedback

   You'll find most developers are very willing to provide feedback. All you have to do is ask them and provide a method for them to respond. Gathering feedback can happen through:

   - Your support channels – Set up a channel for feedback, and monitor your channels/forums for comments.

   - Survey your community through online survey forms.

   - Talk to them at events by deliberately asking them – How are we doing? What can we do better?

   - Host regular Office Hours for them to ask questions.

   - Host developer focus groups.

   - Review your support tickets.

2. Friction Logging/Friction Audits

   Friction logging is the process of actually walking through the developer journey to audit its effectiveness. The goal is to "step into the shoes" of your target developer. Whether you are building this journey map prelaunch or reviewing your existing journey, make use of your personas to think about how "Mark" or "Jackie" might first discover you and what they experience throughout their journey.

   We suggest doing periodic tests with developers that don't know who you are and have never been to your site or have not previously used your product. That way, you can effectively gauge their "first impressions." Provide the developers with a couple of URLs to start and/or keywords (your brand, product name, product category, use case) for a Google search and set them off to find and document their journey and impressions. The Developer Journey map is then created from their actual observed experience to ensure your map is not just a theoretical exercise.

If their first impression is negative, they likely won't get beyond two or three touchpoints. Your friction logging will likely uncover issues like missing or inaccurate documentation, problems with the product, unclear messaging, and the level of responsiveness and effectiveness of your support. You'll be able to identify your highlights too!

3. Journey Data Evaluation and Measurement

It's essential that you have set up your Developer Hub and product with data collection and analytics mechanisms (Google Analytics, Mixpanel, Marketo, etc.) to see how and when users engage with your site and with your product. By reviewing your data, you will be able to see the path your users take and where you have friction points leading them to stop or leave your journey, informing you to take appropriate action. You'll learn more about this in the Chapter 26.

Remove Bias

Even with the best will in the world, it can be difficult for your team to be completely free of bias when they are involved in reviewing something they are so close to and invested in.

People have a tendency to seek out information that supports something they already believe (confirmation bias), or believe fault lies in things outside of their control (self-serving bias), or attribute behavior to unfounded stereotypes (fundamental attribution error). Also, when something is seen many times, the steps along the way are often forgotten (generalization).

It's human nature to sometimes "not see the forest for the trees," if you are too close to something. In addition, it is common that teams get defensive around their contributions which can create internal problems. Getting a fresh perspective from those detached from the product is imperative. External experts should also bring an "industry perspective" with a view on best practices and how you benchmark against them, which might not be present within your own company. Using data and analytics also supports this.

Involve the Stakeholders

Once you have the feedback and data of your journey, we suggest hosting a cross-functional internal workshop. This achieves two goals: it educates and level-sets everyone on the experience and helps create commitment to fix the issues uncovered.

You may also invite your current customers or prospective customers to come in and participate in the workshops. There is nothing better than hearing it directly from the horse's mouth. While bringing them into "the mothership" may help to make them feel valued and part of the extended team, be sure they won't hold back in their criticism so you get to the heart of any potential issues.

Summary

Your Developer Journey is one of the most important documents you will create.

It can be used to document and level-set the understanding of your Developers' interactions and their experience with every facet of your company. It also signposts the key external (or earned) places your customers and prospects spend time.

Your obsession should be to constantly refine the goals and key questions you need to answer, to move the developer along the journey through the stages. The majority of Developer Programs will only start to produce meaningful revenue when the Developer makes it to (and stays in) the Scaling stage.

You can also use your journey to inform improvements required in your Developer Experience and go-to-market execution. It is a living document and should be revisited with every major release or change in your offering to identify stumbling blocks to move the Developer from discovery through to scaling as quickly and efficiently as possible.

Remember to use the personas you created to think about how your core audience like "Mark" and "Jackie" might find your portal and what they might experience throughout their journey.

In the next few chapters, we will dive deeper into the stages and touchpoints of the Developer Journey and give you practical information to use.

Discover

Is This of Use to Me?

The developer's journey begins when they first learn about you, which we call the Discover stage. If we look back at the Developer Journey Map, we see the goal of the developer at this stage is to answer the question – **Is this of use to me?** The task of DevRel is to answer that question and move the developer along to the next stage of the developer journey as quickly as possible.

In this chapter, we'll review the ways developers discover you and considerations for you to create effective awareness campaigns as you move them to the Evaluate stage.

While we rightly focus on the developer audience for this book, remember it is impossible to guarantee that 100% of the people discovering you will be developers. It is therefore important to consider this when creating your journey and experience. Other job roles could include product or technical managers who will evaluate you based on their needs and from their perspective in their organization. They may be doing this independently of the developers in their company or in a coordinated manner as part of a company-wide evaluation. We defined this broader group, who all contribute to the buying decision, as the developer decision-making unit (DDMU).

While we do not advocate diluting your overall Developer Experience to cater for your nontechnical visitors, it is best practice to create and make available less technical content to help them find the answers to their questions, enabling them to also reach the decision to adopt your technology.

© Caroline Lewko, James Parton 2021
C. Lewko and J. Parton, *Developer Relations*,
https://doi.org/10.1007/978-1-4842-7164-3_16

Awareness and Outreach

The process of getting the attention of developers is called outreach, which typically falls under the functional area of developer marketing. The Discover stage is where the developer will experience their **first touchpoint** with you. You'll want to make a good first impression as they tend to decide pretty quickly if you are interesting enough to invest their time to learn more.

Raising a developer's awareness of your company and product can occur in a number of ways such as advertising, getting a referral from another developer, reading about you on a blog, or meeting one of your advocates at an event.

The developer will use these interactions to gain an initial understanding of:

- What are you offering?
- Is it compatible with their existing technology stack?
- Is it a tool that could solve their current problem?
- Are you credible? Has anyone else used it?

The answers you give, or perhaps the impression you create, will help them decide if you deserve their time to explore further.

Discover Touchpoints

You have many different options for outreach, and we have not comprehensively included them all on our developer journey framework. Successful touchpoints have something in common – they all start with a clear understanding of the target developer they are trying to speak to.

Identifying the type of developers you are trying to reach is achieved via your segmentation (Chapter 12) followed by identifying individual representative developers to form your personas (Chapter 13). Now you know the "who," you can then tailor your messaging (Chapter 14) to appeal to them and answer the "how" and "why."

As mentioned in Chapter 15, there are two types of touchpoints used for outreach – internal touchpoints, sometimes called owned properties, and external touchpoints, sometimes called earned properties. Here are some examples that are relevant for the Discover stage.

Internal touchpoints are those which you can directly control, or affect, to increase awareness and discovery, such as:

- Search engines – SEO and paid advertising.
- Content marketing – including social media, blogs, newsletters, webinars, etc.
- Your own events.

External touchpoints are those which you don't wholly control, but can influence indirectly to help grow your reputation, such as:

- Blog posts or articles that someone else has written that mention your products.

- Public relations activity leading to press coverage.

- Analyst relations activity leading to favorable positioning in research reports.

- Product search sites like Product Hunt, G2, etc.

- Online developer communities and resources.

- Events run by others, where your own people or people independent of you are discussing your product. These interactions take place face to face or online and in different formats like conferences, meetups, hackathons, and more.

- A referral from a friend/colleague.

Top Developer Discover Sources

You likely don't have an unlimited budget or staffing resources, so you probably want to know the short answer of where to focus. Based on research from Developer Media,[1] along with discussions with clients and our own observations, we recommend the following.

Search Engines

Online searches are the number one way developers find out about new tools. This, of course, is dominated by Google, which continues to enjoy over 80% of all search traffic.[2] Optimizing for this type of discovery is essential and typically achieved in three ways:

1. **Search Engine Optimization (SEO)** – This includes writing good copy with the right keywords and metadata on your website. It is also vital that your docs can be indexed by Google to aid discoverability.

---

[1] https://www.codeproject.com/Surveys/2343/Where-do-you-find-info-on-new-developer-tools

[2] https://www.statista.com/statistics/216573/worldwide-market-share-of-search-engines/#:~:text=Ever%20since%20the%20introduction%20of,share%20as%20of%20January%202021

2. **Paid search** including bidding on your company and product name, keywords related to the searches your target audience use, and bidding on searches for competitive products. You might also consider retargeting ads on other platforms like social media. Remember that developers are heavy users of ad blocker software,[3] so research before going all in with your marketing budget.

3. A **content strategy** including blogs, whitepapers, video content, etc., which help drive traffic, time on page, conversion, create thought leadership for you, and create authority for search engine algorithms if others are linking and sharing that content.

Peer Referrals

Developers like to learn about new tools, as well as get answers to problems, from trusted sources – their peers. Peer referrals can come from one-on-one conversations, but most often come through mentions on various online developer communities, programming sites, and platforms, such as Slack, Discord, Subreddits, Stack Overflow, GitHub, Code Project, and many others. You will need to discover the groups that are most relevant to your product and audience. Your developer persona work can help here. It is vital that your DevRel team is actively listening and engaging in these communities.

Your Developer Advocates

Your own team may be the first touchpoint with developers. This often starts with a conversation with a developer advocate at an event (either in-person or online). Remember, first impressions are everything. It is crucial that everyone who has the potential to make contact with developers be prepared with detailed product knowledge, the messaging associated with it, the call to action (CTA) the developer is encouraged to take, and that the team member is empowered and willing to take ownership of any feedback or issues.

The typical CTA for all this initial activity is to encourage the developer to visit your Developer Hub. If you've done a good job, you need to be prepared for what comes next.

---

[3] https://marketingtechnews.net/news/2018/mar/13/developers-use-adblockers-and-dont-engage-online-ads/

The Developer Hub

Regardless of the developers' initial touchpoint with you, you will want to get them to visit your Developer Hub as quickly as possible so you can present the right information they need on a property you control. If you've managed to catch their interest through any of the preceding activities, they'll also want to check you out on your home turf.

Where they land on your website must be a **key focus of your developer journey.**

The developer will find and arrive at your hub in a number of ways (not all are ideal):

- **A URL from your inbound marketing** – Typically for simplicity, this is your default homepage; however, it is worth experimenting with custom landing pages containing specific content related to the campaign you are running. This approach is popular as many developer hubs are complex, and rather than leave to chance where the developer clicks, a custom landing page provides better focus for that initial interaction and improves the chances of conversion.

- **A URL found through a search engine** that may take them to your developer hub's landing page, *or it may take them somewhere else you hadn't planned or expected*.

- **A URL from a referral** – As this is out of your control, be prepared because they may be directed to a nonstandard entry point or, worse, an outdated page or HTTP 404 error. A good CMS is your friend to avoid these types of issues.

- **If you are part of a larger Developer Plus company**, the developer may land on the URL to your main corporate site, not your Developer Hub, so ensure you have an obvious link to your Developer Hub to get them to the right place as quickly as possible.

- **developer.yourcompany.com or yourcompany.com/ developer** – These are standard formats for URLs to developer hubs, which many developers directly type into their browser bar or search engine.

Your developer journey must be prepared for all of these scenarios to ensure the developers' first touchpoint with your Developer Hub is a positive experience. A good Developer Hub first touchpoint experience, like any website, comes down to about 50ms.[4] You have a very short amount of time to make an impression here. Your chances of success are heightened if you have designed your page for your target audience. You don't need to design for the general public, you design for your niche audience.

It's hopefully obvious, but ensure all your online and offline marketing efforts contain your URL. As we mentioned, this URL may be customized by campaign or event to further tailor the message the developer sees when they arrive and should be trackable so you can correctly attribute traffic and conversion to each campaign and touchpoint.

Once the developer lands, help them to quickly understand what your product does, answer their questions, and remove any doubts, thus enabling them to reach the conclusion that you are worth investing even more time.

Always use plain language, recognized terminology, and only make claims you can substantiate. We recommend creating simple phrases that convey what problem your product solves and how. Be aware of your competitors and how they are positioning themselves so you have a distinctive and unique take. We went into more detail on this in the messaging chapter.

Have they lingered for more than a few seconds? Congratulations – you've piqued their curiosity to find out if your product is worthy of their time.

Are You Credible?

As developers continue on their discovery journey, they will likely conduct their own desk research, review your product pages, and check out your case studies to find out who else is using it and to verify that your technology works in practice (because very few want to be the first to use an unknown tool). They will also be looking for evidence that your product is being actively developed, maintained, and supported.

This is also the stage where developers start to make a judgment on your reputation using external sources beyond your control to get an unbiased view on the quality and adoption of your technology and the speed and elegance of resolving any issues. Blogs, meetups, social media, Stack Overflow, GitHub, Product Hunt, and Hacker News are all examples of the places they will go to conduct this research, along with asking their peers directly.

---

[4]Google's research, https://research.google/pubs/pub38315/

A direct quote[5] from a developer about a new tool:

It is a good tool but when we look at the GitHub repo of 'company x', there's not much activity and no future goals set. There are only two contributors and just 201 stars. So my advice is to think twice before depending on it too much and recommending it to others. Just for the sake of comparison, 'company y' has 20,500 stars with and around 1500 contributors....

Also, remember you are selling to a highly technical audience, so your site's usability, look and feel, navigation, responsiveness, and load times also factor into their first impression of you and your competence.

Seeking reassurance on the adoption and popularity of your product, or the technologies your product depends upon, is important to answer questions such as:

- Is there a healthy pool of skilled developers familiar with the technology that I can employ directly?

- Is there a choice of outsourcing agencies that support your technology?

- Most importantly, will developers find help if they hit problems (both from you and the wider non-affiliated community)?

You may think your offering is the best thing since sliced bread, but it would be a serious business risk for the developer to pick a cutting edge or, conversely, a declining technology with a small associated developer community.

Brand-new technologies can be unstable and subject to rapid change. Older technologies can be deprecated. A small community usually means a lack of peer support and expensive talent. For example, the JavaScript community goes from strength to strength, holding the number one spot as the world's most popular programming language (used by 67% of developers) for eight years in a row. In comparison, once in the top ten as recently as 2017, Ruby has declined to just 7% of the developer population. It pays to stay on top of developer trends.[6]

So, unless the developer is highly motivated to learn more due to a positive first impression, or they are being told by their boss they have to use your product, you need to work hard to be relevant and engage them. If their experience at any one of these touchpoints falls below their tolerance threshold, they will be gone, unlikely to return. There's an even better chance they will tell their peers about their "bad" experience.

---

[5] Found on a YouTube channel of a developer program. Name withheld for privacy.
[6] https://insights.stackoverflow.com/survey/2020#most-popular-technologies

Summary

Discover is the first stage and first step a developer takes in engaging with you. Being able to quickly answer their key question – is this of use to me? – is critical in your outreach campaigns. Once the developer has made a cursory review of your Developer Hub, has this initial question answered, and decided you are credible, then they are ready to dig a little deeper.

In the next chapter, we'll review the Developer Experience and the all-important "docs" and how they fit with the next stages on the journey: Evaluate, Learn, and Build.

Developer Experience

Product and Docs

If you have passed the developer's "sniff test," they will be incented to invest a little more time with you, dig a little deeper into your resources, and take your product for a test spin and the next stages in their journey which are Evaluate, Learn, and Build.

However, before we explore those three stages further, let's pause and discuss Developer Experience (or DX) which is critical to your ultimate success with developers. We'll explore first what DX is, its components, and why it is an important part of Developer Relations.

Developer Experience (DX)

We defined DX earlier as:

Developer Experience (DX) is the experience developers have when they interact with your *product* and *documentation*.

© Caroline Lewko, James Parton 2021
C. Lewko and J. Parton, *Developer Relations*,
https://doi.org/10.1007/978-1-4842-7164-3_17

You'll note on the Developer Journey map in Figure 15-2 that we highlighted and identified DX with a dashed box around the area encompassing Evaluate, Learn, and Build.

Getting the DX right is the most important part of **converting engagement into adoption, a process often called onboarding**. As mentioned in Chapter 8 on DevRel business models, adoption is the holy grail. That decision point where a developer shifts from experimentation to deciding to use your product in production. It's also likely the point where they become a paying customer.

> There is such a great range of skills, tactics and techniques involved in Developer Relations, and it's hard to say one is more important than the other. One of the fundamentals in my opinion is around DX or Developer Experience. It doesn't matter how good your outreach is, or how many developers you are getting to your website, if your product is either difficult to set up or get started with you are likely to fail. The journey for both new and existing users needs to be smooth to make sure they stick around. I worked at Symbian where the barrier for entry was just too high for developers with a complex programming framework and onerous certification programme, and this really scared off a lot of developers. If you look at the programming frameworks and processes that Apple and Android have for their stores now they seem normal, but they broke down a lot of barriers at first.
>
> Whilst your journey can't always be perfect it's a good idea to do a comparison with a similar service or product, you need to make sure you can do better than that.
>
> —Rod Burns
> VP Ecosystem at Codeplay Software
> Formerly DevRel roles at Inmarsat, WIP, Marmalade, and Symbian

A frictionless DX that leads the developer to adoption is a significant differentiator for a successful Developer Relations program. We've witnessed this in companies like Stripe that focused entirely on having a great Developer Experience while doing little or no marketing outreach.

DX however is also the easiest to screw up and is often neglected. You can spend all the money in the world advertising to developers, tweeting, and sponsoring events to get attention, but when developers finally reach your Developer Hub and interact with your product, you will lose them if you can't meet their DX expectations.

This is the first time the developers see your product in great detail and try it for themselves. The developer may be ready for you, but is your product ready for the developer?

Product

Product is one half of DX, but that isn't usually something that DevRel professionals take an active role in creating or owning. It is, however, something that DevRel absolutely supports and influences.

For specific DX with the product, DevRel professionals are there to advocate for the developer in a number of ways:

- Act as an information valve (Figure 2-3) educating developers about the product and any changes to it in a timely manner and bringing developer feedback to the product team.

- Work with the product team on the development and use of personas, so everyone is creating for the same user types. Your internal developers can then base their user stories around the personas for which the DX is being designed.

- Encourage the product team to measure the developer journey inside the tool/product to identify areas of friction.

- Ensure the requirements of your developer community are front and center when discussing product road maps to ensure those needs are being met. This can also include identifying potential "breaking changes" and what the community must do to avoid or prepare for them (e.g., download updates, switch to a new API version, perform a set of migration steps, etc.).

- Research and keep up to date with community and market trends to help advance and improve your DX.

- Consult with the product team to ensure they understand what DX encompasses and that there is buy-in from the management level.

Documentation

Documentation, or "docs" for short, are the other half of DX. They are the technical details developers will review and use to evaluate and learn about your product and then build something with it.

If the developer has a good first impression of the docs (clear, simple, clean), then they immediately have a positive impression of the product. It's dangerous to make assumptions about the reader's prior knowledge. Everyone wants simple, even developers. Some DevRel programs we work with actually hired school teachers into their DevEd teams as they have the necessary training in how to present new subjects and knowledge in the most accessible way.

Docs cover a range of resources and information including installation and reference guides to understand any specific languages or frameworks that are needed, FAQs, code samples, getting started guides, tutorials, and changelogs.

Best practice is to ensure your docs, code samples, and tutorials are written for multiple programming languages so you appeal to the broadest audience, with a selection mechanism to switch between languages.

See Figure 17-1 for the most common types of docs.

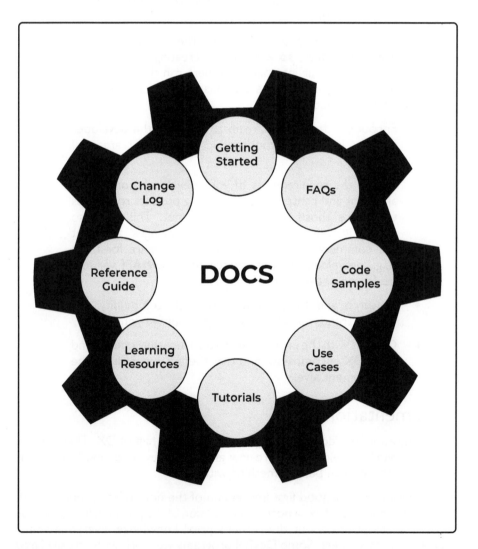

Figure 17-1. The many types of developer documentation or "docs"

These resources are imperative to offer during the Developer Journey so developers better understand what they can accomplish with your product and, just as importantly, how easy or difficult your product is to use.

Docs Span All Stages of the Developer Journey

Depending on where the developer is in their journey, the amount of time they spend on each resource will vary. Typically, in the Evaluate stage, developers give quicker glances to overviews and quickstart guides to gain a general understanding of what is being offered and what they need to get started. When they move into the Learn and Build stages, they take deeper dives and look for specific information and answers to their problems in resources like tutorials and reference guides. We'll do a deeper dive on some of these docs in upcoming chapters.

What Makes Great Docs?

Producing great documentation requires attention to detail and of course an understanding of the information your developers need and when. In general, well-written docs cater to a variety of developer types with a range of experiences, from those who are coming to your product for the first time to those who are already using it.

One of the first things to ensuring that you have great docs is to make them publicly accessible – a step toward boosting your chances of being found in the Discover stage and to remove friction from the Evaluate stage. If the developer has to create an account to read them, download a monolithic PDF, or worst still provide a payment method to access this documentation, you will lose them.

Your docs should also be in an easy-to-read format. Many developer programs use a content management system (CMS) like Readme.io or GitBook, which are designed for the creation of developer guides and API documentation. CMS tools like these also allow various team members to contribute and maintain the content. Such tools generate web-based documentation that is searchable and indexable, providing SEO opportunities and an integrated table of contents structured in a way that is familiar to most developers. Each of these features greatly helps developers find information faster. There is a move toward open source docs as a representation of openness and to encourage feedback and contribution with links such as "Improve this page."

Other developer programs use plain markdown or more recently MDX files that are then processed and rendered via a docs solution or custom-built docs platform.

Try to avoid document formats like PDF files for your technical documentation as they are static, difficult to search, and require downloading. Once published, PDFs continue to be circulated out in the wild, giving you significant version control problems.

By generating your content in a web-based format using a CMS or on GitHub or GitLab, you **ensure that the content is up to date – this is critical**. Nothing undermines confidence in your offering or builds frustration faster than out-of-date or inaccurate docs. As part of your versioning strategy, organize your documentation by product version, so developers always know which version to reference, corresponding to the version of your software or API that they are using.

The look and feel and quality of your docs makes an impression, which is an important part of delivering your messaging in your company voice. Poor docs practices like broken links, dead ends, inaccurate or missing information, or poorly written lexically dense content – common with large corporations governed by complex communication rules – create the sense that working with your technology will likely be a long and difficult process.

Simple clean layouts that start with basic installation steps – common with open source solutions – go a long way toward showing just how easy your product is and that your docs and product have been created with developers in mind. Also ensure that your site renders well on mobile, as developers often start their journey on their mobile devices.

Who Should Create the Documentation?

Often, the job of creating the documentation falls on the engineers that created the product. They need to be involved; after all, they know the product best. However, being the closest to the product can also be a major disadvantage. Here's why. The product development team has spent the last months (maybe years) intimately involved with the build. They know how it works, and they might have discovered quick workarounds to get to a certain point to save them time. Be mindful they may suffer from generalization because they innately know all of the steps and forget to list some of the critical points or steps an outside developer needs to know.

A common approach, which we highly recommend, is to have a technical writer or team of technical writers. These writers are often part of the Developer Education team, who work in conjunction with the product and engineering teams to build the documentation. Strive for technical writers from a relevant technical background (like software or hardware engineering). They will know the questions to ask and how to bridge the gap between internal engineers' knowledge and the information that the prospective developers need. Moreover, such technical writers can often create or work with code samples, demos, and provide other types of highly valuable learning resources.

In general, developers consider your documentation to be a component of your product; hence, they both fall under the umbrella of Developer Experience. It would be wise for you to consider this too.

Summary

Developer Experience, comprised of the product and its supporting documentation, is one of the key components of Developer Relations. DX can be a differentiator for your program or, if neglected, can signal a program's downfall. DevRel is there to support and influence the product based on the best interests of the developers. That support includes the creation and maintenance of docs, as well as other resources and activities to educate developers throughout their journey.

In the next chapter, we will pick up on the next stage of the developer journey, Learn, and review some of the specific touchpoints and resources DevRel provides.

Evaluate

Will It Meet My Needs?

When the developer moves into the Evaluate stage, their primary motivation is to find out if your product will meet their needs. They are looking for any "red flags" that give them reason to walk away. Your task is to pique their interest, answer their questions, and remove any doubt, via a range of resources that **move them toward some type of activation with you**.

In this chapter, we'll review the questions developers want to answer and their expectations of the touchpoints they will encounter.

Activation

Activation is something you can measure; it could include creating an account, signing up to your newsletter, participating in a webinar, reading your use cases, or upvoting one of your comments on Stack Overflow. This is the beginning of a developer's engagement with your program.

In order to encourage activation, some of the first questions you need to help developers answer include:

- What can I do with this tool and will it solve the problem I have?

- Does it look easy to use or complex to implement?

© Caroline Lewko, James Parton 2021
C. Lewko and J. Parton, *Developer Relations*,
https://doi.org/10.1007/978-1-4842-7164-3_18

Evaluate Touchpoints and Developer Education Resources

Your Developer Hub now has its opportunity to shine which includes the entry points for your docs and product. It's also the start of your Developer Education and the many resources your team will need to develop from simple use cases to more extensive workshops.

Some of the touchpoints and resources that you'll want to have ready in the Evaluate stage include the following:

Product Pages

Regardless of the number of products you have, you'll need a place to describe each of them. They may demand their own pages, or you may group them by categories. Be sure to present what you feel will best serve your developers. We've seen many DevRel programs just list SDKs or APIs without adequate descriptions of what they are while having completely obscure naming conventions. Regardless of how you describe your products, the developer needs to understand at a glance exactly what they are and how they fit into the grand scheme of things. Remember, they are still trying to decide if what you have will meet their needs.

Documentation Landing Page

At the Evaluate stage, the developer's first step is often clicking your "Docs" button. At this point, the developer is just reviewing what you have to get a sense of the scope of the resources you've made available. Documentation, as we've noted in the previous chapter, covers a range of different types of information and often forms a mini-hub within your Developer Hub.

Hopefully, you've made Docs easy to find. As we noted, developers may directly land on specific topics within your information architecture[1] by using links returned from search engine results. Make sure there is a clear navigation mechanism to get back to your Docs' homepage wherever they land.

The Docs' landing page should provide a map of your topics to make them easy to navigate. This is typically done by providing a well-thought-out table of contents that is always present as the reader navigates the topics. Every individual developer evaluates and progresses at their own pace and in their own style. Catering for this in the developer journey boosts your chances of success and demonstrates empathy.

---

[1] https://www.usability.gov/what-and-why/information-architecture.html

FAQs

FAQs (frequently asked questions) are answers to common questions in a short and simple way with hyperlinks to aid discovery of the right content, including what the product is, what it is used for, and what its technical requirements are. FAQs should ideally be limited to no more than a dozen questions. You can use data from your support tickets to help inform what should appear here.

Use Cases and Case Studies

We've included use cases and case studies together, because they are often confused.

Use cases illustrate common uses of your product, giving the developer an idea of what is possible and what kind of problems your product can solve. Use cases could be as simple as a couple of paragraphs describing what could be created for a given audience in a particular vertical or as a more in-depth article with technical details on how to derive a result. We encourage you to provide some of your use cases with code samples and tutorials so they are practical and encourage the developer to cross into the next stage of the journey.

Case studies, on the other hand, describe a real-world solution implemented by one of your customers using your product. They are meant to inspire through examples of how other developers have implemented your technology and are used in part to determine your credibility via the types of customers you have and the creativity of their implementations. For example, profiling a Fortune 500 reference customer imparts a sense of trust, while a high-profile startup imparts the sense that your tech is powering something innovative. They are also a way to reward your community by showcasing their work and their company.

The most successful developer-oriented case studies are those that go beyond the traditional marketing-led case study we have all seen, containing customer quotes and smiling faces. Developer-oriented case studies often show code and typically review a problem a developer had and how it was specifically solved with your product, including any development challenges they encountered or other integrations that were needed.

Marketing-style case studies do have a time and place however, and depending on the sophistication of your DevRel program, you can offer both types, targeting the respective technical and business audiences.

Forums and Community Messaging Tools

Your own forum may be hosted on your website, or you may offer support and interaction through a tool like Slack or Discourse. Your online forum should always be visible and accessible for developers to review regardless of their involvement with you. If you use Slack or Discord, display clear instructions on how developers can find it and join. We've seen many forums hidden behind registration or permissioning requirements which doesn't portray an open or welcoming impression to new users. Don't be afraid to actively seek dialogue with new and existing customers – the answers to their questions will be there to help others with the same issue further down the line.

This can be the first test of your support, and it can make or break a decision to move forward. Consider creating a specific onboarding or getting started area within your forums for developers new to your product.

Webinars

The term "webinars" covers a number of different formats, from the traditional playback of a prerecorded presentation + live Q&A session through to live streams of coding on platforms like YouTube and Twitch. They tend to be an hour or less. They represent a scalable option to reach a large audience without high cost or the logistical complexity of traveling to an offline event. Depending on the subject matter, webinar recordings also represent evergreen content, meaning they have longevity, and provide great "Google juice."

External Touchpoints

GitHub

GitHub has achieved global popularity as a revision control system for a variety of reasons, notably that it's revolutionized team-based version control and enabled collaborative coding at scale. As such, most developer programs have added their resources to this platform enjoying features like version history, "diff" comparisons, and a workflow built around integrating contributions from multiple collaborators.

As a GitHub presence has now reached a mandatory state, developers will search for you expecting to find code samples, SDKs, binaries, and docs. By having these resources on GitHub, developers can view the change history, pull requests, and commits to gauge how actively your product is being updated and maintained. This also allows developers to see how engaged your community is through product contributions (e.g., branches from community members which have been merged into the main line), responses to bug fixes, and integrations of feature requests. By being able to view all of this activity, developers will gain insight into how well their input and feedback will be welcomed once they become users.

Stack Overflow

Stack Overflow has become the number one developer learning and knowledge sharing resource on the Web, receiving 100 million visits a month with 20 million questions having been asked.[2] In the same way Google has become synonymous with searching, "Stack" has become synonymous with getting community answers to technical questions. Developers will use Stack Overflow to discover you and will continue to use it to find answers to their technical questions across all parts of their journey. It's important your developer program has an active presence on it. Stack Overflow memed themselves for their 2021 April Fools' joke by announcing "The Key" with an accompanying blog post:[3]

> *One out of every four users who visits a Stack Overflow question copies something within five minutes of hitting the page. That adds up to 40,623,987 copies across 7,305,042 posts and comments between March 26th and April 9th 2021. People copy from answers about ten times as often as they do from questions and about 35 times as often as they do from comments. People copy from code blocks more than ten times as often as they do from the surrounding text, and surprisingly, we see more copies being made on questions without accepted answers than we do on questions which are accepted.*

Pricing Options

Before they get in too deep, the developer wants to know – **Is cost a barrier?** While they likely will not be creating a fully fleshed-out business model at this stage, they will have some cost parameters in mind – comparing you to their existing vendors and/or by comparing your pricing to your competitors.

As we mentioned at the top of the chapter, they are looking for red flags – anything that causes concern in the evaluation of your offering or slows them down to give it a test. Remember that developers are often the decision maker for the adoption of new technology or a decision influencer as part of a wider team. Offering free or discounted trials helps move them along in the evaluation process.

While providing free trials and service credits is a well-used marketing tactic to encourage experimentation, you need to be transparent and upfront with

---

[2] https://stackoverflow.com/company
[3] https://stackoverflow.blog/2021/04/19/how-often-do-people-actually-copy-and-paste-from-stack-overflow-now-we-know/

the actual cost of using your products at scale. This is vital to building trust and a long-standing relationship with your customers. Nothing is more irritating and off-putting than not displaying any pricing on your developer hub, but having a "call sales" call to action, to learn more.

It is always advantageous to link your success to the success of your customers; in other words, if they become successful, you become successful. For example, many API companies charge on a transactional or "per-dip" basis. This means that the cost is low to customers in the early stages as their transaction volume is small. As they grow in volume, so does your revenue – a win-win. Just be ready with a volume discount plan to ensure they are not penalized for their success further downstream – you absolutely want to retain and grow your most successful customers.

Best practices include providing usage calculators to help developers make an informed judgment on the likely cost of using your product. Tiered bundles of functionality is another popular tactic, presenting an impression of value for money linked to an increasing commitment.

Summary

In the Evaluate stage, the developer is still dipping their toes to see if you will meet their needs. Give them the information they need in a well-laid-out format, so, at a glance, your offering looks complete, they feel confident to give it a trial run, and that pricing isn't a barrier to get started.

Next up is the Learn stage, where they take their first look at your product.

Learn

How Does It Work?

The Learn stage comes next. At this point, the developer is now satisfied that your product can meet their needs, they have the relevant skills and the prerequisite tools, and cost isn't a barrier. It's now time for them to give your product a test and figure out if they can make it work.

Your task is to continue to engage them by building their confidence in your product, so that they understand they can create something in a timely and cost-efficient manner.

Onboarding and Engagement

You'll recall from Chapter 5, one of the key developer traits is that they like to experiment and learn by doing. Additionally, the vast majority of developers self-teach when adopting new technologies. As such, you need to present a simple path to get them hands-on with your product and seeing results as quickly as possible. Their motivation may vary from needing to solve a major problem for their company, implementing a new feature within their current project, or simply just exploring to satisfy their intellectual curiosity. Regardless of the context, they'll want to get up and running with your product as quickly as possible.

© Caroline Lewko, James Parton 2021
C. Lewko and J. Parton, *Developer Relations*,
https://doi.org/10.1007/978-1-4842-7164-3_19

Time to "Hello, World!"

Developers will start by determining how easy and fast it is to get to their first "Hello, World!"[1] milestone with your product. "Hello, World!" is usually the first program developers write when they learn to code. The goal is to output those words as confirmation that they were able to understand the syntax, build the program, and see the expected output. Developers continue to use it as a test to see how a product works, how easy it is to use, and, most importantly, prove that they can get it working.

Time is important in this test. You may have seen these abbreviations – "TTHW" and "FTTHW" – which stand for "Time to Hello World" and "First Time to Hello World." Often, the benchmark is to complete a TTHW within five minutes or less. Developers may be OK spending more than five minutes, as long as they deem it a worthwhile or reasonable investment of their time given the product's complexity.

Learn Touchpoints and Docs

To achieve a fast TTHW, developers expect high-quality docs that are easy to follow, free of errors, and bring to their attention any potential pitfalls a new developer may experience. Moreover, developers will appreciate it if you have taken the time to document what "hello world" looks like for your product and the steps to achieve it.

The docs a developer will review include:

- Getting Started or Quickstart Guide
- Tutorials
- Code samples

Getting Started or Quickstart Guide

The "Getting Started" or "Quickstart Guide" (QSG) is typically where a developer who is new to your product begins on their way to a working "Hello, World!". The may have peeked at the QSG in the Evaluate stage, but now it's time to try it out for real. The QSG should contain the minimal steps to achieve this, with the least verbosity possible, starting with the minimal installation.

---

[1] https://en.wikipedia.org/wiki/%22Hello,_World!%22_program

If you find your QSG is excessively complex, this is a sign that:

- Your product is too complex.

- You need a new technical writer.

- Or you need to provide more preprovisioned resources like sandboxes, sample data, provisioned virtual machines (VMs), interactive tutorials, etc.

Perhaps more than one is true!

For this guide, you'll want to clearly identify the different editions of your tool, such as free vs. premium, community vs. enterprise, etc., and write the content to deliver the shortest TTHW. It can be helpful to collaborate with developers who have a variety of skills and experience to observe and time them following your documentation and building their TTHW. This will help you further optimize your instructions.

Tutorials

Developers will also be looking to see what tutorials you provide, in both video and written formats. It's therefore critical that you've thought about the different personas of developers evaluating your product, including their prior knowledge of your product as well as their knowledge (or lack thereof) about your product's external dependencies (e.g., database systems, third-party cloud services, industry knowledge, etc.) and their preferred learning method.

Tutorials should take the developer to the next level by showing how to accomplish common tasks that go beyond those illustrated in the getting started guide(s). Ideally, your tutorials should show how to accomplish a good number of common use cases that are possible to achieve with your product. If certain aspects of your product apply to different types of developers (e.g., back-end vs. front-end developers), be sure to clearly identify and label who the use case content is intended for.

Code Samples

Just as with the QSG, the code samples shown in the tutorials must not only work if copied and pasted but must be accompanied by extensive descriptions and with explanations of the most important parts. Each sample should be prefaced with a description of the problem it will solve and the expected output. If the code sample requires extensive setup to get working, then you should provide for this (e.g., provide a sandbox or an installable container with everything needed to get it working).

Signup and Registration

To work toward a TTHW, it is likely and expected, the developer will have to complete at least a limited registration to gain the necessary access to things like an API key, download an SDK, or get cloud access to your product.

Keep in mind that the speed of your registration is a critical part of the developer's journey. Since the developer is still exploring your product at this stage, delay the requirement to register until absolutely necessary. When they get to registration, fight the temptation to collect unnecessary data, and have a clear privacy policy that states why you need the data you are requesting and what you do with it. Focus on gathering the bare minimum for them to progress. If you ask for too much too soon, you may lose them. Today, there are technologies like OpenID Connect which integrate with third parties like Google or GitHub to make registration and user authentication even faster.

Ensure that the signup process does not introduce a delay or a dead end, like making them wait for manual approval. The process should be self-service from start to finish, requiring no intervention on your part.

Developers should not have to overthink or work too hard to get to "hello world" as part of their evaluation, so don't put a barrier like complex registration in their way.

Education Resources

At the Learn stage, a developer will be very happy if you provide additional resources beyond the basic docs. Additional education resources not only assist them in their learning but it also provides more opportunities for them to get to know you and start to have affinity for engaging in your community. You may even have specialized DevEd team members who are responsible for creating and managing these resources.

Resources that you'll want to have ready in the Learn stage include the following:

Forums and Community Messaging Tools

We saw Forums in the earlier Evaluate stage, and they continue to play an even larger role in Learn. Developers will look for answers to particular issues as they start getting hands-on with your product. They will note whether any questions went unanswered and who provided information (e.g., the developer community, or your company's support team, etc.) – these are all important signals of the popularity of your product and the level of engagement in it.

They will also note how easy it is to search for specific topics, so the presentation and organization of your search results is important to the developer's evaluation. While this can be a lot of work, it will instill confidence that your product is actively supported, worthy of further investigation, relatively easy to use, and actively (and happily) used by others.

Learning Resources

Depending on the size and maturity of your DevRel program, you may have created additional learning resources including ebooks, whitepapers, video tutorials, podcasts, games, project submissions, and other types of content. Many programs have a dedicated learning resources section of their developer hub where these extra resources can be found.

As with your docs, be sure that these resources are searchable and easily found. Note that version control can be more challenging with these types of resources than it is for docs, as these resources may exist in many different stand-alone formats like PDFs and video or audio files. It's therefore good practice to ensure that all such resources are clearly marked with their publication date and any specific product versions, so that developers can quickly identify content relevant to them. Regardless, as we've heard from developers, you can never have too many learning and educational resources!

Office Hours

Office hours are where you set aside time for developers to ask you questions directly. There are lots of methods to choose from – you may invite them to an online video conference call, host an AMA (Ask Me Anything) session on Reddit, stream on Twitch, or make yourself available on your community forum or Slack at a specific time. The point of hosting office hours is to be available for developers to directly ask you their questions and get to know you. If you host them at a regular time, this encourages developers to "meet" with you when they need to and lets them know you are there for them.

Training

To supplement the self-learning style approach of the content outlined earlier, you may want to consider formal training programs. There is a huge variety in the style and type of training you can deliver. From short-lived coding sessions streamed on Twitch to gamification to tutor-led classroom academy–style courses. Training tends to offer a specific learning outcome for the attendee and offers interactivity where a developer can get their specific questions answered immediately.

To help developers with their professional development, offering certification is beneficial, allowing the developer to demonstrate their skills are current and officially recognized. Microsoft is a market leader in this area offering a comprehensive range of free and instructor-led paid certification courses.[2] As well as your own training offer, there is a vibrant third-party DevEd ecosystem including players like General Assembly, Code Academy, Udemy, Treehouse, and many others.

Technology Dependencies

Often, the biggest barrier to entry when learning a new product is the setup process, especially in today's packaged and componentized development environments. From operating systems and system updates to compilers, external packages, and a myriad of build systems, today's developers must navigate and install the correct versions of a whole ecosystem of interdependent components before they can even begin working on a project. On top of this, they may also need a degree of knowledge about these components which goes beyond their core domain of knowledge.

Don't assume that your developers are familiar with your product's technological dependencies. Often, we see docs and other education resources make sweeping assumptions about the developer's prior knowledge and jump straight into the specifics of their own offering.

Take the time in your docs (e.g., QSG) to explain how to set up your development environment, highlighting any dependencies or any prerequisites, why they are needed by your product, and provide links to external resources where developers can learn more if they so desire (e.g., Homebrew, Docker, Linux, Java, etc.).

If you clearly label this as introductory content, your content will accommodate both the more experienced developers and the newbies. Experienced developers will be able to "ground" themselves in the content by quickly understanding how your offering relates to those dependencies, while newbies can easily get up to speed by following the links that you've provided to those external resources.

Summary

Once you've built their confidence and developers have proved to themselves they can get up and running with your product by building a simple "Hello World," they will then enter the next phase of their journey – Build.

---

[2]https://docs.microsoft.com/en-us/learn/certifications/

Build

Can I Build a Proof of Concept?

Having moved past a Hello World, and deciding to proceed, the developer reaches the Build stage. Now they are ready to create something specific with your product for the problem they are trying to solve.

The developers' activity has moved from exploring to building. Your mission is to continue to engage, encourage, and motivate them and remove friction so they can reach their (and your) ultimate goal – scale.

Engagement and Support

At the Build stage, the intent of the developer changes from browsing and experimenting to attempting to build something more meaningful. "Something meaningful" will be to build a lightweight version of their product called a proof of concept, prototype, or MVP (Minimal Viable Product) depending on the scope of what they are eventually trying to build.

Remember, however, they aren't fully committed to your product just yet. This can be a frustrating point for Developer Relations, where there is often pressure from executives or sales teams to push the developers a little harder to convert them to paying customers. Hold your ground and remind them that the developers' adoption of products is unique, including this Build stage of going deeper with your product.

© Caroline Lewko, James Parton 2021
C. Lewko and J. Parton, *Developer Relations*,
https://doi.org/10.1007/978-1-4842-7164-3_20

Continued inspiration and motivation is required from DevRel to suggest fresh ideas on what can be achieved, backed with your educational resources to solve adoption issues. Community activities (discussed more in a later chapter) also figure as a strong influence at this stage.

Build Touchpoints and Resources

Developers will continue to rely on the docs and education resources they used in the Evaluate and Learn stages. There are no dramatic changes you need to make.

However, there are two touchpoints that will see increased usage – your product and forums:

- **Your product** will be put to the test, and there will be little tolerance for broken code, missing features, poor performance, or insufficient information. Devs still want to get their idea built as quickly as possible, so keep friction at bay. A great product experience is table stakes. Keep versioning and any changes well communicated via emails and your changelog (more below). Be especially open to product feedback collected from developers that needs to be relayed back to the product team.

- **Forums** continue to play an essential role in supporting the developer. They want the creation of their proof of concept to be fast, so hopefully your forums are able to address any questions in a timely manner. If they don't, or aren't specific enough, developers will rely on your Support, which we outline in the following.

Here are a few additional resources that are particularly valuable during the Build stage.

Extensions

A key element found in many of today's technology offerings is their "extensions" – the components that allow for integration and customization, expand functionality, and provide extensibility. Extensions can take many forms including libraries, webhooks, callbacks, and other types of event handlers and proprietary plugin architectures specific to your product. Developers will be particularly interested in how easy (or difficult) it is to extend your product. Like the product itself, your extensions should be well documented and frequently revisited to ensure that the process remains smooth as the product evolves.

Sandbox and Tools

A sandbox is an environment that accurately reflects your live environment. Common examples include test servers with fake data, downloadable containers and virtual machines, interactive "playgrounds," console windows embedded in your docs, etc. Your sandbox can allow the use of other supportive resources like compilers, profilers, debuggers, etc. These can be stand-alone tools provided as part of your product or third-party offerings which your product depends on or supports.

All of these are vital tools to enable smooth testing and can get developers to their proof of concept or MVP quicker by reducing or even eliminating setup and installation steps during the Build stage. Any inaccuracies will create a negative impression and impede the developers' progression to the Scale stage. You also do not want to create a burden for your support team by generating unnecessary inquiries and cases.

Reference Guides

Often found toward the end of your docs' table of contents, reference guides are those invaluable topics which provide detailed information about technical specifications, APIs, architectural details, etc. Unlike other topics which focus on concepts, tasks, and achieving goals, reference guides supplement the rest of your documentation, so it's not uncommon for them to be comprised primarily of lists and tables, additional code samples, formulas, and diagrams.

During Evaluate and Learn, developers may glance through the reference guides to get additional details, but it's really in the Build stage where developers often investigate the reference guides in detail. However, all docs, including QSGs, should link to reference guides where possible, to help developers regardless of where they are at in their journey.

Developers in the Build stage use the reference guides to find those "supportive" details which will enable them to successfully experiment with more aspects of your offering. This includes gaining an in-depth understanding of its architecture, learning about all of its APIs, identifying valid parameters, etc. More generally, an in-depth collection of reference guides assures developers that you've thought about all of the information they could possibly need to know and that they will be well supported when it comes to those little details that make a big impact when trying to scale something with your product.

Changelog

Publish and maintain a changelog. As we have stressed throughout, having simple, clean, and accurate documentation is one of the key ingredients to success with developers. A changelog is another vital component of that strategy. Simply, developers need to be aware of any changes you have made to your product, including major releases and patches. For this, a simple list will suffice but is best augmented with links to any relevant release notes or docs associated with each change. Highlighting changes in your newsletters and your Forums is also important so developers don't run into surprises.

Support

While developers may have encountered your formal Support offer in earlier stages, now is a good time to explore Support more thoroughly. Developers need to know where to find "official" support when they need it. We use the word "official" to differentiate from the independent community-led support they may seek from peers and places like Stack Overflow. Forums or tools like Discord and Slack are common channels for official Support, which can grow over time into a searchable knowledge base or Wiki-style database.

Be clear and upfront with your hours of support coverage. Set expectations on your average response time by defining this up front, as it helps to defuse frustration in this increasingly "on-demand" world. Your response time may vary by channel, which is fine, as long as you are clear. Remember we highlighted in Chapter 5 that developers' working hours can be well outside the normal hours of business operation, and of course you will have developers working in multiple time zones around the world. Unless you have reached the point of having a 24 hour/365 days a year support operation, inform the developer up front so they can plan accordingly.

Your support team needs to be attentive and empowered to resolve issues quickly, to own feedback, and champion it within the organization back to Engineering, Product, and other teams. They also need to be able to use their judgment to keep customers happy by offering service credits or other acts of kindness.

You also need to remain current, by providing support in the channels your audience expects. This is getting increasingly complex to manage for support professionals. Things have moved quickly from providing simple help articles, email, and phone support to chat (both live and bots), Slack, Discord, and similar platforms and monitoring third-party sites like Stack Overflow and Reddit. Focus is key. You can't be everywhere in equal quality, so pick the channels you are going to focus on and always seek to bring the conversation back to official channels where you can capture the conversation, track engagement, and close the loop with customers. Your support team should be coordinated with DevRel to ensure both teams are driving developers back to official channels.

Remember customer support is not just the support team's job. Anyone that interacts with developers in the field needs to be proficient in dealing with support issues and have a broad understanding of common issues. This especially applies to Developer Advocates who will be seen by developers as a representative of your company and product. They don't want to hear "Sorry I don't know, can you raise a support ticket?" We strongly recommend your Developer Advocates spend time answering support tickets and shadowing the support team to get a deeper understanding of issues and to build empathy with users of the product they are out promoting.

> *Providing support to developers is very different to providing support for B2B or B2C customers. You have no idea what they are going to do with your product and what they are going to connect it to. So you have to be expert in your own product and be a jack of all trades in order to understand what the customer is attempting to do.*
>
> —Jason Nassi
> Director Customer Centric Engineering at Salesforce

The Developer Relations team can assist the support organization by collecting and sharing common use cases they are seeing in the field, so that support can use analogous examples when troubleshooting issues with customers.

Finally, depending on a company's maturity level and growth strategy, the support team can be a powerful acquisition channel in its own right. One of the key considerations in setting your support strategy is how far down the rabbit hole do you go? Troubleshooting code is complex, and often your technologies have been combined with those from other vendors by the developer. Where do you draw the line? To drive adoption, your support organization could help with anything and everything in a very welcoming way, but of course this stretches your support team as you grow in popularity and the volume of support tickets increases. Also, not only do your volumes increase, but the persona of the developer evolves. You will find yourself providing support for enterprise developers working in large organizations with complex architectures and dependencies, legacy systems, networking policies, and governance policies in place. The stakes are raised, and greater amounts of revenue are at risk.

Adoption Is Still in the Balance

The important thing to focus on during the Build phase is the developer is now within touching distance of adopting your product and becoming a significant customer for you. In other words, depending on your business model, they are about to become revenue generating.

Here, it's important to review your touchpoints both qualitatively and quantitatively. Your qualitative relationship touchpoints (events, support interactions, etc.) can pick up signals of when developers are crossing this threshold, as they will likely be quite open to share and discuss either directly with you or on social media, or on sites like Stack Overflow.

Capture and analyze your usage data to paint a quantitative picture of your developers. Use data to spot important signals like the developer beginning to read more advanced content, any spike in API transactions, redeeming a promo code on their account, downloading an SDK, or making API calls in your sandbox.

You should be able to tag an individual developer's position on the journey within your CRM and/or business analytics tools, so you can run reports on the health of your developer funnel and measure the average time to progress through the various stages, how active they are, and where you lose developers. More on this in our chapter on metrics.

Summary

You will see a natural continuation of many, if not all, of the touchpoints we described in previous chapters during the Build stage of the Developer Journey. This is by design. As we stated in the introduction to the Developer Journey in Chapter 15, the stages of the journey indicate changes in the developers' intent. It does not imply that touchpoints only come into play at specific times – if only things were so cut and dry.

In the Build stage, continue to engage, encourage, and motivate your developers and remove friction so they can reach their (and your) ultimate goal – scale.

Next, we explore the Scale stage, where the developer moves into production and what comes next in their long-term relationship with you.

Scale

Can I Build for the Long Term?

Playtime is over. The developer is now releasing a product of their own into their production environment. Your product was chosen to be part of this release, as the developer is confident that it solves their problem. Prelaunch, their focus is on optimizing, testing, and shipping. Post launch, their gears shift to operations and maintenance of that product.

It may look like you are at the end of your journey with them, but your interactions now couldn't be more crucial to their success and yours.

Retention and Growth

How you approach your relationship with your developer at the Scale stage is often dictated by your business model. It's typically the point where they have made a revenue commitment with you, or their primary product supported by your tool is ready to ship. They are now categorically a customer.

As we saw in Chapter 8, the revenue of many developer programs is delayed until the developer's final product is distributed and sold. In this case, you may only start to generate value and return on investment (ROI) when the developer starts to create meaningful transaction volume and revenue. And most importantly, you want your developer to continue to create volume and revenue over an extended period of time. Additionally, as we all know, a

© Caroline Lewko, James Parton 2021
C. Lewko and J. Parton, *Developer Relations*,
https://doi.org/10.1007/978-1-4842-7164-3_21

software-based product is never truly complete. If there is an end, it's the end of life of that product. Otherwise, there is always a new feature or upgrade.

For these reasons, the Scale stage cannot be neglected. A retention and growth strategy is critical to the success of your program and your company. In many ways, Scale is the start of a new phase with your developer as their success, which is tied to yours, becomes your overarching focus. Scale also requires a team approach from those working in Support, Account Management, Community Management, and Developer Success.

Scale Touchpoints and Resources

During the Scale stage, your Developer Experience (DX) is back on center stage. Your product has to work, and your Docs have to be up to date and be accessible. Devs will want to know your Forums or Support teams have the answers they need when they need it – after all, they are on deadline and have their own customers to please. It's also time to celebrate their success.

Let's take a look at some of the touchpoints and resources required to retain your developers as they scale.

Developer Success

Once the developer's product is out the gates, your relationship with the developer may shift. As they operate and maintain their product, their focus often includes new teams inside their organization, like Operations, DevOps, DevSecOps, or MLOps (a new term which has arisen regarding managing the machine learning product life cycle).

We recognize that the term DevOps can mean different things to different people. Here, we use it to highlight a new audience that the DevRel team needs to consider. You are still working with a technically savvy audience but with some subtle differences. For example, it is likely the operational teams will be more focused on automation of the development and release process, observability, and monitoring.

As your developers' commitment and dependency on your technology increases, it is table stakes to provide dashboards and other tooling to ensure they can monitor performance and measure their usage of your services.

It's important to remember, as we noted in Chapter 15, the Developer Journey stages indicate significant changes or stage gates in the developer's intent and actions, but do not imply elapsed time. The reality is the operational teams within your customers' companies will be active at all stages of the journey and will be a key stakeholder in any purchasing decision before new vendors and technologies are adopted within their organizations.

Typically, your product docs, quickstart guides, and code samples are all oriented toward a developer who needs to understand a specific method to achieve a stated goal. Now storytelling comes to the fore, explaining how your technologies fit into the big picture, sharing new ways of working, and defining best practices. AWS Well-Architected[1] is a good example of this kind of approach. An emerging role in Developer Relations is the Developer Success Engineer, who plays a big role in this phase and is often assigned to support a customer long term.

Support

Support was important in the Build stage, but now it requires deeper attention.

Timing is everything. Be thoughtful with how and when you communicate with them. If they are pulling all-nighters to hit a deadline, the last thing they need is to be interrupted by your "exciting webinar this Thursday afternoon." Be available when they need it. If you have an account management or success team, you may be required for some on-demand one-on-one support. It may be sufficient to hold regular office hours, which they can attend as and when, and continue to keep your forums and any knowledge base you have up to date.

Maintain a frictionless experience as you release new features and versions of your tools. For example, a new release of your product that breaks their implementation would be a disaster to their product and revenue, therefore damaging their confidence in you and affecting their likelihood of staying with you long term. Your primary job is to inform them of what's on offer while maintaining accurate documentation and associated resources like changelogs, code samples, and new learning resources.

The DevRel team is also required to see the big picture and be the key channel as the "voice of the developer" back to engineering and product development teams. Feeding back feature requests, improvements, and bugs requires a thoughtfulness about the scope of the issues, commitments that can or can't be made, and the effect on sales teams as well. For example, as your engineering team enhances the product, and pays off any technical debt,[2] strategize how you will balance rolling out breaking changes with the need to force existing customers to upgrade. Be thoughtful in how you prioritize support tickets to both answer questions in a timely manner and protect engineering time as they either fix breaking changes or work on new product releases.

---

[1] https://aws.amazon.com/architecture/well-architected/?wa-lens-white papers.sort-by=item.additionalFields.sortDate&wa-lens-whitepapers. sort-order=desc
[2] https://en.wikipedia.org/wiki/Technical_debt

SLAs

SLAs, or service-level agreements, are one example of performance that is stated and measured and agreed upon between you and your customer and may be monitored by an Ops team. SLAs can range from metrics specific to a product's performance such as uptime or latency, security metrics, or support-related metrics such as time to answer a support ticket. SLAs are also metrics that feed into your planning and evaluating, which means they require a way to be adequately measured.

Product Road Map

Your developer's success is attached to your longevity, and any changes you make will directly affect them. Therefore, it's incumbent on you to let your customers know where your product is heading through sharing your product road map. Indeed, it is now common to publish your road map so potential customers can appreciate your direction and if your direction aligns with their long-term needs. A great example of a public road map is Slack, which first published theirs in 2016 on a Trello board.[3] Their information includes their reasoning, the road map, and something they call an Ideaboard. Some companies let their developers vote for their most wanted features.

Inspiration and Community

In addition to the purely technical resources, inspiration and community go hand in hand to retain and grow the relationship with existing developers and go full circle to bring new developers into the fold. Your goal is to engage your developers in your community to make the relationship with them more "sticky" and meaningful and have them contribute to the ecosystem. This engagement is very much centered on the depth and quality of your relationships with your developers. We dig deeper into community management in Chapter 25.

During the Scale stage, the DevRel team inspires developers with new features to adopt or new use cases to create. This expands your footprint within your existing customers, increasing the revenue from their account. This is often referred to in sales as cross-selling and upselling. Tailor your messaging and activities around these themes through methods like customer workshops, internal hackathons, events, blogs, forums and community messaging tools, case studies, podcasts, videos, etc.

---

[3]https://medium.com/slack-developer-blog/the-slack-platform-roadmap-34067b054177

The Developer Relations effort also has the opportunity to inspire your own product team to incorporate complementary services or add new features and use cases that have the potential to solve more of the customers' problems while, of course, generating more revenue for you in the long term.

Showcase

We have referenced the need for case studies to inspire throughout the book. Well, where do these case studies come from? Your developers and customers of course. Case studies are the stories of the developers that have created something meaningful with your products. This is good for you, but it's also good for the developer — showcasing their achievements within their community and within their own company. Refer back to Figure 5-1 — "**I made that**," the central motivation of most developers — a pride in the fruit of their labor.

There are other ways to showcase and acknowledge developers. Look for opportunities to build meaningful relationships with them via events and parties — make them feel part of a larger positive movement. Provide opportunities for them to share their knowledge and improve their craft, by offering speaking slots at your events, writing guest posts for your blog, and offering certification programs. In this way, growing their expertise with you becomes a recognized skill furthering their own career opportunities.

Ambassador Programs

Ambassador Programs, sometimes called Champion Programs, are a way to recognize, empower, and reward community members that go the extra mile in promoting and supporting your program. Along with your own forums, monitor external resources like GitHub and Stack Overflow for the individuals being helpful and attentive.

Meetups or community groups sometimes spring up organically around your technologies, or YouTube and Twitch channels may start to feature your product. Thank these external advocates by arming them with swag, bring them in to meet your engineering and support teams so their knowledge and impact builds, involve them in road mapping sessions, and capture the feedback and sentiment they are hearing in their communities. You can have a formal Ambassador Program and showcase them on your website or keep it lowkey. Whichever you choose, identifying these individuals is a key part of your community building activities.

Partner Programs

As your community and ecosystem grow, your company may wish to establish a Partner Program. Partner Programs vary but typically represent a new channel to market that would not be possible without the partnership. It may be making your tools available in another ecosystem through an official integration (like an app store), or it may be enabling and training third parties (e.g., ISVs) to increase the chance they build solutions for their clients using your technologies. Either way, it is a means for your collective companies to go to market together with a better or stronger offering for prospective customers.

The go-to-market activities to promote the partnership might include joint PR, advertising, co-attending conference and trade shows, or other joint marketing. Depending on your company's size and type, the Partner Program might functionally be part of your Developer Program, or it may be a sister program in a different department requiring internal collaboration.

Certification

Finally, you may create a certification program for your product. Microsoft[4] has one of the longest and broadest certification programs that recognizes a developer's skills and knowledge and which provides career benefits. If recognized by the industry and prospective employers, certification gives the developer a leg up in a job they may be applying for, enhances your own ecosystem, and creates lock-in for those that become certified, leading to more product sales.

Business Decision Makers

Don't forget about the business decision makers. In a company that has multiple decision influencers and decision makers, you want all of them to be in agreement that your product is the answer to their problem. The ideal situation is both the engineering team and the management team are all advocating your product.

Your potential audience widens from just pure developers; best practice is to create and clearly label content for decision makers from a nontechnical background.

Business people will also be open to speaking and blogging opportunities you might offer to them and will attend customer dinners and roadshows. It is

---

[4]https://docs.microsoft.com/en-us/learn/certifications/

common to see both technical and business tracks at conferences, for example, which is something the DevRel team may be responsible for delivering. Business people will also join Advisory Boards where early access to things like your road map will help in their planning.

Summary

We're not quite finished on our Go-to-Market part, but thought we should pause to reflect on the Developer Journey. Through Chapters 15–21, we introduced the concept of the Developer Journey and drilled into the five stages Discover, Evaluate, Learn, Build, and finally Scale.

The Developer Journey is one of the most important tools for you to use to set up and monitor your program because it views the activities through the eyes of your developer.

Getting this journey right provides the path to the success of your program, alignment with your stakeholders, and informs your go-to-market strategy and your metrics.

Getting it right also requires a functional approach. Although we referred to the parts of the Developer Relations framework (Developer Marketing, Developer Experience, Developer Learning, and Developer Success) throughout the journey chapters, you might still be wondering how it all fits together. Figure 21-1 presents the 30,000-foot view of how the key DevRel functional areas, first described in Figure 1-1, span the end-to-end journey. We'll take a look at various team roles to round things out in Chapter 27.

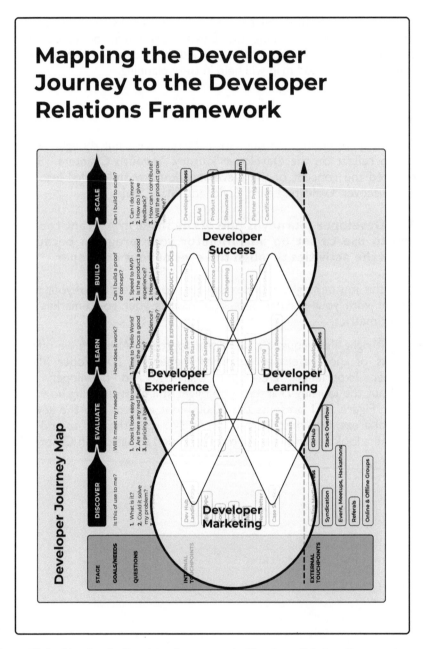

Figure 21-1. Mapping the Developer Journey to the Developer Relations Framework

Our Go-to-Market part will continue with a deeper look at Marketing, Events, and Sales, along with a chapter on Community, which truly spans across the entire Developer Journey.

Developer Marketing

Tactics for Awareness, Lead Gen, and Relationship Building

When we explored Chapters 15–21, you probably noticed that marketing interventions occur throughout the Developer Journey. Developer Marketing starts at the Discover stage and supports and encourages developers as they adopt your product and scale.

This chapter will touch on some of the key marketing tactics and best practices deployed by successful DevRel programs.

Marketing Tactics for DevRel

There is a range of marketing tactics used within DevRel, many of which are typical for any marketing strategy. There are also a few tactics specific to DevRel. However, any good marketing professional will want to understand and create tactics specific to their target market, rather than recycling standard B2B or B2C tactics.

© Caroline Lewko, James Parton 2021
C. Lewko and J. Parton, *Developer Relations*,
https://doi.org/10.1007/978-1-4842-7164-3_22

As we noted in previous chapters, Developer Marketing is one of the key branches within DevRel. It can functionally sit within the DevRel team, the marketing team, or sometimes even product. As such, there can be overlap in the activities.

For instance, developer marketing activities are distinct from the DevEd activities, whose primary focus is education and enablement. That said, there is no doubt that a by-product of high-quality DevEd is also attracting and converting developers into long-term customers, complementing the more overt marketing, advocacy, and sales efforts. And vice versa, using messages and content that helps developers learn is an effective marketing tactic. We refer you back to Chapters 12–14 for a refresher on developer segmentation, personas, and messaging.

All of the developer marketing tactics are typically designed to achieve one of three things:

- Create awareness
- Create leads and ultimately revenue
- Build relationships by nurturing prospects and existing customers

We reviewed several marketing tactics in Chapter 16, specific to various touchpoints in the Developer Journey. Below we'll do a deeper dive into the most significant developer marketing tactics.

Note that because event marketing is intrinsically linked to Developer Advocacy and building community, we have dedicated Chapter 23 to it.

Developer Hub

We reviewed the Developer Hub in Chapter 16, but want to refer to it again as it is your most significant marketing asset and presence on the Web. Having a high-quality website that identifies who your product is for and the value it delivers is table stakes in your marketing toolkit. Once a developer becomes aware of you, it's the first place they come to learn more.

Your site will quickly grow in complexity, especially if you have multiple products and multiple target audiences. The age-old challenge is keeping the call to action (CTA) simple to clearly map out the desired journey you want the developer to take as they navigate your content. Allowing the visitor to self-identify tends to be the preferred method to accomplish this. Example paths include navigating the content by their chosen programming language, use case, role responsibilities (e.g., technical or business), or experience level with your technology.

Every organization is different, but the "front end" of the Developer Hub is often the responsibility of marketing. The "back end" of the hub, which houses the Developer "Console" or "Dashboard," the actual tool, and usually includes the functionality behind product registration and login, falls into the realm of Developer Experience and the product teams (Chapter 17). Depending on the size of your organization, you might have yet another team that looks after the overall corporate site and controls brand guidelines.

You'll also want to make sure you track the developer journey from the start of a marketing campaign through to product usage. This can be the trickiest part given split teams, and often the tools used that track marketing and tool usage are different and not compatible.

If your organization is splitting responsibilities, ensure coordinated thinking and open lines of communication to ensure a seamless and frictionless experience for the developer regardless of where they land and the best tracking possible for all teams.

Social Media

Any modern business understands the importance of an active and authentic presence on the social media channels used by their target audience. These channels allow you to project the personalities of both your brand and individual team members. Use both the official company account and those of your employees to engage the community. The company's overall stance will set the tone of voice of your corporate account. There is usually a little flexibility to allow your staff to bring their style and personality to bear within certain parameters.

It can be increasingly difficult to separate business and personal on individuals' social media channels, so it is vital that social media training is provided to all members of staff, regardless if they are in a customer-facing role. Like it or not, you are all representing your employer 24/7, 365 days a year. If you are spending more time ranting about the difficulties of traveling for your job at the expense of building a positive image for you, your company, and your product, you may be wasting a valuable asset. Having a disclaimer in your bio like "*views my own, not of my employer*" is worthless at that point.

SEO and Advertising

As we highlighted in Chapter 16, search engines are the primary discovery channel for developers to find out about you. It is, therefore, vital you have a good SEO (Search Engine Optimization) strategy and that your Marketing and DevEd teams are writing search engine–friendly content at all times to boost the chances of discoverability.

To supplement organic search discovery, you will need to consider using paid advertising to build awareness and generate leads and look for opportunities to post on the external sites as the inbound links will help your Google juice. If you have fine-tuned your Developer Experience, you can create a well-oiled machine where developers discover you via search, visit, engage, and register/buy within a few clicks and a few minutes, with no interaction required from your company. Achieving a self-service approach is the key to scaling your program.

You'll use the messaging and keywords you put together from Chapter 14. Buy search terms related to your company and product name, keywords related to the searches your target audience uses, and searches based on competitive products. Use retargeting on other platforms like social media and paid placement on social media to highlight company/product news, key content, an upcoming event, or other engagement techniques like a competition.

Depending on your target developer and industry focus, look for other advertising or placement opportunities on websites, newsletters, YouTube channels, etc., that attract the audience you are targeting.

Content Marketing

Even before the COVID-19 pandemic hit, the use of content marketing has grown. For some companies, it is their primary means of marketing. Most of the growth is due to recognition of how developers want to receive information and, equally important, that messaging needs to be available for developers wherever they are, whenever they happen to demand it. In many ways, content marketing has surpassed event marketing, once considered a key way to attract developers. Not all the best developers can afford, or take the time, to attend your event. And as we know, developers are now located worldwide.

If the intent of your content is to promote to and convert users (vs. say enable), or establish thought leadership,[1] we label this marketing content. Where the primary responsibility for content production sits varies with the company. It may be the role of a generalist, the marketing team, the DevEd team, a Developer Advocate, technical writer, or video production team, or you may have a dedicated content team.

There is a broad range of content formats including case studies, product fact sheets, brochures, whitepapers, webinars, presentations, newsletters, blog posts, podcasts, and videos in various formats. Depending on the maturity of your organization and the resources at your disposal, you may have to

---

[1]https://en.wikipedia.org/wiki/Thought_leader

prioritize where to focus your efforts. Some of the content will reside on your own properties, and you'll want to identify opportunities to provide new content or syndicate your existing content to other sites where your target audience spends time.

Be guided by your target audience to understand where and how they consume content. Run experiments to measure effectiveness of content before going all in on something that doesn't convert. We also recommend being consistent in your output. There is nothing that shows less thought leadership than having a blog that hasn't been updated for the last two years or a "monthly" newsletter that comes out every six months! As we mentioned in Chapter 14, be sure to define your audience's reading level and have a consistent style and tone of voice across all of your materials.

Your content strategy should create material that adds genuine value to your target audience while simultaneously positioning your company as thought leaders and thus driving leads. If you have content, especially data points, that are unique to the industry that you can share, this can be a home run.

A great example was the Mobile Metrics Report produced by the mobile ad network pioneer AdMob between 2006 and 2010.[2] Their target audience was mobile app developers, who would integrate AdMob and share in the revenue generated from the placement of ads within their apps. Due to the amount of traffic passing through AdMob's servers, they realized they were sitting on a gold mine of previously unavailable data detailing the market penetration and usage patterns of mobile phones. In a stroke of genius, they freely published this data in regular reports. In turn, this positioned them as leaders in the field establishing their brand with everyone across the mobile and app ecosystem and beyond. The data was also regularly cited by the mainstream press, like the *Financial Times*. Google acquired AdMob for $750m in 2009.[3]

We spoke with Russell Buckley who was Managing Director of Europe at AdMob:

The goose that kept laying golden eggs

We asked ourselves would this data be useful to the wider community, and the answer was yes. We were quite surprised by the reaction to it, and we called the report the goose that wouldn't stop laying golden eggs. Every quarter when we released a report we saw similar coverage and attention, and it was probably the single most important marketing thing we did.

---

[2] https://techcrunch.com/2010/06/30/admob-android-apple/
[3] https://techcrunch.com/2009/11/09/google-acquires-admob/

We didn't really spend anything on marketing. We did some evangelism in the community and spoke at conferences, and then we had the report. The only other thing we used to have was a ticker on our homepage showing the number of ads we had served. It was a vanity metric, and a stupid one at that, if anything it should have been the number of ads clicked, but we realised our ads served number would be the biggest number we could ever quote, and when we hit milestones like 50 million, 1 billion, 10 billion, 20 billion there was a PR opportunity.

You can tell when you are winning when you go to conferences and your competitors are saying "We are like Admob, but we do this…."

—Russell Buckley
Partner at Kindred Capital
Previously Managing Director, Europe, at AdMob

Automated Nurture

Configuring email nurture campaigns can be effective to remain at the front of your developer's mind, giving that little bit of inspiration and nudge to action, ultimately turning them into a customer or more active user. Typically, successful nurture programs define key triggers in the Developer Journey and then define associated nurture campaigns to begin when the developer activates that trigger. The campaigns send several emails spread out over several weeks. You can run A/B tests to find the optimal times to send and space emails.

Examples of nurture campaigns may be:

- The developer completes an event registration form. An associated nurture campaign could share relevant content in the run-up to the event and reminders to attend, and then post event send content and materials used in the event, and then signpost what to explore next.

- A developer registers for your product. This could trigger a series of nurture emails that provide links to the quickstart guides, docs, use cases, and inspirational content of what others have built with the same product.

- A developer has registered for your product, but after a predetermined amount of time and/or activity on their account, they are tagged as dormant or have failed to complete onboarding. This could trigger a campaign to attempt to reengage them and probe for any issues they may have encountered. Those emails could include similar content to the preceding example, plus links to support or FAQ content, or a short survey to understand what has happened.

Marketing Partnerships

Relationships with other organizations in the ecosystem are vital. Good partnerships will enable you to extend the reach to your target audience more effectively and cost-effectively than if you had to build a channel from scratch.

For example, if you wanted to reach developers working inside larger corporations using IBM technologies, it would take significant marketing effort to target, engage, and convert them directly yourself, especially if you were a new brand with no track record. A more sensible approach would be to partner with IBM Cloud to get your product featured in the IBM Cloud catalog. This immediately puts you in front of your target audience with next to no marketing expenditure. For less established brands, you may experience a credibility boost, being positioned alongside a trusted brand like IBM.

Many vendors offer an ecosystem, catalog/store, or partner program where you can position your offer as a simple complementary add-on like Salesforce AppExchange, Rakuten RapidAPI, Google Cloud, etc.

These partnership opportunities are not just limited to technology ecosystems. If you recall our segmentation and persona work in Chapters 12 and 13, you may well have decided to target the CTOs of early-stage startups in New York, London, and Hong Kong, for example. How do you efficiently reach them? Where do they cluster? Reaching the CTO through their technical communities is one approach highlighted earlier. The other would be reaching them via other intermediaries that operate in the startup ecosystem. For example, you could partner with startup accelerator programs, coworking spaces, VCs, and sometimes local government agencies. By offering discounts, talks, access to your people, and other benefits, these relationships can develop into useful channels to build awareness and adoption.

Developer Communities

One of the more effective marketing strategies we have used is becoming an active member of other developer communities relevant to your audience. If you have been around for a while, you might refer to them as user groups. There are the obvious large general communities like Stack Overflow, but there are thousands of smaller, very targeted ones. These communities can be online only or groups that sometimes meet in person. Some of the communities are product specific like Kubernetes, some are gender specific like Women Who Code, many are location specific, some are technology specific like the Subreddit for machine learning, and others are sharing sites like Indie Hackers. It's best to start with a community where you, your team, or some of your developers are already members.

Working with communities is a task that can take a lot of work and time and can only be done one on one, usually by your developer advocate. There is no tool to engage with communities. But this is the reason they are so effective because as a member of a community, you become a trusted source. You can't be greedy in these groups. You have to support other members with your knowledge, in addition to sharing information about you or your company. The trick to using these communities as marketing channels is that you must become a genuine, active, and respectful member.

Summary

Marketing plays a significant role in creating awareness, leads, and building relationships within DevRel. Activities range from typical marketing tactics like SEO, social media, and advertising. There are also developer marketing–specific tactics like engaging with external developer communities. Content marketing has grown over the last several years and in many ways has surpassed event marketing in one of the best ways to create awareness with developers.

Events

In-Person and Online Events

Events have historically been a cornerstone of Developer Marketing and the primary channel to deploy your Developer Advocates in front of the developer community. Events are also a way to extend your developer education channels. They come in many forms, from large conferences and trade shows to small meetups and hackathons to online and in person. Your team will be attending events that someone else has organized, and you will also create and run your own events in a variety of formats.

Post COVID, it will be interesting to monitor if the historical importance of in-person events returns. Or will we see a long-term correction toward online or hybrid-style events (which blend in person and online) and greater investment in Developer Education and content?

We believe events will endure because face-to-face remains unmatched for creating the personal and community connections we all crave and offers spontaneity and experiences that online can just not deliver. In-person events also require being fully present, providing a higher quality of engagement away from the distractions of screens and other interruptions.

This chapter will provide a high-level strategy for events and offer checklists to help you plan and execute them. Let's start with a reality check.

© Caroline Lewko, James Parton 2021
C. Lewko and J. Parton, *Developer Relations*,
https://doi.org/10.1007/978-1-4842-7164-3_23

Event Reality Check

Of all the many outreach tactics in the toolbelt, events are often incorrectly perceived as an easy, quick win. Why?

- They are visible – internally and externally.

- Many can be delivered on small budgets within a short time frame.

- They often don't require complex organizational buy-in compared to launching a new product (except for creating your own large conference, of course).

- For a corporate, you are perhaps excited by the feeling of positively positioning your brand as edgy and community centric.

- If you are worried about falling behind your competition, you feel compelled to "keep up with the Joneses."

The reality check is events are the most resource-intensive marketing you undertake to reach developers. And to the uninitiated – the return on investment for running events can be the hardest to articulate back to your stakeholders.

Our advice regarding events is always:

Invest the time up front to create a common understanding of your intent with events, thus avoiding that scratching your head moment as you struggle to figure out exactly what you got in return for your money, time, and effort.

There were too many developer events pre-COVID, and a lot of them were undifferentiated, so the quality wasn't holding up. It was a self perpetuating problem as events can be a boon for marketing and DevRel teams under pressure to perform. Ask what's in it for developers?

—Matthew Revell
Founder and CEO, Hoopy

Choosing Which Events to Attend

There is no shortage of events to attend, whether in person or online. Events also come in many forms, such as conferences, trade shows, meetups, hackathons, and live coding sessions, with many variations like geography, technology, developer audience, business audience, private, public, professionally organized, community-run, etc.

Be clear on why you want to attend an event:

- **Learn** – About the topic, the community, the organizers, the venue, scout competitors, and network.

- **Speak** – Keynote, panel, etc., to showcase your technology and thought leadership.

- **Educate** – Demo or workshop.

- **Presence** – Run your own booth or be part of a partner's booth.

- **Sponsor** – Which in addition to brand association will likely include many if not all of the preceding options.

Before leaping in on an event, know the answers to these basic questions:

- **Is the event credible?** It won't look good for you to be involved in an event with a poor reputation or a declining level of interest. The golden rule is never to sponsor an event you haven't been to before. Ideally, you will have team members that have attended to understand how it is run and to pick up signals on its quality and reputation or, at the very least, be able to research its reputation via your developer community. Does the event have a solid code of conduct, and do they have a program to support underrepresented groups? Check its previous sponsors and speakers. Does it attract quality and diversity? Other sponsors and speakers have to make the same decisions as you, so a consistently high-quality lineup of sponsors and speakers is a positive sign. Even if you can't get hard attendance data from the organizers, you will be able to make your own judgment by reviewing photos, engagement on social media during and after the event, and attendee sentiment on back channels. Watch videos of talks from previous events to gauge the production quality, size of the crowd, and the level of engagement.

- **Is it our audience?** You need to ensure that by attending, you will get to meet your developer target audience. As we covered in Chapter 12, understanding the audience for your product is fundamental to be successful with any marketing activity. Events are no different. Research its audience – will this event get you in front of the right type of people?

- **Can we properly represent ourselves?** Can you customize your sponsorship and representation? Is it a pay to play for a decent speaking slot, or are they genuinely interested in your opinion on a topic? Is there an opportunity to demo our product? Are any of the sessions recorded/streamed to reach a wider audience during or after the event? Are our competitors there? How can we position ourselves vis-à-vis them?

- **Can we resource it?** Check you have the people, the bandwidth, the preparation time, and the budget to ensure you can commit. Create an annual event road map. If it's an in-person event, ensure you are not creating an impossible schedule of travel for your people working in the field and that you have the right staff available in the right places. There is no point committing to a Python event in Berlin and London on the same day if you only have one Python person in your DevRel team.

Event Preparation

Now that you have decided to commit, achieving success from an event investment entails more than just showing up. Here are some must-do pre-event activities:

- **Budget** – Set and track a budget for the team, resources, and expenses you are going to need.

- **Pre-event promotion** – Run a pre-event marketing campaign to ensure you have high levels of engagement at the event.

- **Pick your team** – Match your team's skills with the expected audience. In other words, never put a nontechnical sales or marketing person in front of a developer crowd or a Java developer in front of a Ruby crowd. First impressions count – and you are making lasting impressions. Ensure your spokespeople are trained for public speaking, have stage presence, and deliver content in an impactful way. They should be fluent in your product, processes, pricing, and messages so they do not freeze when questioned.

- **Create an event plan** – Document everything in advance and brief the team working on the event. Include information like where they need to be and when, venue address, booth location, team contact information and travel itineraries, and who is responsible for bringing gear like banners, laptops, merch, etc.

- **Create your perfect product demo** – At most events, there is normally the opportunity to pitch on stage. The time available varies considerably, but it is a key opportunity to create interest in your offer and drive traffic to your booth or to your people working the show for a more detailed conversation. Not every product caters to it, but if at all possible, show a live experience that ends with some "magic." Magic could be a transaction across your API, changing the state of something, pretty much anything that engages the audience, allows participation, and proves your demo is live and not slideware. The goal is to show the crowd that getting started and seeing results is fast and easy. **And practice your pitch!** (See inset below on the craft of speaking.)

- **Steal the show with a stand-out booth** – Like the classic property cliché, it's all about location, location, location. Work in advance with the event organizers to review the floor plan, or in the absence of a plan, at least discuss where your booth will be. Depending on the style of event, pick a high-traffic area where you have a better chance of pulling people in to chat with you or to at least see your brand. It doesn't matter if your booth is just a table and chair or a major installation at a global trade show. First impressions count. Create a way to engage folks to come and talk to you.

- **Treat each event as a separate marketing campaign** – Identify your existing content relevant to the event subject, or create new content to fill gaps. Identify customers in your existing community that could be interested in the event and make them aware you will be there. Call to actions could include signing up for the event, scheduling a meeting with your team at the event, downloading your content (e.g., a cheatsheet relevant to the event topic), or entering into a contest to win free tickets to the event.

At the Event

- **Arrive early and test EVERYTHING** – Power, AV connectors, microphones, slides, videos, Internet, etc. Set and enforce booth etiquette rules – dress code, no eating and drinking on or around the booth, no working or checking your phone when staffing the booth, take breaks away from the booth, no chatting to colleagues. Your booth crew should be attentive and welcoming at all times.

- **Promote your attendance and content on the event hashtags** – Position your social channels as worthwhile to follow. For example, post content from interesting speakers, including quotes, photos, and video – don't just flood the hashtags with your own marketing – be helpful to the community.

- **Lead capture at the event** – It's the reason you are there. Ensure you are capturing every prospect and conversation you are having at the event. Depending on the event, you may or may not be provided with tools to capture leads by the organizers. Remember, every lead is not equal. You may already have a qualification methodology in your company, which you can plug straight into your event process to allow prioritization of post-show follow-up and increase the chances of conversion through personalized follow-up.

- **Gather feedback** – Use the event to gather feedback from attendees on their knowledge and sentiment of your product and company. You can use formal methods like a short survey or informally based on conversations.

- **Organize activities outside the event** – Take people out to dinner or a concert. Host a reception. Host them at your office if the event is in your hometown.

Post-Event

- **Follow-up** – Priority number one is timely and relevant follow-up with the leads gathered at the event. Consider a high-touch follow-up for your hot leads, and automate the outreach to those less likely to become a customer.

- **Repackage and recycle any content created at the event** – An example engagement tactic is to post photos from the event to your Instagram page and encourage people to make comments. Publish an event post on your blog, publish videos of talks your people gave at the show, and continue to reference the event hashtag to increase relevance and improve discoverability.

- **Run an internal debrief with a self-reflective event report** – Involve all the teams that worked the event to ensure the contents are representative. Collect all the key metrics and data points, together with the qualitative highlights. Brainstorm with the team the things that worked and the things that didn't work. The objective, while things are still fresh in the memory, is to double down on the good stuff and fix and improve the stuff that didn't work for next time. This exercise establishes a culture of continuous improvement. As you build up a history of these event reports, they are incredibly useful when event organizers reach out to you in six months, asking for you to get involved in their event again. At your fingertips, you'll have an informed opinion before saying yes or no.

Online Events

When you read the preceding advice, you probably had in your mind that you are attending an in-person event. Read it again and consider an online event. Except for a couple of instances, the advice is similar. For example, even for staffing your online booth, first impressions still count.

We are, of course, experiencing an explosion in online events since COVID-19 flipped the focus from in-person. But online events are not new for DevRel. Many programs have been successfully running online events for a number of years to extend their reach to more developers in more cost-efficient ways.

Our experience of attending and participating in conferences and running training and workshops online is that it's harder to capture attention and engage the audience than in-person events. Also, virtual online exhibitor halls or "meet the sponsors" breakout rooms that attempt to replicate the in-person event experience are typically poorly implemented, poorly attended, and feel awkward. They also lack the spontaneity of browsing at an in-person event that allows for striking up natural conversations.

Here are some additional considerations and tips for online events:

- Provide direction that you and your team will follow about how you will appear on camera regarding the level of appearance, tone, dress, room setting, any virtual background image, etc.

- Be sure any presentation you do will be recorded and that you will have access to use it or refer to it in postmarketing activities and for self-reflection on your performance.

- Confirm access to your virtual booth and your marketing assets (logos, marketing collateral, demos, downloadable content, etc.) before and during the event. Test, test, test – if you can. Some online event platforms can be complex to use or may not have features or final results you were expecting.

- Confirm the technical specifications of the marketing assets you'll use, like logos, banners, and copy length, in advance to ensure your presence looks as professional as possible.

- Be well staffed. You and your team will need to work hard at an online event to capture attention. Someone will need to monitor the virtual booth at all times and spend time in event chat channels and associated social media channels driving engagement. Time zones can make this challenging.

- Look for opportunities to provide blog content to the organizers for posting on their site pre- and post-event for additional attention.

- Assure the quality of your connection and equipment like camera, mics, and lighting before the event.

- Always start with a clear agenda of your talk to ensure the audience is aware of what is coming up. This helps combat them straying to their email or allows them to dip back in at points they find most relevant.

- As there is a lower bar to attend an online event (e.g., no travel requirement, typically free or low-cost tickets, etc.), we have found that the audience can be different from what you expect. Ask qualifying questions at the start of your talk like "Who has heard of...", "How many of you are...", "How experienced are you with..." to ensure that your content matches the crowd, and you can adjust on the fly.

- Don't rely on slide visuals in the same way you would for an in-person event – recognize that many people leave online events streaming in the background, only listening to the audio as they multitask on other things.

- Ask questions, take polls, and use similar techniques to engage your audience.

- Make your online events shorter than their equivalent in-person version. There are just too many distractions, and no one wants to be stuck staring at a screen for hours on end. Aim for a maximum of two hours and three or fewer speakers.

- Consider the best channels and tools to reach your audience. There are a growing number of specialist online event platforms (e.g., Hopin, BigMarker, vFairs, etc.), online meeting tools (e.g., Zoom, Google Meet, Microsoft Teams, etc.), and content platforms (YouTube, Facebook Live, Twitch, Clubhouse, etc.). Ensure you are recording your event and making it available for full replay and/or edited sessions.

We found conferences and events a great way to gain visibility for our startup and meet new people, but with lots of events and limited budgets, we needed to do our homework. The best value for us came in the form of promoters that were willing to customize our sponsorship, went above and beyond with introductions, and helped us gather a mailing list. We did experience a mismatch in what we thought our 'virtual booth' would look like to what is reality – we were unable to change our content during the event, so weren't able to put our best foot forward. On the other hand, we also experienced the importance of the platform being used for the event. Platforms like Grip makes it very easy to update your content at any time, communicate with attendees, and having a great time during the virtual event.

Also, don't be afraid to negotiate upfront for what you need, or as we found negotiate following an event, to get an extra blog or something to make up for promises that weren't kept.

—Martin Isaksson
CEO and Co-Founder, PerceptiLabs

Organizing Your Own Events

At some point, you will organize your own events – online and in person. It's a natural step as organizations desire to set the agenda and provide a tailored experience for their community.

The majority of your events by volume will be smaller-style events like meetups, workshops, office hours, etc.

Larger companies with hefty budgets often decide to host their own branded conferences for their developer community and the wider ecosystem. Vendor examples of these large conferences include Apple's Worldwide Developers Conference, Dreamforce, AWS re:Invent, F8, Microsoft Build, Twilio's Signal, and Samsung Developer Conference. These take a year or more to plan, have budgets in the millions of dollars, and usually involve hiring several professional firms to support the planning, production, and execution.

Regardless of the size of your event, doing a reality check as mentioned earlier and setting an intent are important starting points. As well, much of the strategy and advice outlined for attending others' events applies equally to your events. You have the same challenges and considerations when assessing which events to create, how to engage the audience, how to follow up post-event, and how to measure ROI.

Event Journey

The major difference between organizing an event and attending is the additional burden of planning, logistics, and execution. Established marketing wisdom is to put yourself in your customer's shoes and see things through their eyes. As with the Developer Journey, you'll want to create an Event Journey.

The Event Journey is the complete sum of the experience, or touchpoints, that the developer will have from discovering your event through to the eventual follow-up after the event.

These touchpoints affect a developer's feeling toward your company and your product. Their complete experience will influence whether they choose to engage with you during and after the event. Your goal is to remove any friction or barriers. Nothing is worse than attending an event whose layout and format is confusing and where you feel alone.

You can uncover potential issues by asking questions like:

- Have we made the registration process easy?
- Do we need to help them get manager approval?
- Have we given them enough time to prepare?
- Do we greet them when they arrive (online and offline)?
- Are our speakers prepared?

Figure 23-1 highlights the touchpoints to consider for your attendees.

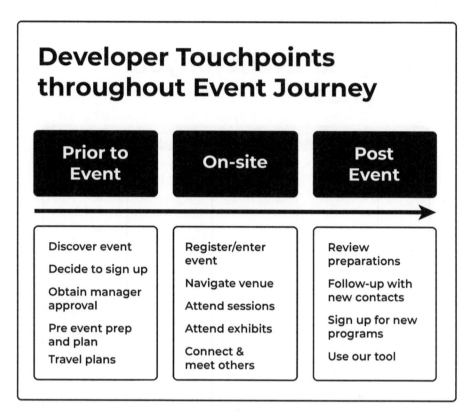

Figure 23-1. The Event Journey from a developer's perspective

We recommend you create a journey for each of the personas you expect will attend your event. For larger events, it may well be beyond developers to also include business job titles, the press, and investors. Focus on what each persona will see, hear, learn, and meet based on their motivations, as shown in Figure 23-2.

Plan your Event for your Personas

	INDIE	STARTUP	BRAND	ENTERPRISE
SEE	Any new tech, partner tech, demos	Any new tech, partner tech, case studies/demos	Any new tech, partner tech, demos	Any new tech, partner tech, demos
TOUCH	All our technology and SWAG	All our technology and SWAG	All our technology and SWAG	All our technology and SWAG
LEARN	Coding	Overview of technologies, how to commercialize	Overview of tech, marketing with us	Coding light, tech overviews, tech security/architecture
MEET	Peers, rock star devs, our tech people	Peers, rock star devs, investors, our people - tech and BizDev	Partners, startups, our BizDev	Partners, our BizDev and tech

Figure 23-2. This chart identifies the senses each of your persona will experience to aid in planning your event

Hackathons

Hackathons are hands-on technical events, where individuals or teams compete to create software and/or hardware projects. There is normally a theme set by the hackathon organizers and often a requirement to use a designated set of developer products. The developer products are typically those of the sponsoring companies. As with other developer events, hackathons can be online or in person and require alignment with your personas, clarity around your intended outcomes, and the marketing and logistical preparation that goes into delivering any successful event. Hackathons can be private invite-only events, for example, with the developers of one of your major customers or your own internal developers. They can be public events that are open to all or hybrid events where you invite a few developers from your community to work side by side with your own developers.

Here are a few tips specific to hackathons:

- **Be clear on why you are running a hackathon** – Are you interested in validating and getting feedback on your new product, building your community, generating buzz for your product and company, scouting for talent or partners, or gathering ideas for your product? Know your intent and plan accordingly.

- **Check your expectations** – The size of the event and prize is often inversely proportional to the quality of projects that will be generated. Bigger is not always better. Hosting a large, open event with big prizes in Silicon Valley will attract serial competition attendees, who have no real interest in a long-term relationship with you; they'll simply want to win a prize. In very specialized/ commercial markets, smaller, more focused events that allow for higher-quality interactions between your team and participants can generate better outcomes. Remember the Salesforce $1 million hackathon controversy we covered in Chapter 10.

- **A hackathon is a technical event with coding** – It is crucial to have technical staff on hand to answer developer questions, inspire the teams, and help them with their code throughout the event – this is not an option.

- **Be mindful of constraints of time that the teams are working under** – They often are new to each other and have a short amount of time to deliver something that works. Don't expect miracles.

- **Do not expect to get any IP or own any of the output** – Developers retain the right to their work.

- **Share your details in a timely manner** – The sooner you can get information out to developers to give them time to understand your product and what types of project you are looking for or give them an opportunity to "play" with the module, SDKs, API, etc., the better your results.

- **Provide focus and context** – The better you can focus developers on a topic and provide them with context, the better your results in terms of focused and polished apps or products. Loosely defined topics may generate more out-of-the-box ideas and unusual innovations, but more highly focused topics, categories, and specs will generally create more polished and complete ideas that are relevant to your product and company. We recall a hackathon where many great apps were created, but at judging time over half were rejected because 'legal won't allow them'. It's kinder to provide developers with those type of restrictions upfront to avoid wasting their time and yours.

For the community view on what it takes to ship a great hackathon, check out the Hack Day Manifesto.[1]

Event Return on Investment

The first question you'll be asked the day after any event is: "How did it go?"

Be prepared and data driven in how you assess the return on investment of your event marketing spend, but don't overwhelm yourself with data. Pick which metrics are meaningful for your business, and as we explore in greater detail in Chapter 26, avoid vanity metrics when at all possible.

Suggested metrics include:

- Engagement with your brand and content pre/during/post-event. How did blog traffic, website traffic, etc., convert into engagement (e.g., downloading content, contacting sales, or registering for a product). Your share of voice vs. competitors and sentiment analysis.

- Ticket sales, attendance-to-registered ratio (aka no-show rate), the number of prearranged meetings.

- Leads collected at the event and the percentage qualified as "hot."

- How those leads convert into sales opportunities, the elapsed time to convert, the number of opportunities that close, and the monetary value of those "won" deals.

Although data is king, don't exclusively focus on the data. Also, create a system to collect anecdotes, quotes, conversations, and feedback. These qualitative data points are all supremely valuable by-products of getting out of the office, adding color and insight to your event investments.

---

[1]https://hackdaymanifesto.com/

Summary

Events of all varieties are still a cornerstone of developer marketing and are used for developer education as well. However, be aware of the perception that all events are a quick win. The execution of events, whether you attend or organize an event, encompasses many details which require well-thought-out plans. Creating an event journey, much like the Developer Journey, can provide great insight into your developers' experience with your event. Finally, along with data, consider qualitative ways to measure your event ROI to determine the results for both you and your community.

Sales

Myth-Busting — DevRel and Sales in Harmony

You are in sales.

There we said it.

It's vital to understand that everybody in their company is selling. All the time. To deny this does a disservice to the impact your work has in creating value for your company.

Explaining how your product works at a meetup is selling. Writing a blog post about a cool use case is selling. Writing your API specification is selling. Chatting to a friend about how great the culture is in your startup is selling. Face it – you're in sales.

This chapter will address the stereotypes of what exactly sales is and show how to optimize it for DevRel. You won't have to be afraid of sales anymore.

Understanding Modern Sales

Today, sales is about solving problems. You have to intimately understand the client's needs, including their problem, their context, their environment, their resources, and their industry vertical. You have to inspire them and open their mind to new ideas and the art of the possible.

© Caroline Lewko, James Parton 2021
C. Lewko and J. Parton, *Developer Relations*,
https://doi.org/10.1007/978-1-4842-7164-3_24

You can't solve someone's problem if you don't understand it, which is why listening is so important, combined with strong technical and business knowledge. There is nothing worse than trivializing your customer's problem because you don't understand the complexity and nuance of their situation.

For example, while much of Twilio's Developer playbook turned into a de facto standard for DevRel, Twilio made its fair share of mistakes. For every "Ask Your Developer" billboard, there are examples of strategies that didn't work, such as the launch of Twilio Flex with its claim that you could build a contact center in "a few lines of code." While this felt on-brand with Twilio's "simplicity" marketing message, it completely glossed over the complexity, dependencies, and mission-critical nature of building and operating contact centers inside large organizations. Unintentionally, this lack of understanding of the customer made some contact center professionals feel undervalued and led them to question if Twilio understood the contact center space at all.

A modern sales approach also reveals why a sales team would want to work with a DevRel team, given where the expertise lies in supporting the customer.

Beyond Self-Service

When you first launch your product, you may believe you can build your business solely on a self-service model.

This belief may be true initially, but as word spreads and you begin to scale, there will be certain triggers to make you consider the creation of a formal sales operation or stronger alignment with your existing sales team.

Some of those triggers include:

- Large organizations begin signing up via self-serve channels. Sometimes, this happens in "stealth mode" when an employee of a large company registers using a Gmail account rather than a corporate email account to avoid signaling interest from their company. It could also be a developer experimenting on their own time. You need to be vigilant. Engage them to understand their use cases and seek to win them as a customer. Once they are ready to sign up with a corporate account, a sales approach may be necessary.

- Large companies may discover you via self-service and experimentation. However, for them to make a meaningful purchasing decision, they will likely have specific needs, like adding you to their preferred vendor list, running a tendering process, adding privacy and security stipulations, and negotiating on terms and price. These requirements are very different from the standard DevRel approach and need new skill sets and teams.

- If they have an existing relationship with your company, customers may automatically approach their sales rep first. To be effective, sales will need to be briefed on your product and understand where a handoff can take place. Salespeople who work on commission can get very territorial, so they'll want to have confidence in your ability to service "their" customer.

- As awareness of your product and brand grows, you will start to move (intentionally or unintentionally) beyond the hardcore developer audience. You will attract a broader technical and nontechnical audience. As they likely won't be writing code directly, this new audience requires a different experience and style of content. Job titles vary from company to company, so they often want to engage with a sales or business development person rather than a developer advocate. Or if they identify as technical, they will want to talk to a solutions architect, technical presales, or sales engineer.

- As your company revenue grows, so do the expectations. Your current and future investors want to see quarter-on-quarter revenue growth and ensure you are identifying and capturing the full market potential of your company. This situation is especially true if your company is on a path to IPO. Along this journey, companies target higher value and more complex sales. Then an outbound sales motion is added to start proactively prospecting for new customers, complementing the inbound self-serve channel to accelerate revenue growth and market share.

DevRel and Sales Synergies

So how do DevRel and Sales work together? We've seen DevRel and Sales work exceptionally well together when there is the will, an appreciation for each team's strengths, and joined-up departmental leadership. Figure 24-1 shows how DevRel activity and Sales activity can act in harmony to influence, win, and grow opportunities.

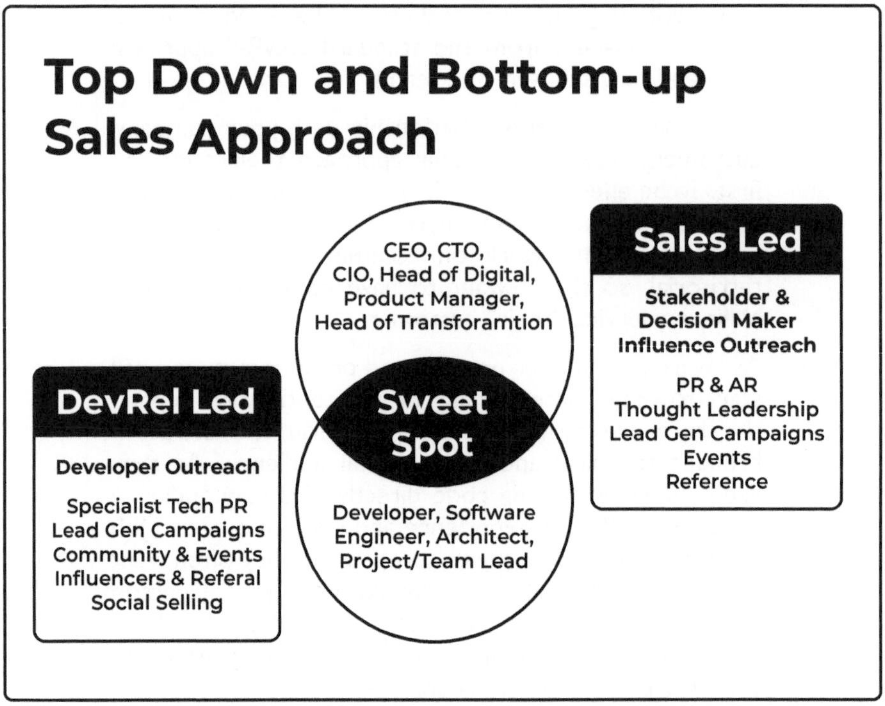

Top Down and Bottom-up Sales Approach

CEO, CTO, CIO, Head of Digital, Product Manager, Head of Transforamtion

Sales Led

Stakeholder & Decision Maker Influence Outreach

PR & AR
Thought Leadership
Lead Gen Campaigns
Events
Reference

DevRel Led

Developer Outreach

Specialist Tech PR
Lead Gen Campaigns
Community & Events
Influencers & Referal
Social Selling

Sweet Spot

Developer, Software Engineer, Architect, Project/Team Lead

Figure 24-1. The sweet spot of a top-down and bottom-up sales approach

Your activities as a DevRel team are predominantly focused on Developers and related technical job titles inside an organization. Your tactics, messaging, and channels are optimized to reach this audience, covered in previous chapters.

Sales (in conjunction with marketing) will operate in parallel to your DevRel activities to find, reach, and influence the "business job titles" inside the same company. They use messages, tactics, and channels appropriate to that audience.

It all comes together in the "sweet spot." Here, all the relevant decision makers and decision influencers in the company are aligned and advocating for your product.

Ameer Badri has led Sales Engineering teams at several high-growth companies, including Netlify, Twilio, and Salesforce. He's gained extensive experience operating a sales motion alongside a Developer Relations play. This combined approach is a strategy he's used effectively:

DevRel and Sales working in harmony

At Twilio we went into a number of customers where the DevRel team had warmed up the opportunity. We frequently heard, Oh I saw someone from

Twilio speak at this conference or meetup. It created a familiarity. Of course we still had a lot of work to do, but it gave us a foot in the door.

Over the past 5 years I have seen significant changes, and the days of DevRel and Sales mixing like oil and water are gone. At Netlify the DevRel team attend customer meetings alongside Sales and help with sales related content production. Both teams are focused on solving customer problems and driving revenue.

—Ameer Badri
Sr. Director Global Solutions Engineering at Netlify

DevRel and Sales Alignment

Every company will find itself in its unique situation dependent on different stages of maturity, organizational structures, business models, and monetization strategies. However, the frameworks used to plan and monitor the Go-To-Market strategy remain the same, with room for variations.

In DevRel, there are three frameworks we follow:

- **The Developer Journey stages** – Covered in Chapter 15, the journey reflects the objectives of the developer. The needs of your customer, the developer, are always number one.

- **The Developer Relations objectives** – These four objectives (Awareness, Activation, Engagement, and Retention) reflect the DevRel team's high-level mission as you go to market. We reviewed them at the start of Part IV and saw them in Figure P-IV.

- **A typical sales funnel** – There are many variations of sales and/or marketing funnels, with slightly different terminology and stages. We have used a funnel example inspired by Salesforce and HubSpot as they are commonly used tools. It is a simple task to substitute in your preferred sales funnel to suit your situation. The funnel is typically managed by a combination of the marketing team, sales team, and customer success team.

Figure 24-2 shows how the three frameworks work together for your own understanding of their alignment and sequencing.

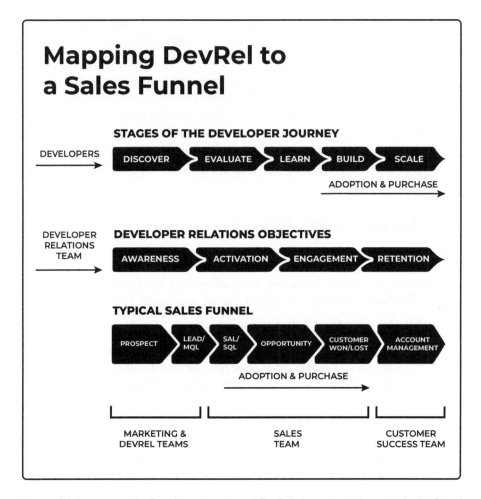

Figure 24-2. Mapping the Developer Journey and DevRel objectives with a typical sales funnel (**Note:** The stages do not align perfectly and are shown for illustrative purposes only.)

Alignment and Sequencing Example: Direct Revenue – Self-Serve Operation

To better understand how DevRel and Sales align, here's one example.

Let's look at an organization that has a self-serve operation with a direct revenue model. Here, the inbound marketing motion is managed by separate sales, marketing, and DevRel teams. This combination introduces a high degree of complexity, so it is important to understand how this all aligns.

Here is how the teams and frameworks would work together in this example:

- At the start of the process, the high-level DevRel objectives naturally align with the sales funnel. **The objective for everyone is to create awareness that attracts prospects**.

- Because most Developer Programs have some kind of zero-risk trial, a developer can become an active user (i.e., they complete registration) without spending money. **This is why activation comes before engagement in our DevRel objectives**. If you don't have a "try before you buy" offer, it may be more appropriate to place engagement ahead of activation.

- While the developer is at the experimentation stage (Learn), they are considered an opportunity in sales parlance because there is still a chance they never implement anything in production or buy your product. **Developers may experiment for a long time for various reasons, so we indicated under the DevRel Journey that Adoption and Purchase could take place anywhere along a continuum**.

- **They only become a "won customer" when they start spending money**. This is why the sequencing of the Build stage aligns with Customer won/lost. As we discussed in Chapter 20, this is where the rubber hits the road, and it becomes clear if the developer has serious intent to adopt your technology.

- Once the developer has successfully implemented something in production, the focus switches to nurturing and retention to ensure they remain customers over the long term, and additional revenue generation opportunities are explored. This is why **Scale aligns with Retention, Account Management, and Customer Success**.

If executed properly, there should be no need for sales intervention with the majority of customers. As previously discussed, if you have a frictionless Developer Experience, a prospect could appear, be qualified, and be won in a matter of hours, if not minutes.

However, in many large organizations with a DevRel play or working with large customers or very fast scaling customers, working with a Sales and/or Business Development team can be synergistic. They often speak "corporate" and are skilled in negotiations. The corollary is that they will need you to speak "dev," providing them with support on calls and their own sales documentation.

Summary

Modern sales, which is about solving customers' problems, is an important component in DevRel. Creating a formal sales operation in your startup or a stronger alignment with your existing sales team can create synergies required to influence, win, and grow opportunities as you and your customer scale.

Community

You Are Here to Serve

We've purposely anchored this chapter on Community at the end of our Go-to-Market part. Community, a vital component of DevRel, is a central theme we hope we've carried throughout the book. However, community is a topic that is often misunderstood, misused, or simply not acknowledged at all, so we believe it is fully deserving of its own chapter.

Because Communities are so vital to DevRel and the success of your program, we represented them as the tree trunk and roots in our Developer Relations Framework (Figure 1-1). A strong, healthy trunk supports a tree's growth, and the roots provide crucial information and nutrients shared between the tree and its surrounding ecosystem, forming complex networks and connections that are often hidden from view.[1] We liken this as a metaphor to describe a developer program and the community of developers it seeks to serve. It also takes into account your community activities in their various guises, which will benefit both your individual program and the surrounding ecosystem.

---

[1] According to the book *The Hidden Life of Trees* – https://goodbooksummary.com/the-hidden-life-of-trees-by-peter-wohlleben-book-summary/

© Caroline Lewko, James Parton 2021
C. Lewko and J. Parton, *Developer Relations*,
https://doi.org/10.1007/978-1-4842-7164-3_25

Community can mean many things in the context of DevRel. It could refer to a structured managed activity, a descriptor of a formal or informal group of like-minded individuals, or a management philosophy for your program.

You can see why the word *community* and its implications often get mixed up regarding developer programs. For example, just because you have a developer program does not mean you have a healthy, vibrant developer community. Similarly, talking about "your community" doesn't imply you have one or that you understand how to harness it. On the flip side, you might have a community and not yet realize it!

Let's unpack these concepts.

What Is a Community?

Several developer programs claim to have more than one million community members. This number sounds impressive and aspirational. However, the devil is always in the detail. When you dig below the surface, you may find they have one million emails on their newsletter's mailing list, of which less than half have registered for their product, only 10% of them are active users, and there is little contribution from any of those "members" nor any appreciation for them. In this case, would you still argue they have a community of one million members?

In DevRel, there is no standard definition of what a community member is nor transparent reporting or auditing of the community numbers reported by companies. So be aware you are not comparing apples with apples.

The most **general definition of a community is a group of people that share a common interest**. The commonality can be a topic, the place where they live, a brand they like, or a product they have purchased. With such a loose definition, you *could* claim to have a million members in your community, but we believe that is a disingenuous claim built on a vanity metric. (See Chapter 26 for more on vanity metrics.)

A community – at least one that has value to your organization, your DevRel program, and the members – is much more than just a common interest. Community is a philosophy. And as we'll also see, it needs to be architected and managed to create value for you and its members.

Community Is: A Philosophy

First and most importantly, as it relates to DevRel, Community is a philosophy. It's a philosophy of appreciating the value of your current, potential, and previous users, as well as the wider ecosystem. Your role is in service to them.

Community is a Philosophy – You are Here to Serve

Have this concept at the forefront of your work. You are not just serving a faceless entry in a CRM system, but real people with real issues, building real applications. As we outlined in Part II, one of the key differentiators of DevRel is the link between the developer's ultimate success in using your technology and your own success. This symbiotic relationship necessitates a deeper ongoing connection so that the developer can be inspired, educated, and nurtured. Quite different from a typical B2B or B2C style relationship.

These people form more than just a mass of users; they, plus other members of your ecosystem, form your community. As we indicated in Chapter 1, the whole point of your program is to engage, serve, and nurture your community. This is the essence upon which your success will be built. Without a healthy, sustainable, and active community, you have little chance of success.

But before we get carried away with calling everyone a community member, we need to understand the practicalities of what a community is and how you manage one within the DevRel context.

Community Is: A Relationship

You can call your active users, or members of your mailing list, or your Twitter followers "your community," but **what's important is whether they share that sense of identity with you**.

In the preceding example, just because you have a developer program with users and understand you are there to serve, this does not mean you have a developer community. There must be a shared understanding, a self-identification on the developer's part, where they acknowledge they are part of your community. This understanding is heavily dependent on how their relationship with you is defined and activated as we'll see next.

Community Is: A Subset of Your Developer Program

In 2004, Tim O'Reilly coined the term **"Architecture of Participation,"**[2] to describe systems designed for effective user contributions. Doug Belshaw, then at Mozilla, riffed on this ten years later expressing, *"Any time you're asking someone else to chip in who doesn't have an obligation to help you, then you need an architecture of participation."*[3] **In essence, that's the role of community management.**

---

[2] https://web.archive.org/web/20120208001626/http://www.oreillynet.com/
   pub/a/oreilly/tim/articles/architecture_of_participation.html
[3] https://dougbelshaw.com/blog/2014/10/10/episodic-volunteering/

To form a community that flourishes, your job is to create an environment for interaction and contribution, and to nurture those relationships.

In this regard, your developer community is not an alternative name for your developer program; rather, community management is a function within your developer program, as shown in Figure 25-1, which requires its own resources, activities, and goals as it reaches critical mass.

A Community is Managed as a Subset of Your Developer Program

Developer Program

Community Management

Figure 25-1. A community is a subset of your developer program

We've seen the sequencing of community formation and the creation of a DevRel program vary. Sometimes, a product is released and gains popularity with developers who form an informal community. Recognition of this informal community leads to a DevRel program being reactively created to formalize the product's promotion and manage/grow the nascent community. We've also seen individuals tasked with starting a developer community where no DevRel program exists.

In reality, not all Developer Programs have a formalized community program, due to a variety of reasons like program maturity, culture, budget, etc. We do believe that all programs can benefit from at least acknowledging an informal community that requires minimal management. This may include encouraging and recognizing ad hoc versions of various types of community contribution as outlined in Figure 25-2 that may or may not be on a touchpoint that you own.

In our view, the **best practice is to set up the basics of the developer program first** if you are serious about developers as your customer. Otherwise, you risk friction in your journey and in your relationship with your developers. We've seen communities turn on companies with negative comments because their needs like Docs, Developer Education, and other support weren't met. We've seen developers start to write the documentation for a product out of frustration when there was none. That might seem like a great way to get someone else to do the work, but in reality it left negative sentiment for the company which was very difficult to repair.

A DevRel program, as laid out in this book, provides the foundation upon which the community is built and maps the journey your developers follow.

The Benefits of Community

As we reviewed in Chapter 1, the focus on developers as a route to market is relatively new, as are the frameworks and concepts in formalizing a DevRel program. So it's not surprising that we have seen a disconnect between how DevRel and community management coexist. This is often due to a lack of understanding of the benefits and impacts a community brings as part of your DevRel program.

Benefits of formalizing and taking responsibility for a community may include:

- Attracting new users
- Retaining existing users
- Increasing engagement with and between current users
- Enhancing product support
- Gaining new product or feature ideas
- Enhancing brand reputation

In essence, having a community supplements and amplifies what your team or company can do on its own in three significant ways:

1. A community can expand on the capacity of your team.

2. A community brings their own authentic experience with your product, free of any corporate bias you may intentionally or unintentionally bring. This is especially beneficial in identifying use cases your team would probably never think of.

3. Developers trust their peers, so make great advocates for your product.

Community contributions exponentially enhance what you do.

Still, not everyone recognizes the benefits a community can bring to a company and its developer program. We've noted in some situations, the company strategy is more product and engineering focused and often measured on the next new product launch, rather than supporting the current product. Thus, they don't actively think about the management and stimulation of their users within an associated community. Others are unclear how DevRel and Community work together or are measured.

Here are some community metrics to consider:

- Referral programs – Are your biggest fans advocating and recruiting more people into the community?

- Do your active community members have lower churn and higher lifetime value vs. standard users?

- How many community members support other members on your owned properties or external properties like Stack Overflow and Reddit? Are you recognizing and encouraging this behavior?

- Are your GitHub repos growing?

- How many feature requests/contributions are coming from your community? Are you recognizing and encouraging this behavior and implementing their suggestions?

- Are community members contributing to positive brand sentiment or amplifying your messaging?

Community Management Is: Members and Contributions

A managed community is about activities, especially activities that contribute to the betterment of the group. We call these *contributions*, which come in many forms. A few of the more common contributions are shown in Figure 25-2.

Figure 25-2. Types of Developer Community contributions by active members

There will be a range of contribution types, quality of contributions, and the cadence to which members contribute; that's just human nature. The 1% rule[4] suggests 99% of your community will be lurkers rather than active contributors.

The most valuable members of your community are typically both users of your product and contributors back to the community. If they are already product users, they will have a better appreciation for what other users need. Therefore, they can make the most valuable contributions.

Within your community, there will be a hierarchy of the members, as shown in Figure 25-3. The goal of community management is to move members up the pyramid to become active contributors to the community.

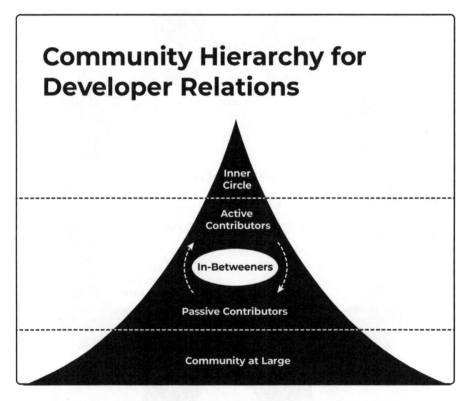

Figure 25-3. Community hierarchy for Developer Relations is focused on the participation and rewarding of the community members

---

[4]https://en.wikipedia.org/wiki/1%25_rule_(Internet_culture)

Note the community hierarchy is often mistaken for a sales funnel, but it is not. There is no relationship between where a community member sits in the community hierarchy and their potential or actual revenue contribution. We reviewed sales funnels in Chapter 24 if you need a refresher.

The community hierarchy is focused on the participation of community members.

The sales funnel is focused on users and customers.

Let's review each part of the Developer community hierarchy and the role of community management.

Community at Large

As we discovered in Chapter 5, there are around 21–25 million developers in the world today. These developers plus other relevant job titles like product managers, solutions architects, and others make up the community at large.

For one of them to become part of your community, they first need to know about you. Your sales and marketing activities will build awareness in the market and bring people into the Discover stage of the Developer Journey (Chapter 16). In sales funnel terminology, they would be defined as a prospect.

To become a community member, the individual will need to understand and agree to the benefits of engaging as a community member, delineating it from just a buyer relationship.

Passive Contributors

Once you've been discovered, an individual takes a step that associates them with you in some capacity – the "joining of the community." This could be signing up for your newsletter or following you on social media, but they may never actively publicly engage on social media, forums, or other community channels.

Even though they are not actively participating, passive contributors still benefit from lurking and absorbing information and tips from others as they learn about your product and become active users.

Not everyone needs to contribute to be considered part of the community. However, your job is to help them understand that contributions, big or small, have value and that all members are respected.

In relation to the Developer Journey, they will be in the Evaluate and Learn stages, and in terms of a sales funnel, they will be a prospect, lead, or opportunity.

Active Contributors

Active contributors regularly contribute in a variety of ways (see Figure 25-2). They likely answer questions regularly in the various channels where people seek help, and they attend your webinars or other events. They may even contribute ideas or code or volunteer to beta test. If they are active product users and have reached the Scale stage of the Developer Journey, they may have been featured in a case study.

In relation to the Developer Journey, they will be in the Build or Scale stage. In terms of a sales funnel, they will likely be a won opportunity and generating revenue.

Remember, don't confuse active *product users* with active *community members*. You may have a very active product user who has never contributed to community activities and may never contribute. That's OK. Their reasons vary from not having enough time, just not being interested, or not thinking they have anything valuable to contribute. Your job is to encourage and show easy ways to contribute.

In-betweeners

The in-betweeners range between passive and active contributors. Depending on the size of your community, this group can be very broad and rather elusive. These individuals float on either side based on their current situation, interests, or time availability. They can be product users or not. You may have heard from them once, or they have spikes of activity, and then go quiet.

It can be useful to survey this group to dig deeper into their variable participation. Are they no longer interested in your product? Have they found another job? Are they frustrated by your lack of adequate documentation? Do they feel like their contributions weren't adequately recognized? Do they just need a nudge of encouragement?

Your job in community management is to continue to nurture them and to show them easy ways to contribute.

Inner Circle

Members of your inner circle are the most valuable community members.

They are active product users having reached the Scale stage of their developer journey. They are also active members of your community.

These community members could be part of your Developer Advisory Group that meets with you regularly or someone you or your product team feels like they can reach out to at any time for feedback. You have likely showcased them in your newsletter, offered them a speaking slot at a conference, or perhaps even featured them in a larger media campaign.

As illustrated in the diagram, not everyone makes it this far in the hierarchy. At this level, it's about quality over quantity, as the most worthy contributors have proven that they can actively and continuously provide the most value while having the most to gain from their participation.

How to Start a Community

Every successful community starts with hand-selected and hand-nurtured one-to-one connections. You want to start with the willing, but more generally, building communities is also about building relationships.

These initial community members are easier to find than you might think. For many, they self-identify because they are the ones already asking and answering questions on your forums or talking about you in other channels like Stack Overflow and Reddit. Through your product adoption analytics, you might spot customers that are starting to gather momentum using your technology. Because these people are already supporting you, you may already have an informal community and just don't know it yet. They may have even reached out to you personally to ask a question or suggest a feature. You can be proactive and do a call for beta testers or host office hours to identify individuals interested in getting involved and contributing.

A successful community requires you to create a culture of openness and respect where people feel comfortable contributing and where you accept criticism and feedback graciously. A formal community also requires Community Guidelines[5] and a Code of Conduct that determines how individuals contribute and set behavioral expectations.

Where Is Your Community?

Wherefore art thou developer? Your community could identify as being part of your community, or someone else's! Your community may spend time on your Forums or community sites, or they might spend more time outside of the touchpoints you own, such as Stack Overflow, Dev.to, or a Slack or Subreddit Group. They could be part of one community or a member of several.

Community is a hot topic these days and in many ways is reaching a saturation point of the number of communities a developer is part of due to time and interest. Developers have a ton of choice when it comes to communities.

---

[5]https://docs.github.com/en/github/site-policy/github-community-guidelines

It's best to serve your community where they are, rather than trying to force them to come to your preferred location. However, do be prepared to host or ramp up your community as needed by your users, as their demands for specific support and feedback regarding your product increase.

Gamification

Gamification is often the first thing that comes to mind when managing a community. Gamification is used to encourage individuals to contribute, to gain peer recognition through badges or titles and earn tangible rewards, like T-shirts, gift cards, dinners, etc. The in-between group is often the most engaged with a gamification model and most influenced by it.

We recommend that most communities do not need to be gamified. Much depends on the type and size of the community and your intent with it.

We have seen gamification programs work very well when the incentives and expectations map to your developer personas. However, be aware gamification programs can backfire, especially when they are emphasized over more important resources like technical documentation and the Developer Experience, or where a community member only engages if they receive something first. Here, you run the risk of your developer program and your product not being taken seriously.

Community Recognition and Experiences

As you build your community, it's important to reward those that participate, as a strong preference over gamification. Random acts of kindness help recognize and reward individuals and demonstrate you appreciate and invest in your community.

Examples might be sending them a care package of swag for a social media shout-out or for helping someone on Stack Overflow, hiring a cinema for a movie premiere, throwing community parties, showcasing their work in your marketing materials, making an introduction for them, or inviting them to speak on stage where you have a speaking opportunity as part of a sponsorship package. There is no shortage of ideas!

More formal examples include launching an MVP program on your support forum recognizing individuals' skills and community support. Or you may consider inviting them to join customer panels to enjoy early access to your road map and feedback directly to your product and engineering teams.

Being thoughtful and going the extra mile is appreciated and makes a tangible difference. Often, a simple "thank you" is enough.

The above is a very quick look into what developer communities are and how they can be set up. A successful and active community program can be a ton of work, requiring dedicated resources to set up, nurture, and grow it. There are many sources to learn more about community management, including CMX,[6] a hub for community management professionals. There are also tools which are being developed to track developer community activities like Orbit.[7]

Open Source Communities

This chapter, and much of the book, has focused on building developer communities for organizations looking to profit from their activities. We'd be remiss if we did not briefly mention Open Source communities here.

There are two key differences with Open Source communities:

1. Open Source communities have implicit trust in the product as they can see the code and understand how it works.

2. Contributions to open source add clear value to both the project and the contributing individuals. For example, developers are often asked about their open source contributions in job interviews, so having a track record of contributions provides an advantage. A clear win-win for both parties.

When working in DevRel for an open source organization, the orientation is shaping and pointing a community of smart people in the right direction. Success is based on the technical leadership of a community, not selling. The theory is that the combined weight of eyes will find and fix everything. The key is not to discourage contributions.

Summary

A Developer Program is not the same as a managed Developer Community. However, all developer programs can benefit from having a community program as part of it, whether you have a formal or informal community.

Community members can be significant contributors to a developer program, providing benefits from awareness to support to new innovations that allow everyone to flourish.

There is much to learn about managing a community that cannot possibly be covered in one chapter. If we have provided you with an understanding of the philosophy of community, that you are here to serve, which is the cornerstone of having a successful Developer Program, then we have done our job.

---

[6]https://cmxhub.com/
[7]https://orbit.love/

Managing and Growing Your Program

Metrics, Team, Phasing

You're a whiz now at DevRel, and your program is set. Your developers are going to have the most amazing frictionless experience.

Our final part is about managing and growing your program. We'll first look at metrics, crucial to measuring your performance and being accountable. Then we will explore how to build a team, finishing off by exploring the growth phases of your program.

Let's do this!

Metrics

Measuring and Monitoring Goals and Activities

A fundamental component of managing your program is to measure its performance. Metrics, as we have seen, can be a murky area for many developer programs. You can guarantee any conference on DevRel will have a speaker or section dedicated to metrics. There is also no shortage of data to measure and opinions on what you should measure!

Problems arise when programs don't know what to measure, don't know how to measure, aren't measuring the right things, or aren't making effective use of the metrics they do collect.

Being able to articulate the impact of your work is vital. It's something you want to own rather than have imposed on you.

   Run towards metrics and crave accountability.[1]

This chapter will review those topics.

Metrics Hierarchy and Clarity

Creating effective developer program metrics requires alignment and clarity.

When properly aligned and clarified, metrics allow you to:

---

[1] We are thinking of creating a T-shirt with these words!

© Caroline Lewko, James Parton 2021
C. Lewko and J. Parton, *Developer Relations*,
https://doi.org/10.1007/978-1-4842-7164-3_26

- Clearly communicate priorities and motivate your teams

- Measure progress toward your goals and objectives

- Forecast if those goals and objectives can be reached

- Make improvements to your strategy and tactics

- Demonstrate to the team and company as a whole how Developer Relations contributes to the overall business

- Negotiate resources for next year

Let's see how you accomplish this.

First, Alignment

We reviewed company and interdepartmental alignment in Chapters 10 and 11. Overarching the developer program metrics are the company-level goals and metrics (see Figure 26-1), which emphasize what is important to the business.

Your **Program Goals** and accompanying metrics should be aligned with the company's overall goals and agreed with your stakeholders. Underneath this, you can get more granular with goals and metrics for your program activities and community interactions.

Your Lead Program Goal forms the "Why?" of your existence and helps the team focus, driving everyone in the same direction. If you have a team member that is unsure what they should be doing, point them back to your company and Program goals.

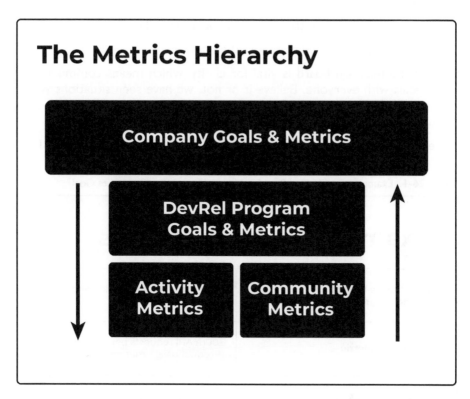

The Metrics Hierarchy

Company Goals & Metrics

DevRel Program Goals & Metrics

Activity Metrics

Community Metrics

Figure 26-1. The metrics hierarchy ensures all goals and metrics are aligned

Underneath those, the **Activity metrics** are the "How?". They outline the ways you will achieve your program-level goals and metrics. If you can't figure out how an activity rolls up to your program goals, you should probably stop doing it. You can take this one step further when measuring your team. All team members should have a set of activities that they commit to at the start of the reporting period (quarter, year, etc.) that roll up to one of the Program goals.

Community metrics measure the health of your community – how your program interacts with it, supports it, and vice versa. If you haven't figured out why community matters, go back and read Chapter 25.

Next Is Clarity

Metrics are the way to measure progress to achieving your goals. To achieve clarity, each of your metrics should include:

- The end goal (what do you want to achieve)
- The target (the number)

- The time frame (by when will you achieve it)
- The source used to report the number

Getting the team on board is vital for clarity, which means communicating these goals with everyone. Believe it or not, we have seen situations where the team lead knew the goals and metrics, but for whatever reason, chose not to share with their team. Don't be that person!

Here's an example of a properly aligned and clarified metric in Table 26-1.

Table 26-1. Example of a Clarified Program Metric Aligned to a Corporate Goal

Example Program Metrics

Corporate Goal or Lead Program Goal	To become the market-leading payments API
Program Metric	300m API requests per day (Product usage metric)
DevRel Objective	Engagement & Retention
Time Frame	by Q4
Data Source	Product Reporting (PAS - Product Analytics Software)

DevRel Program Metrics – The What

Your DevRel Program metric identifies the "**What?**". What needs to be achieved to reach the goal and show the results of your activities? Having a metric attached to your work ensures you are accountable and gives you and your team a very clear target on which to drive toward.

At the program level, you are going to want to identify and track metrics that align to the four Developer Relations objectives of:

1. **Awareness**
2. **Activation**
3. **Engagement**
4. **Retention**

At this level, keep things simple to avoid going in too many directions (i.e., lack of focus) and to communicate to all stakeholders what is driving your work. Designate one metric as your lead metric (or top-line metric) to target, as we did in the preceding example. You might also want to include strategic statements so your team and stakeholders are clear on your priorities for the time period in question.

You'll also want to track at least one metric for each DevRel objective to track the progression and conversion of your prospects and customers through the stages of the Developer Journey. Figure 26-2 identifies the Program-Level Metrics that most programs will use and shows them in relation to the Developer Journey, DevRel Objectives, and Sales funnel.

Resist the temptation to dream up unique metrics to measure your program. **Defining metrics is not a creativity test.** If your stakeholders don't understand your metrics or can't compare them to the metrics of other departments or investments they are responsible for, it can create frustration and suspicion.

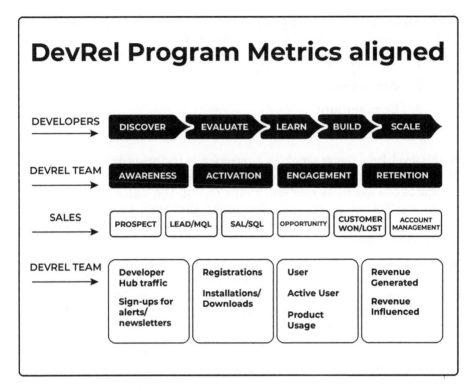

Figure 26-2. Example of DevRel Program Metrics aligned with the Developer Journey, DevRel objectives, and Sales team

You will see that the metrics shown in Figure 26-2 are, in many ways, the calls to action (CTAs) you are seeking from your developers. Have they checked out your Developer Hub? Downloaded or tried your product? Became a customer? Actively use your product?

Product-level metrics are based on quantitative funnel metrics that you own and track from a reliable source (more on data sources in a bit).

Your lead metric and others will depend on many things, including the type of company you are, expectations from corporate for reporting, where your DevRel program fits within your organization, as well as where your product or company is in their life cycle. For instance, if you have just launched your product or are an unknown startup, your Awareness metric might be the most important one right now. If you've been around for a while and your growth is stagnating, you might see what you can do about converting your free users to a higher level or value of usage within Engagement.

Define your metrics further based on your situation and point in the Journey. For example, an active user could be defined as a time-based metric like Monthly Active User (MAU), or it could be activity-based like the number of apps pushed to production. Product usage, particularly for products like APIs, is typically measured in requests, but you can also track the percentage of accounts that send a predefined number of transactions per month or hit a predefined spending threshold.

Activity Metrics – The How

As mentioned earlier, your **Activity Metrics** are the "How?". The tactics of your strategy. They allow you to track the things you do day to day and their performance. The results of these metrics roll up to provide additional insight into your Program-Level metrics, as mentioned earlier. You can also track these metrics by the DevRel Framework or practice category to better manage how and where your team is spending their time.

Some examples of Activity metrics are shown in Table 26-2.

Table 26-2. Sample Program Activity Metrics by DevRel Objective and Practice Area

Sample Program Activity Metrics

Activity Metric	DevRel Objective	DevRel Practice Area
Search Engine Ranking	Awareness	Dev Marketing
Social follows	Awareness	Dev Marketing
Paid advertising perfor-mance (e.g. impressions, clicks, signups)	Awareness	Dev Marketing
Number of newletters opened and links clicked	Awareness Evaluate	Dev Marketing DevEd
Number of blogs written and links clicked	Awareness	Dev Marketing DevEd
Number of events attended, and developers reached	Awareness	Dev Marketing
Number of quick start guides written and their performance	Evaluate	DevEd
Number of use cases written and their peformance	Awareness Evaluate	DevEd
Number of demo videos produced and viewed	Evaluation Build	DevEd
Time to 'Hello World'	Evaluate	DevEx and Product
Number of code samples available	Build	DevEx
Number of case studies written	Retention	Dev Success
Product improvement suggestions captured	Retention	Scale

If you need ideas for activities, revisit the Developer Journey. However, always be sure to focus your activities. More is not always better.

Note, some of these activities may be performed by people outside of the direct DevRel reporting structure. Therefore, it is critical you have agreement between teams on how the impact is going to be measured and reported.

Community Metrics

Community metrics illustrate your community's size and depth and its synergies with your program.

Community Metrics can be gathered with **quantitative data**, for instance:

- The number of questions/mentions on Stack Overflow
- The percentage of answered/unanswered questions on Stack Overflow
- The number of GitHub project starts
- The number of forks for company-hosted GitHub projects or projects that use a product library as a dependency
- The number of community-answered questions in your Forum
- The number of Stack Overflow or GitHub activities vs. your competitors' stats
- The number of content pieces written by a community member

They can also be measured by **qualitative data** such as asking your developers direct questions either informally or with a formal survey to find out:

- Product reviews
- Overall company, program, or product sentiment, including NPS scoring[2]
- Tool usage

---

[2]https://en.wikipedia.org/wiki/Net_Promoter

You should also understand the **value of your community** by analyzing the data to find out:

- Churn rates of community members vs. noncommunity members
- Lifetime value of active community members vs. active users
- Referrals by active community members

Assessing Your Metrics

When defined, and applied correctly, your metrics should help you see how your program strategy contributes to the overall business and how your tactics contribute to your program's success.

Keep in mind there is no one uniform set of metrics suitable for every program and every company. Assessing your metrics is a cross-functional dialogue to agree on what is best for your situation.

As you develop your metrics, ensure each one passes these two tests:

1. **Ask, "So what?" after every metric** – What does the number tell us? What does it mean? Is it meaningful? For example, does it really matter how many followers your program has on Twitter? Can you prove a link between your performance on social media and your product adoption or revenue growth? That's not to say your social media efforts may not be important; just question if it should appear in your Leading metrics dashboard or if there are other metrics more important.

2. **Ask, "What do I adjust?"** – This will establish if the metric is actionable. Is there a clear action you can undertake to influence the metric? What can you tweak? What change can you make? What experiment can you run? What do you need more or less of?

Here, we acknowledge the work of Eric Ries in defining "actionable" and "vanity" metrics. If you are not familiar with the concepts, we recommend you read Ries' blog posts on the subject.[3, 4]

---

[3] https://tim.blog/2009/05/19/vanity-metrics-vs-actionable-metrics/
[4] http://www.startuplessonslearned.com/2009/12/why-vanity-metrics-are-dangerous.html

The chances are the metric isn't relevant if it doesn't have a "material" effect on the success of the program, and if you can't answer the preceding two questions.

If you can't clearly identify an action linked to the metric, it's not actionable.

Testing Your Metrics and Conversion Metrics

You may not hit upon the best metric the first time around, so find ways to test them. Creating time-based cohorts and monitoring progress through your Developer Journey stage gates enables you to track the impact of outreach campaigns and the effect of tweaks in your Developer Experience on your conversion rates. Split testing or A/B testing are your friends here, allowing you to run smaller experiments to find the optimal result.

Reviewing the conversion metrics between your DevRel objectives is a must-do and can be very revealing. After your Lead Program metric, your conversion rates are most important.

Take a look at the following figures which provide an example of tracking conversion metrics. In Figure 26-3, we see from the initial 1000 prospects, only 2% (21) become customers. Figure 26-4 takes this one step further to show possible issues or problems occurring at each DevRel Objective and the accompanying metrics to monitor and adjust.

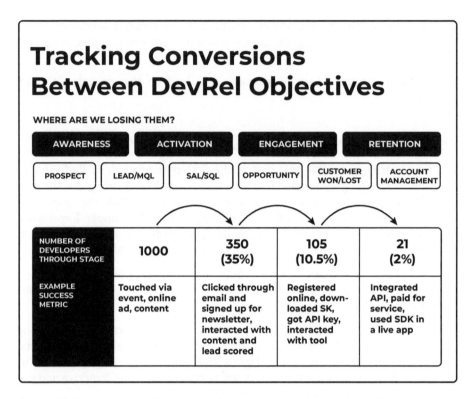

Figure 26-3. An example of tracking conversions between DevRel Objectives

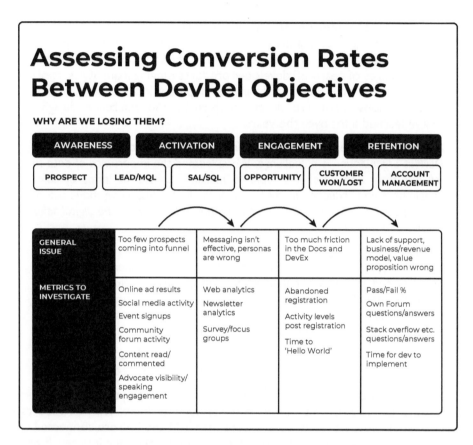

Figure 26-4. An example of assessing conversion rates between DevRel Objectives

Data Sources and Challenges

Half the battle of determining metrics is in determining the source of your data. Unfortunately, you might only be able to collect some of the data you need, or perhaps none at all, which can be unfortunate and frustrating. Below we list some of the common sources. You might have to get innovative in tracking down the data you need.

When deriving your sales funnel metrics, the best source is your company's CRM, such as HubSpot, Salesforce, Marketo, etc. If that's the tool your company uses, use your best efforts to use it too. Your access to the data should help you both determine metrics for some of your activities and feed your own leads into it. If you tag these records as they enter the CRM with DevRel and their source (event, PPC, etc.), they can be tracked through the funnel as a DevRel-influenced prospect, and you will be able to understand which of your awareness activities provide your most valuable customers.

Qualcomm Developer Network (QDN) is one of the oldest developer programs dating back to the BREW[5] application development platform in 2001. Its current incarnation supports one of the most complex ranges of nearly 60 developer products ranging from SDKs, tools like profilers and debuggers, hardware development kits for IoT, robotics, XR applications, hardware developer boards, and reference designs. They've learned a lot over the years:

Positioning a DevRel program and the importance of developers inside a large DevPlus organization is a challenge. We've learned the importance of data to tell our story and have been able to measure DevRel in terms of sales enablement and reduction in support tickets. To do this, we've made use of our corporate CRM and marketing automation tools to track the digital sales journey and participation of developers.

You don't sell by being salesy. We create technical content for developers and provide it how they want to consume it, which helps them evaluate our products and give them confidence they meet their requirements. This is especially important today due to the preference for self-service, regardless of the size of the company. We are very conscious of developers' needs and the importance of respecting and serving the community.

Ana Schafer Muroff
Senior Director Marketing, Qualcomm Technologies, Inc.

To determine product-related metrics, you should talk to your product team and use Product Analytics Software (PAS) such as Mixpanel, API Metrics, Keen.IO, PostHog, etc. If possible, ensure the CRM and PAS are connected so you can properly see the path a developer takes across your journey. If not, you may only be able to track trends. For instance, if you have just run a marketing campaign and there is a significant rise in product signups, you can infer some of that success. Cultivate a good relationship with the owner of the PAS tool!

The usability of these kinds of tools is vital. We have seen situations where it's required to write SQL queries to pull data. This process adds friction to your reporting, immediately limiting how many people in the organization can access the data and the frequency of reporting.

Web analytics tools like Google Analytics and Optimizely allow you to configure and track your awareness goals and make conversion tracking easier across the Dev Journey, such as tracking the performance of content like your blog posts.

Some external analytics companies will have reports you can buy to compare your results to your competitors.

---

[5] https://en.wikipedia.org/wiki/Binary_Runtime_Environment_for_Wireless

If you survey your developers for input and sentiment (and you should), tools like SurveyMonkey or Typeform can be used, and consider using a Net Promoter Score[6] to get a snapshot of sentiment and satisfaction in a single figure.

Determining tool or product usage via a community survey is also possible. This might be a surprise to you, but a bigger surprise is realizing that many programs have no insight into how their tools are used. They can measure something like SDK downloads, but have no further data because it's either not tracked, or they have no access to the data. So a developer survey, while not direct quantitative real-time data, can provide important insight into the types of developers, their companies, and how and why they use your product.

It's not always easy to find a tool to track and monitor all of your activities from the number of blogs written to informal developer feedback, etc. We've seen many DevRel programs use spreadsheets, and more are using one of many project management tools available like Notion, Airtable, etc. But note – these are manually maintained and not automated. So pick a tool that makes it as easy as possible to input the task, keep track of your data, and be able to quickly refer to the numbers you need for reporting.

Reporting Your Metrics

An often overlooked consideration is how to best present your metrics and data within your organization. You can have the best set of metrics in the world, but how are you sharing that information?

First, keep in mind the consumer of your reports. For your managers and above, they'll want to see your top-line metrics first (Program-Level metrics), and perhaps that's all they want to see or have time to review. Next, report on the Activity and Community metrics that back up your top-line metrics. You don't need to report on all of the metrics you track. Choose your backup metrics that most clearly add insight to your top-line metrics.

The ultimate goal is to have a web-based tool with a set of predefined reports that can be run across configurable time periods with the functionality to run custom queries from a simple interface like picking from lists and tick boxes, similar to the Google Analytics experience. This tool should be available to everyone inside the organization, providing the best possible transparency to the performance of your program at any given time, meaning you are not a bottleneck for any inquiries. Ensure these reports can be exported into a variety of formats so they can be incorporated into other departments' reporting.

---

[6]https://en.wikipedia.org/wiki/Net_Promoter

If you are using more traditional methods like a spreadsheet, slide deck, or written report, take the time to design and present the information clearly. Treat your reporting as a product, not a chore or an overhead. Your reporting represents your reality within the organization. It's your number one internal sales tool to demonstrate the impact and importance of your team's work.

Understand how other teams in the organization present and report, align where possible. As we have mentioned before, you shouldn't be seeking to reinvent the wheel here. A uniform approach reduces frustration and friction with your stakeholders.

Finally, don't assume that just because you provide a link to a reporting tool, or you diligently email out your monthly report on time every time, anyone actually reads them. Everyone is busy. Ensure that you have a slot at the most senior stakeholder meeting appropriate in your reporting structure to present your performance and highlights each month or each quarter. This ensures your key internal audience has heard you and provides an opportunity for them to ask you questions and for you to make suggestions or requests.

We would recommend you review the AAARRRP framework[7] by Phil Leggetter which is designed to help you have a conversation with your stakeholder to agree on high-level directional goals. It also helps DevRel professionals map goals to activities and identify which activities will really help achieve the goals.

Metric Accountability

Being accountable shouldn't feel scary or something you should be seeking to avoid. Being transparent and upfront about what you are doing and why it is important for your company is Business 101. The leaders that clearly define the "why" and are transparent and generous with the distribution of their performance data are the most successful in any industry.

There are three dangerous signals to watch out for:

1. Self-perpetuating the myth that DevRel is hard to measure.

2. DevRel practitioners acting like having targets applied to their work will somehow stifle their creativity or dampen the impact of their work.

3. DevRel practitioners who believe they need to constantly invent new metrics and new terminology.

Put yourself in the shoes of your CEO, line manager, your investor, or your peers. Empathy, a critical trait for DevRel professionals, isn't just toward the

---

[7]https://www.leggetter.co.uk/aaarrrp/

developers in the community you are serving. It's also inward to the people you're collaborating with inside your company.

You are asking them to give your program their personal and financial support. To secure and maintain this support, you will need to demonstrate why investing in your program is a better use of their time and money (and reputation) than other competing ideas. You can guarantee there will always be more good ideas than resources.

Demonstrate why this is good for them, forecast what their return on that investment looks like, and benchmark yourself against your competition (both internally and externally). You will not be successful by inventing new metrics or using language that your stakeholders don't understand. That comes across as avoiding accountability by blinding people with science or failing to understand the importance of integrating into the core business so all investments can be benchmarked on a level playing field.

Finally, don't forget your perception with colleagues in other teams across your company. We have seen firsthand the culture problems created when there is a perception that the DevRel team has a set of vanity metric targets to hit while they travel the globe tweeting about the latest party they are attending or the free airline upgrade they have bagged. All this while engineering has pulled an all-nighter to ship a release, or salespeople are being fired for missing their quota. Be self-aware!

Summary

As a manager of a DevRel program, you need to be accountable for your work and show its impact to the rest of your team and stakeholders. Metrics allow you to do just that.

Identify Lead and Program Metrics to set the *why* and *what* of your program, and Activity and Community metrics to back those up with the *how*. Metrics is not a one-time exercise. Review and test them regularly for insight into program adjustments.

Don't confuse a metrics exercise as a test of your creativity.

It's a test of your impact.

The right metrics enable you to make better decisions as you manage your team, which is the next chapter. Well-defined metrics also point out the maturity of your program, a topic we will see in Chapter 28.

Team

Getting the Right People on the Bus

You may be sitting back and chuckling to yourself. "Team? I wish!" Or you finally received some budget to hire a new team member, and you're not quite sure of the exact role to fill.

You are not alone. The genesis of many DevRel programs comes from an individual or a small group of people looking to lead the charge within the company. And often within that company, DevRel is an unknown quantity, so the investment profile doesn't fit the company norms. One lucky person is anointed to start and lead the program and do everything – the classic jack of all trades.

In this section, we will outline the various roles and describe "what good looks like" as you build out your DevRel team. This will help you benchmark where you are on your particular journey, where DevRel roles sit inside a typical organization, how to go about building a team, the skill sets required, hiring, and how the interactions work with other departments.

Generalists Get You Started

In the early days of a program, you are likely operating with a group of generalists who chip in to various activities, have that "can do" attitude, and are great at calling in favors across the organization to supplement the lack of dedicated resources in the DevRel team.

© Caroline Lewko, James Parton 2021
C. Lewko and J. Parton, *Developer Relations*,
https://doi.org/10.1007/978-1-4842-7164-3_27

The 2020 State of Developer Relations Report shows us the typical daily tasks of a "jack of all trades" DevRel person.

The Typical daily tasks of a "Jack of all trades" DevRel Person

OVERALL	
Content Developement	61%
Strategy and Planning	46%
Events	39%
Evangelism	29%
Outreach	25%
Research/staying up to date	18%
Marketing	17%
Social media/SEO	17%
Product Developement	16%
Support	14%
Asking for funding	6%
Other	6%
Portal Management	4%

Figure 27-1. *The typical daily tasks of a "jack of all trades" DevRel person*

Often, we hear it is this variety of tasks that makes DevRel such an appealing and exciting career choice. We struggle to think of another role that gives you such a wide scope of activities and influence. You operate across the organization, are involved in all the facets of bringing a product to market, and have the opportunity to engage and interact with customers (the developers) out in the field.

As your product gains traction, your developer community grows in size, and as growth expectations rise you must start planning for the expansion of the DevRel team and the creation of specialist roles and groups within the DevRel organization.

Specialists Help You Scale

As everything gets dialled up to 11, let's take a look at some of the specialist roles DevRel organizations typically hire as they expand their operations.

Developer Advocates

In most companies, the Advocate role represents "the boots on the ground," the "human face" representing the company and product out in the relevant technical communities. Think of Advocates as engaging their target audiences in a "one-to-many" fashion. They attend in-person or online events to network and to speak. They learn about and engage developers in various online communities. They provide product demos and help developers get hands-on with their company's technologies. They help overcome basic adoption issues at hackathons and bring developer feedback to the company.

Depending on the size of the DevRel organization, there will be a variable amount of content responsibility, for example, writing technical blog posts, contributing to the docs, and putting together the quickstart guides. There may also be contributions to production code and responsibility for providing and maintaining SDKs, etc. Where the technical responsibilities are significant, you may see job titles like Developer Experience Engineer or Developer Relations Engineer.

Often, they will be known within their own technical community via their open source contributions, authoring books, or organizing meetups. They may also visit customers to help them get up and running, depending on the sales team's technical skills.

Typically, an Advocate is the first hire a company makes when they start a formal DevRel program. You will see from the data in Figure 27-1, there is a danger they are seen as a technical and marketing Swiss Army knife and get unrealistic expectations heaped upon them. No one can realistically be an expert in all these disciplines simultaneously.

There is also a misconception that DevRel starts and ends with Developer Advocacy. This is perhaps unsurprising as Advocates are the most public-facing role within a DevRel team. However, in most DevRel programs, there is a team back at base driving the digital output and enabling team members out in the field, so the Advocate is never truly alone.

There is no doubt this can be a high-pressure role. It's challenging to perform such a dynamic role, understanding how to prioritize and project-manage everything that is expected. Being the "face" of the company out in the wild can be highly rewarding if your company and product are seen as cool and valuable. However, if there are issues, you become the scapegoat when things are not going well. There is the pressure to "perform" on stage via public speaking and perhaps live coding, and added to all of that is the fatigue of travel to attend the events all around the world. Compounding this is the fact that many DevRel professionals are early in their careers (27% have less than two years of experience, and 47% less than five years). Additionally, as there is no formal training for DevRel, 82% learn their role on the job.[1]

Companies should therefore be realistic on how much one person can achieve. It is also a reason that burnout is a real and serious problem. To help avoid this, expansion of the number of Advocates employed and the creation of additional specialist roles help lighten the load.

We have written this book during the COVID-19 pandemic which has led to the disruption of the global event circuit. This has forced the DevRel profession to rethink how they engage their communities. Only time will tell if the industry fully resets back to the previous norm or if the mix of in person vs. online has fundamentally changed for the long term.

Most would agree that nothing replaces in-person interactions for their quality of engagement and the serendipitous nature of being in the same place at the same time as a number of like-minded people. However, a long-term reduction in travel would contribute to lowering pressure and fatigue on individuals, reduce costs, and provide environmental benefits.

Speaking is a craft, and hard work!

Speaking is like any other craft or thing that needs discipline, some people may have a gift for it but practice and work are more important. Think about professional athletes or musicians. You can be good at it but it still can be hard and exhausting and sometimes awkward, especially in the beginning. But I promise you, it will get more comfortable over time. Try different speaking styles, and get feedback. I was once doing a show with a junior advocate where we both gave talks. Walking to dinner after our talks she said "I don't think I am cut out for advocacy, there is no way I can speak like you." In my head I was shocked, she was already better at speaking than most advocates I knew. I tried explaining to her: "I was a professor and a professional advocate

---

[1] Data acquired from the 2020 State of Developer Relations Survey.

for 10 years. You are a really great speaker — it will feel more natural over time". Unfortunately for our profession, but fortunate for her, she is a functional programming (Lambda) lead engineer at a large tech company now. I think she realized she likes being an engineer more than being an advocate, and that's ok.

One last thing about speaking. For me, it is something I "turn on" for the talk. I start to project my voice, I become much more outgoing and conscious of the words I speak. After it is done, well about 30 minutes after it is done, I am exhausted and want to be alone for the next day. Being "on" in the booth is exhausting as well. I really enjoy and get charged by having discussions in small groups with people I know. Giving talks, working the booth, going to conference social events is draining for me unless I have a small group of friends with me. You DON'T have to be an extrovert to be a speaker, you just have to be able to perform when needed.

—Steven Pousty
Developer Experience Engineer, Tanzu
Formerly DevRel at Crunch Data, Digital Globe,
Red Hat, LinkedIn, deCarta, ESRI

Support and Success Teams

Often, when the team is growing and your developers are engaging with you, it comes time to hire individuals dedicated to supporting your community's technical needs. The Support and Success teams spend time answering internal and external forum questions and may also spend one-on-one time with customers. They liaise directly with the product team to prioritize support tickets and feed developer requests back into the company.

Field Marketing or Event Marketing

In the early days of a program, it is likely your generalists will be attending and speaking at meetups and hackathons in their respective communities to network and spread the word.

However, at a certain point, the event opportunities and your ambitions grow past the grassroots meetups, and you begin to assess larger conferences and trade shows. You may even want to organize your own events or conferences. These events may be specific to particular programming languages and technologies, or they might be more general industry events that your target audience attends. At this point, the workload and skills required go beyond being job number 6 on a generalist's to-do list of 30 other things. The investment in terms of time and money demands a professional focus.

Specialist event professionals are skilled in a number of key areas:

- Which events do our target audience attend?
- What is the reputation of certain events and organizers?
- What is a realistic level of sponsorship and handling of negotiations?
- Ensuring your brand is represented in the right way.
- Handling the planning and logistics around booths, merchandise, etc.
- Handling staff rotas to ensure the right staff are attending.
- Developing a strategy to drive engagement and leads.
- Reporting on the return on investment post event.

This is why an event manager is a key hire within the DevRel organization, or sometimes this person will formally sit within the wider Marketing organization, having a dotted-line reporting structure into the DevRel program lead.

Developer Education

As we highlighted in the Developer Relations Framework (Figure 1-1) and discussed at length while exploring the Developer Journey (Figure 15-2), Developer Education (DevEd) is a critical component of Developer Relations. There is a growing school of thought that DevEd is now the primary DevRel function over Developer Advocacy, perhaps driven by the impact of COVID-19. This is somewhat backed up by research from Phil Leggetter that shows DevEd as the second most popular job title after the more generic "Developer Advocate" role.[2] We are also seeing companies like New Relic, for example, building out a team dedicated to specialist content creation and delivery just via Twitch[3] alone.

As you grow and then engage your community, there is a need to produce clear, well-structured, and error-free technical content to encourage Developers to experiment and adopt your product. In addition, you need to be producing supporting content like use cases or case studies or other thought leadership pieces to inspire developers and their colleagues and to provide the reassurances and trust that others are finding success using your

---

[2] https://noti.st/leggetter/9B23EW/defining-the-roles-within-developer-relations-v0-1-0#sjIQBU7
[3] https://www.twitch.tv/new_relic

technologies. Technical writers are often added to the team to produce and edit this content, either in-house or through an agency.

Your content strategy will be more than just written pieces. DevEd teams produce sample code, demos, even games to showcase the product and other concepts. Often, front-end developers are hired for this and sometimes perform double and triple duty working on UX for the product and the online Developer Hub too.

This team also gets involved in producing video content, which has become more popular in the last few years, so having a YouTube presence is important (or Twitch for some communities). Video content can be a few minutes of quick tips to longer training workshops.

Depending on the maturity of the company, you may progress to offering formal training courses and certifications, so those with formal training and pedagogy are hired. Gamification experts sometimes enhance the team to add creativity to developer challenges and training like TwilioQuest,[4] technical training delivered in an 8-bit arcade-style game.

Developer Marketing

Like any business, your DevRel program needs to be discovered. You will need specific digital marketing specialists that focus on SEO, PPC, and online advertising to build awareness and traffic to your DevRel activities. You will also need a web team. Again perhaps depending on the size of your organization, these roles may sit directly in the DevRel team, outside in the Marketing team, or outsourced to an external agency. If based outside the DevRel team, it will be your responsibility to inform and guide them on the creation and placement of messaging that will appeal to your developer audience.

This team can also be involved in producing direct content sent to your community like developer newsletters and nurture campaigns we reviewed in Chapter 22.

Some DevRel teams add a research and data analysis function that spends time reviewing external sources to keep up to date with trends and competitors to feed back information for product, marketing messages, events, and other community activities. This role also undertakes surveys and focus groups of your own developer community.

---

[4] https://www.twilio.com/quest

Community Managers

As we saw in Chapter 25, community relations becomes everyone's responsibility. However, once your community gets large enough, it requires more management of community-based activities, events, rewards, ambassadors, etc. Having a dedicated person for the community becomes necessary. Larger programs may split online and offline community management responsibilities.

Other Roles

We often say, "it depends," and that refers to the team complement in DevRel too. The age of your program, the size of the product portfolio and community, where DevRel sits functionally in the company, and the type of organization and business model will all affect the roles that are appropriate in your DevRel team.

Consultants and Outside Agencies

From time to time, your team may require some outside assistance to enhance your strategy or perform/supplement any of the roles mentioned earlier either on a part-time, fractional, or project basis. Typically, DevRel professionals in between roles offer short-term consultancy services, but there is a growing number of specialist full-time DevRel consultancies and agencies, which is another positive indicator of the growing maturity of the profession. If you are thinking of engaging an agency to support your program, our advice is ask for examples of their specific DevRel experience and how that translated into success with developers. Over the years, we have seen a number of generic marketing and advertising agencies claim to be developer specialists, but they lack the technical knowledge and industry network necessary to be successful.

DevRel Leadership and Career Path

Who should lead the DevRel team? That's another one of those "it depends" questions. We certainly haven't been shy to express our belief that DevRel functions better when it is led by a person dedicated to DevRel and even better when that person reports at a C-level.

If DevRel is not reporting into C-level, who leads typically depends on which functional department DevRel reports to, for example, you are unlikely to have a marketing person leading if DevRel reports into Engineering. Regardless, it is incumbent on the DevRel lead to share the knowledge of DevRel and collaborate within their own team and with other departments.

One of the challenges with DevRel has been career paths have a reputation of having a glass ceiling as seniority increases. We've heard of engineers who move to DevRel, then aren't able to find their way back to engineering to progress. There are also Developer Advocates who often don't see an advancement path into other departments. These may be symptomatic of several factors, such as:

- The "jack of all trades" approach to DevRel can mean DevRel people may not have the deep expertise to progress from an individual contributor (IC) role to another department.

- Because DevRel teams tend to be fairly small in the majority of organizations and DevRel people are pretty independent and self-starting, people management opportunities are limited; thus, DevRel people struggle to move onto roles requiring line management experience.

- The limited knowledge of DevRel roles and expertise, outside of DevRel circles.

This is changing, and of course we hope this book contributes to the professionalization, recognition, and growth of DevRel. When reporting to an engineering department, we are seeing job titles like DevRel Engineer, Senior DevRel Engineer or Senior Developer Advocate, DevRel Staff Engineer, and DevRel Principal Engineer. When in a marketing organization, we see DevRel Coordinator, DevRel Manager, Director of DevRel, and so on.

Developer Relations (DevRel) is an interdisciplinary role that sits in a border space between product, engineering, and marketing. Cross-functional collaboration is important for any DevRel team, no matter where they sit organizationally, but a company might have particular skills they look for based on how they're organized. For example, DevRel sits in Product at Slack, so I look for candidates who have good product instincts and can synthesize feedback sensibly and clearly.

A mature DevRel org will have a defined career ladder *for Developer Relations (you can see the one we use at Slack[5]). Look for that, or have a conversation with the hiring manager to better understand what skills and responsibilities will make you successful in the org.*

—Bear Douglas
Director Developer Relations, Slack
Formerly DevRel at Twitter and Facebook

---

[5]https://slack.engineering/defining-a-career-path-for-developer-relations/

Team structure and job titles vary by company. The following is an example from Nexmo:

- **P2** – Junior Developer Advocate
- **P3** – Developer Advocate
- **P4** – Senior Developer Advocate
- **P5** – Staff Developer Advocate
- **P6** – Principal Developer Advocate
- **M1** – Developer Relations Manager
- **M2** – Senior Developer Relations Manager
- **D1** – Director of Developer Relations and Directors of Community, Experience, and Education
- **D2** – Senior Director of Developer Relations

The example for Slack can be found in this blog post[5] and Camunda's is here.[6]

Interdepartmental Collaboration

The majority of DevRel teams look to beg, steal, and borrow resources and budget from anywhere they can find them. DevRel professionals tend to be scrappy and creative by nature. Unlocking internal opportunities by building strong ties and demonstrating why their "asks" are essential for the company is crucial. It can make the difference between success and failure. Therefore, it is vital for your program's long-term success that your DevRel team is an expert in building internal relationships and fostering collaboration.

As we explored in Chapter 10, internal politics can be toxic to a program's success, regardless of the perceived popularity or success of the developer communities served. If there are blocked lines of communication with product and engineering teams at the operational level, it is unlikely that the insights you have gathered from developers will be implemented. Developers will quickly realize that your words are hollow, and you are not listening to their feedback. Equally, if you don't have a great relationship with marketing, then you will be quickly frustrated that your messages and campaigns are not landing, or not even running at all.

---

[6]https://www.marythengvall.com/blog/2020/6/29/the-camunda-developer-relations-career-path

Hiring DevRel professionals is hard enough, so don't misinterpret the above and hire a bunch of politically savvy internal operators. This will result in abject failure for your program. However, your DevRel leadership needs to be aware of the need to create excellent internal relationships and ensure they are maintained as people come and go, the company grows, and departments are reorganized over time. If you are with a new startup Developer First company, we recommend instilling this culture from day one.

The importance of collaboration was highlighted in the 2020 edition of the State of Developer Relations research, with examples of the strategies DevRel professionals were using to foster those links as seen in Figure 27-2.

Success Factors of Working with other Departments

Develop Shared Goals	73%
Share Success Together	62%
Foster Trust, Not Competition	58%
Gain Executive Support	57%
Embrace Diversity	37%
Centralized Effective Communication	32%
Measure Performance Regularly	32%
Manage Conflict Head-On Together	14%

"Create situations for informal communication."

"Lead by example."

"Being proactive about reaching out to other departments and creating relationships is key."

Figure 27-2. *Success factors of working with other departments from the State of Developer Relations 2020 Report*

Refer back to Chapter 10 for the extended discussion and strategy around managing Stakeholder-level relationships.

DevRel Demographics

Research is busting some myths around DevRel, especially the cliché that Developer Advocates are all hoodie-wearing 20-something white males, with sticker-covered laptops slung over their back skateboarding to hackdays. We are exaggerating to make a point, but unfortunately there are still misconceptions out there.

Thirty percent (30%) of DevRel professionals are over 40,[7] which actually skews older than the average age of the Developers they serve, as only 16.8% of professional developers are over 40.[8]

As DevRel becomes a more mature practice, the experience levels of DevRel professionals are also increasing, with more than half (52.8%) having 4+ years of experience, as shown in Figure 27-3.

---

[7]https://www.reverecommunications.com/post/state-of-developer-relations-2020-report

[8]https://insights.stackoverflow.com/survey/2020#developer-profile-age-professional-developers5

Figure 27-3. Years of DevRel experience from the State of Developer Relations Report 2020

DevRel is still predominantly male (61%), but the female and nonbinary ratio has increased to 30% over the last several years, a higher proportion when compared to the general developer population, which is reported at only 7.7% and 1.2%, respectively.

Many have claimed that a DevRel professional must have a technical degree. In fact, in the 2020 State of Developer Relations Survey, just over half (52%) of respondents claimed to have a technical degree, and this percentage has remained steady over recent years. If they are required to contribute to the product code base or write highly technical content, then a technical degree is beneficial, but there are many great DevRel professionals without one.

Typical DevRel salaries fall between $100K and $150K, with breakdowns shown by company size in Figure 27-4.

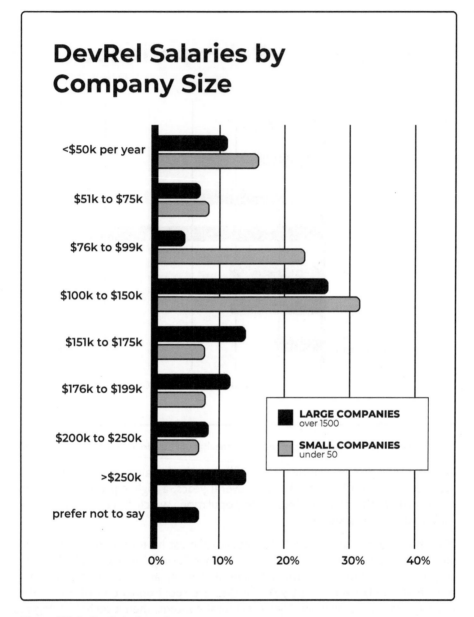

Figure 27-4. DevRel salaries by company size

We believe that average salaries will continue to rise to better represent the strategic value of DevRel in organizations, the unique skill sets required (an unusual blend of technical, marketing, and people skills), and our contention that DevRel should be elevated to the Cx level via the Chief Developer Relations Officer role.

Hiring DevRel

The good news is, compared to 15 years ago, Developer Relations now has a growing pool of experienced practitioners, and the awareness levels have reached a point where there is an element of aspiration from students wishing to enter the profession from universities, thanks to the work of organizations like GitHub Campus Experts,[9] Microsoft,[10] Major League Hacking,[11] and others.

Note however that most student outreach is almost exclusively aimed at encouraging students to adopt the company's technology and to create a positive brand impression, which of course the companies hope translates into product adoption and revenue generation as the students transition into the workplace. DevRel only gets indirect promotion as a career option as students come into contact with the representatives of the companies and sponsor organizations.

A great way to identify potential DevRel talent is to spend time in the communities you wish to target. There you can scout for individuals that have the technical skills you require and stand out from the crowd. Examples include the people contributing to open source projects, the meetup organizers, impressive public speakers/demo-ers, and the natural teachers that help people at Hackdays.

You can also hire internally. As awareness of DevRel grows, we see more individuals from marketing and engineering teams jump at the chance to be part of the DevRel team. They like the challenge of new activities, many like teaching others, and they like the opportunity to influence the product and the chance to interact with developers outside of the organization.

Of course, you will come into contact with DevRel people from other companies on the circuit. Yes, shock horror, it's competitive out there, and people get poached. Perhaps DevRel is unique in the fact that as a by-product of performing a community-facing role like developer advocacy, you are effectively paying for your advocates to build their personal brand. Now this is of course a win-win. The more respected they become, the larger their following, and the greater the opportunities they create for you. Just consider they are consistently performing in the shop window, so have a contingency plan in place should they move on.

Be mindful that reputation is everything, so don't ever do anything untrustworthy, underhanded, or shady in your efforts to attract the right people, or you will soon discover no one wants to work for you or buy your products.

---

[9]https://education.github.com/experts
[10]https://azure.microsoft.com/en-gb/developer/students/
[11]https://mlh.io/

Hiring and Building an Inclusive Culture and Team

It starts from the top – is your leadership and board diverse? Are you sending the right signals, and do you have diversity of thought and inclusion at the heart of what you are setting out to achieve? If you don't have diversity in your positions of power, any recruitment efforts you make will lack authenticity and credibility.

Ensure that you are setting the right cultural tone that treats everyone equally. Pay people of equivalent skill and impact the same, and ensure everyone's opinion is respected and that everyone gets equal airtime to give their opinion without interruption. Think about your company values and how they can help guide the right behaviors.

Ensure your hiring requirements don't fall into the trap of using lazy filters. For example, is requiring a degree *really* necessary to be successful in their role? By requiring a degree, you are automatically excluding a high percentage of underrepresented socioeconomic groups from applying. Wouldn't it be better to specify what skills or attitude you are looking to bring into the business? By asking for too many requirements, you will put off everyone except self-confident males. In fact, don't even call them requirements – instead state "You'd really enjoy this role if you had…." Explain and sell the job in ways such as how much data you will be working with, how many commits you will make each week, how many talks you will give, and describe who will use and benefit from your software.

Avoid building a clone army

When it comes to hiring, the biggest mistake is thinking you can do it without any experience at all. That's a great way to grow a company of people that all look like you, and perhaps don't represent your consumers.

Instead think about who we are building for and go and talk to those communities about why they might want to come and work with you, or go and work with some recruiters that have great networks and can help you and give you a diverse pipeline. If you work with recruiters that just send you candidates that just look like the recruiter, then that's not a good recruiter – talk to them about this stuff, they should be able to help you out.

—Thayer Prime
Founder and CEO, Team Prime

If you don't have the existing networks and relationships to identify and approach potential hires from your target communities directly, be thoughtful about where you advertise your roles and the keywords you use. Maximize the reach of your job ads by using syndication services. There is a growing amount written about the use of language and who it attracts – labels like "ambitious" and "passionate," idioms like "join the rocketship," positioning a foosball table in the office and Friday drinks as company benefits are all demonstrating bias toward young males. Even if it's unconscious bias, it's still bias and will deter diversity in applicants.

If you truly want diversity in age, gender, and ethnic and socioeconomic background, think beyond the clichés. Talk about life and not just work. People in different life stages or personal situations will value different things. Flexible hours, working from home, pension plans, sick pay, health care, maternity and paternity provisions, child care, vacation, etc., are all benefits valued by a diverse workforce.

Summary

The Developer Relations team goes far beyond hiring a Developer Advocate and is broader in scope than hiring one person to run it all. From the start, your program will rely on collaboration between other departments and then will start to add specialists to help you scale.

There are more experienced DevRel professionals than we might have imagined, but it is still a growing field of individuals who learn on the job with activities that range from content creation, strategy and research, online marketing, advocacy, writing code samples, and much more.

Of course, the roles appropriate for your team depend on the age of your program, the size of the product portfolio and community, the type of company and business model, the goals of your program, and where DevRel functionally sits in your organization. We are certain that a strong DevRel program will have a defined career path to attract the best talent and that soon we will see a Chief Developer Relations Officer.

Program Phasing

From Zero to Maturity

DevRel has a large surface area with lots of facets and complexity to consider. It is further complicated by its strategic nature, leading to many strong opinions in an organization on the best approach to managing and growing a DevRel program. It definitely requires you to form and maintain many cross-departmental relationships and have confidence and authority in your plan.

We understand that knowing where to start or what to do next can feel overwhelming. You might have read the book and think, "How do I implement all this? It's just me, on my own!" or "How do I get my stakeholders to comprehend what needs to be done?"

The fundamental approach to tackle any large subject is to break it down into its constituent parts to see exactly where you are on your journey. In this chapter, we examine what makes a DevRel program mature and then review the maturity stages of a program so you can benchmark your progress.

© Caroline Lewko, James Parton 2021
C. Lewko and J. Parton, *Developer Relations*,
https://doi.org/10.1007/978-1-4842-7164-3_28

When Is a DevRel Program Mature?

Every program has to start somewhere. Whatever your scenario, you likely want to improve your program's performance, increase the impact you have, and increase the resources at your disposal.

We've created a framework to show the stages through which a DevRel program evolves to maturity, as shown in Figure 28-1.

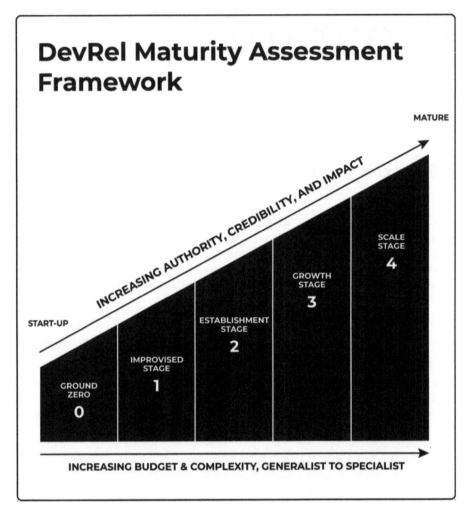

Figure 28-1. The stages of the DevRel maturity assessment framework

Within the framework, there are two categories of influences that determine the extent to which a program matures, shown on the axes, as follows:

- **Increasing authority, credibility, and impact axis**

  This axis plots the key considerations that govern your ability, as the DevRel leader, to influence your stakeholders, gain the support to move to the next maturity phase, or increase investment if you have reached the Scale stage. The efforts of the DevRel team will be centered around boosting the company and products' authority and credibility with your target audience. As these metrics increase, so does your impact on the business. The impact is typically measured in revenue, but as we explored in Chapter 8, revenue is not the only value a developer program creates.

- **Increasing budget and complexity axis**

  It is fairly self-explanatory, but as investment in the program increases, so does the number of people, activities, and customers. More investment is positive news, but it also brings complexity to managing a program. Refer back to our chapters on company alignment, objectives, and metrics to ensure the DevRel activities remain in lockstep with leadership at the company level. As the investment grows, the level of expectation and associated program targets grows as well. This is why we strongly advocate for the role of the Chief Developer Relations Officer operating at the company's executive level.

Appreciating these influences and understanding where your program plots can help you move your program toward maturity. Let's take a deeper dive now into the details of each stage.

Assessing the Maturity Stages of a DevRel Program

So how do you know which stage you are in, and how do you move to the next stage? We're glad you asked!

You'll note from Figure 28-1 the five maturity stages for a DevRel Program are:

- 0 – Ground Zero
- 1 – Improvised stage

- 2 – Establishment stage
- 3 – Growth stage
- 4 – Scale stage

Each stage has ten indicators to measure your program, as shown in Table 28-1. Knowing the indicators and your status of each will help you understand how effective you can be in driving your goals forward and what resources you will need to grow and mature your program. Of course, depending on the type and size of company, there will be variations.

Table 28-1. Indicators of a DevRel Program's Maturity

Ten Indicators of DevRel Maturity

1. PRODUCT	Status and numbers of products
2. DEVREL PROGRAM	Status of program
3. DEDICATED STAFF	Staff complement of program
4. DEVREL STRATEGY	Status of strategy – ad hoc or comprehensive
5. BUDGET	Size of budget
6. INTERNAL AWARENESS & ALIGNMENT	Status of awareness and integration of program inside company
7. DEVELOPER OUTREACH	Complexity from none to formalized program
8. DEVELOPER EDUCATION & DEVEX	Status of learning resources and DOCS
9. METRICS	Type and level of sophistication, impact on company
10. DEVELOPER COMMUNITY	Size of community and level of contributions

Let's take a deeper dive into each stage and how the ten indicators evolve across them.

Stage 0 – Ground Zero

Ground Zero is the point in time before DevRel sprouts inside your organization. This is normally the point where a new developer product is invented or built. Someone is beginning to recognize that developers could become a route to market. This concept is new. It's time to investigate and build a case for further investment.

Maturity Stage 0

1. PRODUCT: 1 (likely alpha)
2. DEVREL PROGRAM: 0
3. DEDICATED DEVREL STAFF: 0
4. DEVREL STRATEGY: None
5. BUDGET: $0
6. INTERNAL AWARENESS & ALIGNMENT: None
7. DEVELOPER OUTREACH: None
8. DEVELOPER EDUCATION & DEVEX: None
9. METRICS: None
10. DEVELOPER COMMUNITY: None

Stage 1 – Improvised Stage

The typical genesis begins when an individual or small team decides some kind of DevRel effort is needed to enhance the chances of success of their new shiny tool, SDK, API, or other developer products. They might not have any preconceived idea about what DevRel is or what activities are necessary. Still, they intuitively know they want to start getting developers engaged with what they have built.

As we touched on earlier, it is often one or two engineers or founders who proactively start answering questions on Stack Overflow or start attending meetups to chat about their work. They become accidental advocates for the product, not typically operating with any "grand plan" or even permission. They are spurred on by their genuine enthusiasm for what they have created. Remember the "I built that" developer truism we discussed in Chapter 5?

Well, that applies as much to internal engineers and founders as it does to the wider developer community you are trying to attract. They have that same pride in what they do, and these pioneers pave the way for a formal program to grow.

No one is quite sure what they are doing, but that isn't going to stop them! They start to improvise and learn by doing.

Maturity Stage 1

1. PRODUCT: 1 (likely beta)
2. DEVREL PROGRAM: 0
3. DEDICATED DEVREL STAFF: 0, 1–3 enthusiasts
4. DEVREL STRATEGY: None
5. BUDGET: $0
6. INTERNAL AWARENESS & ALIGNMENT: Limited
7. DEVELOPER OUTREACH: Ad hoc
8. DEVELOPER EDUCATION & DEVEX: Basic
9. METRICS: Informal
10. DEVELOPER COMMUNITY: <1000

Stage 2 – Establishment Stage

Within the Establishment stage, the company decides that at least one person should spend all or part of their time thinking about DevRel. It's the beginning of formalizing DevRel inside the organization, and developers have been acknowledged as a potential route to market for a product.

The trigger may be due to results achieved by the improvised efforts, a compelling strategic pitch to the board or investors, or perhaps competitive pressure has created the need for a response. Either way, someone now has the responsibility to figure out what needs to be done.

Unfortunately, we often see an individual contributor (IC) brought in to "do developer relations." Understandably, a company is unlikely to go all in without better understanding the opportunity. Here, they tend to go down the path of controlling salary costs while assessing if the "developer opportunity" is worth chasing.

Being the go-to person is exciting and dynamic, for a time. Long term, this scenario is not sustainable if the company is serious about success with developers. Apart from the risk of burnout, it is rare to find an IC generalist that is skilled at the technical and tactical side of DevRel while also having the necessary experience and influence to successfully interact with and lobby the leadership team and build a strategic plan as momentum builds to move to the next stage – Growth.

Ideally, we recommend hiring someone with DevRel experience, seniority, and structure to form a strategy, establish the internal cooperation necessary, and build a budget and hiring plan for the growth stage.

This person develops a plan, creates personas, starts outreach to gather insights from the nascent community, and ensures basic Developer Education, content, and Docs are available. If they are good or lucky or both, they can beg, steal, and borrow support from other departments or secure a budget to hire outside expertise.

Maturity Stage 2

1. PRODUCT: 1 (full release)
2. DEVREL PROGRAM: Infancy
3. DEDICATED DEVREL STAFF: 1–5
4. DEVREL STRATEGY: A plan for a plan
5. BUDGET: < $50k
6. INTERNAL AWARENESS & ALIGNMENT: Growing
7. DEVELOPER OUTREACH: Testing in limited channels
8. DEVELOPER EDUCATION & DEVEX: Basic
9. METRICS: Basic
10. DEVELOPER COMMUNITY: < 5000

Stage 3 – Growth Stage

Based on the learnings of the two previous stages, the company now understands that developers represent an attractive opportunity. After much experimentation in the previous phases, there is a growing understanding of the target developer, value proposition, and/or monetization strategy to employ. The program is ready to grow.

During the Growth stage, program communities typically grow between 10,000 and 50,000 developers with a directly controlled budget of around $1m. One of the ICs is promoted to lead the program, or a DevRel leader is brought in. The team hires additional resources, and we start to see the gradual move away from the generalists trying to do everything to some specialism in roles. There may be growth in the product in terms of features, additional products created, or sales categories added. There is increased interaction with the community for input and contributions.

The timing of this growth is dependent upon the growth of all of the factors. For instance, a program could experience fast growth in two years or less with large budgets, a great team, and corporate alignment. Or they may flail or die, gaining little traction in spite of a great team and attention to Docs, if corporate alignment and budget aren't there.

Maturity Stage 3

1. PRODUCT: < 5

2. DEVREL PROGRAM: 1

3. DEDICATED DEVREL STAFF: < 10, growing

4. DEVREL STRATEGY: Yes

5. BUDGET: < $1m

6. INTERNAL AWARENESS & ALIGNMENT: Improving

7. DEVELOPER OUTREACH: Formalized

8. DEVELOPER EDUCATION & DEVEX: Improving and expanding

9. METRICS: Good

10. DEVELOPER COMMUNITY: < 10,000 with contributors

Stage 4 – Scale Stage

As the developer effort continues to deliver impact, the DevRel leadership team ensures investment flows into the team, allowing it to scale. Specialism continues, and new dynamics like international expansion come into play, affecting everything from the go-to-market plan, reporting hierarchy, individual skills, and geographical distribution of the team.

Complexity increases across all areas of the program, and as the expectations rise, the number of team members grows. Data suggests 15% of DevRel programs have more than 100 people, particularly those with multiple products to support.[1] Budgets may increase to $5m+, leading to more activities, and the size of the developer community rises to hundreds of thousands, perhaps millions of developers.

---

[1] https://www.stateofdeveloperreleations.com

In Developer Plus companies, success may even see multiple DevRel initiatives spring up. In large complex organizations, it is not unusual for other departments to be unaware of your program and start developer-related activities of their own or worse be aware and do it anyway.

Maturity Stage 4

1. PRODUCT: Multiple

2. DEVREL PROGRAM: 1 or more

3. DEDICATED DEVREL STAFF: > 10, growing

4. DEVREL STRATEGY: Yes

5. BUDGET: > $1m

6. INTERNAL AWARENESS & ALIGNMENT: High

7. DEVELOPER OUTREACH: Sophisticated

8. DEVELOPER EDUCATION & DEVEX: Comprehensive

9. METRICS: Comprehensive and impactful on business

10. DEVELOPER COMMUNITY: > 50,000 with active contributors

Comparing Stages and Indicators

We've summarized all of the stages and indicators in Table 28-2 to give you a side-by-side comparison. Likely, the evolution of your DevRel program won't fit neatly into one stage, but use this framework to provide insight into how you can improve your program and, in turn, enable you to provide the best program for your community.

Table 28-2. The Maturity Stages of a DevRel Program

Maturity stages of a DevRel Program

	0 Ground Zero	1 Improvised	2 Establish-ment	3 Growth	4 Scale
Product	1	1	1	<5	Multiple
DevRel Program	0	◔	◑	◕	●
Dedicated DevRel Staff	0	1-3 enthusiasts	1-5	<10 growing	>10 growing
DevRel Strategy	None	◔	◕	◕	●
Budget	$0	$0	<$50k	<$1m	>$1m
Internal Awareness & Allignment	None	◔	◑	◕	●
Developer Outreach	None	Ad-hoc	Testing	Formalized	Sophisticated
DevEd & DevEx	None	◔	◕	◕	●
Metrics	None	◔	◕	◕	●
Developer Community	None	<1000	<5000	<10 000	50 000+

Summary

Knowing where your DevRel program is on the maturity scale helps you to:

- Understand your immediate priorities, allowing you to focus and not get distracted by everything else you might be tempted to do.

- Provide the structure and, along with the book, tools to create and articulate your plan for moving forward.

- Be more structured in your investment requests to your stakeholders as you prepare to transition into the next maturity phase.

- Recognize and celebrate your progress as you graduate from previous phases.

- **Offer the best program to serve your community!**

Epilogue
Turning Theory into Action

The most challenging aspect of writing this book was nailing down the audience.

Who exactly were we writing this for?

Definitely for DevRel practitioners. Some have been in the game for decades, managing finely tuned DevRel teams with hundreds of people and thousands of developers inside the world's leading technology companies. Others are just beginning in young startups with limited resources beyond themselves.

In addition to DevRel practitioners, we believe large sections of this book should be essential reading for stakeholders from the wider organization. Our goal for this book is to improve their understanding of the subject matter and create empathy and a sense of shared purpose.

Developing tools and frameworks that would be helpful to both extremes of experience and everyone in between was a challenge. We sincerely hope there is something in here for everyone.

The least challenging part was agreement on our philosophy for the book. We made an early editorial decision that the book would not be written as the "definitive guide" to DevRel. You may have noted a few instances where our advice was, "it depends." Rather, we wanted a book that put a more visible stake in the ground to establish where DevRel is today, and recognizes that

© Caroline Lewko, James Parton 2021
C. Lewko and J. Parton, *Developer Relations*,
https://doi.org/10.1007/978-1-4842-7164-3_29

there are loads of great DevRel resources already out there, more will be created, and we fully expect our thinking to be refined and adapted by the community.

Whatever your situation, we believe that this book offers, for the first time, a comprehensive and strategic analysis of Developer Relations. One that will help gain recognition for the practice, support its professionalization, and ultimately raise Developer Relations to C-level authority within companies.

What Comes Next? Your Turn

The development of the book has been a collaborative process, and we want that to continue. All of the frameworks have been made available via the book's GitHub repository, or visit us at www.devrelbook.com. Use them and adapt them to your needs. Tell us what you love or hate.

There is a vibrant and supportive community of DevRel professionals, all seeking to progress the practice. We are a small part of that movement. Many of them have been generous with their time and support for this project for which we are thankful.

If your role is DevRel or if you want it to be your job, or you just have an interest in the subject, be sure to explore all the DevRel resources listed on our website, to learn more, add to them, and get connected into this great community.

Good luck!

Caroline and James, August 2021

Correction to: Developer Relations

Caroline Lewko, James Parton

Correction to:

C. Lewko, J. Parton, Developer Relations,
https://doi.org/10.1007/978-1-4842-7164-3.

In Chapter 4, Fig. 4-3 and 4-1 have been swapped per the author request.

The updated version of this chapter can be found at:
https://doi.org/10.1007/978-1-4842-7164-3_4

I

Index